P9-BJM-518

ENDANGERED PEOPLES
of Southeast and East Asia

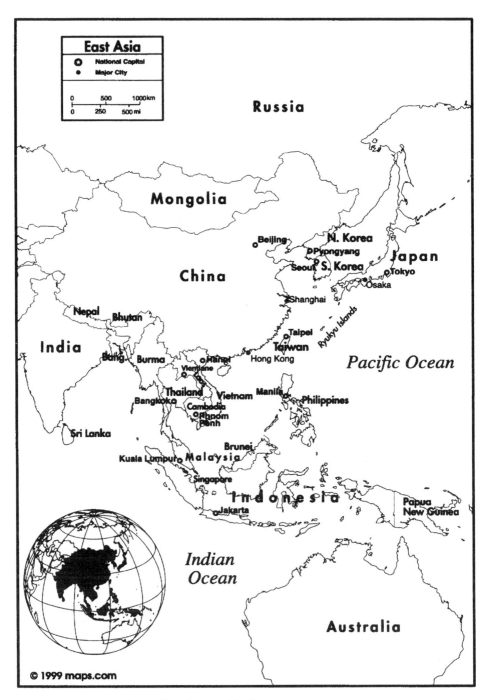

© 1999 maps.com

Used by permission of Magellan Geographix, Inc.

ENDANGERED PEOPLES
of Southeast and East Asia

Struggles to Survive and Thrive

Edited by Leslie E. Sponsel

The Greenwood Press
"Endangered Peoples of the World" Series
Barbara Rose Johnston, Series Editor

GREENWOOD PRESS
Westport, Connecticut • London

Library of Congress Cataloging-in-Publication Data

Endangered peoples of Southeast and East Asia : struggles to survive
    and thrive / edited by Leslie E. Sponsel.
        p.   cm.—(The Greenwood Press "Endangered peoples of the
    world" series, ISSN 1525–1233)
        Includes bibliographical references (p.   ) and index.
        ISBN 0–313–30646–X (alk. paper)
        1. Indigenous peoples—Asia, Southeastern.   2. Indigenous peoples—
    East Asia.   3. Asia, Southeastern—Social conditions.   4. East
    Asia—Social conditions.   I. Sponsel, Leslie E. (Leslie Elmer),
    1943– . II. Series.
    GN635.S58E5   2000
    306'.08'0959—dc21   99–21804

British Library Cataloguing in Publication Data is available.

Copyright © 2000 by Leslie E. Sponsel

All rights reserved. No portion of this book may be
reproduced, by any process or technique, without the
express written consent of the publisher.

Library of Congress Catalog Card Number: 99–21804
ISBN: 0–313–30646–X
ISSN: 1525–1233

First published in 2000

Greenwood Press, 88 Post Road West, Westport, CT 06881
An imprint of Greenwood Publishing Group, Inc.
www.greenwood.com

Printed in the United States of America

The paper used in this book complies with the
Permanent Paper Standard issued by the National
Information Standards Organization (Z39.48–1984).

10 9 8 7 6 5 4 3 2 1

Copyright Acknowledgment

Cover photo: Malnourished Akha children begging in a Thai town, 1987. Courtesy of Cornelia Ann Kammerer.

Contents

Contents

Series Foreword

Barbara Rose Johnston

Two hundred thousand years ago our human ancestors gathered plants and hunted animals in the forests and savannas of Africa. By forty thousand years ago, *Homo sapiens sapiens* had developed ways to survive and thrive in every major ecosystem on this planet. Unlike other creatures, whose response to harsh or varied conditions prompted biological change, humans generally relied upon their ingenuity to survive. They fashioned clothing from skins and plant fiber rather than growing thick coats of protective hair. They created innovative ways to live and communicate and thus passed knowledge down to their children. This knowledge, by ten thousand years ago, included the means to cultivate and store food. The ability to provide for lean times allowed humans to settle in larger numbers in villages, towns, and cities where their ideas, values, ways of living, and language grew increasingly complicated and diverse.

This cultural diversity—the multitude of ways of living and communicating knowledge—gave humans an adaptive edge. Other creatures adjusted to change in their environment through biological adaptation (a process that requires thousands of life spans to generate and reproduce a mutation to the level of the population). Humans developed analytical tools to identify and assess change in their environment, to search out or devise new strategies, and to incorporate new strategies throughout their group. Sometimes these cultural adaptations worked; people transformed their way of life, and their population thrived. Other times, these changes produced further complications.

Intensive agricultural techniques, for example, often resulted in increased salts in the soil, decreased soil fertility, and declining crop yields. Food production declined, and people starved. Survivors often moved to new regions to begin again. Throughout human history, migration became the common strategy when innovations failed. Again, in these times, culture was essential to survival.

For the human species, culture is our primary adaptive mechanism. Cultural diversity presents us with opportunities to draw from and build upon a complicated array of views, ideas, and strategies. The Endangered Peoples of the World series celebrates the rich diversity of cultural groups living on our planet and explores how cultural diversity, like biological diversity, is threatened.

Five hundred years ago, as humans entered the age of colonial expansion, there were an estimated twelve to fourteen thousand cultural groups with distinct languages, values, and ways of life. Today, cultural diversity has been reduced by half (an estimated 6,000 to 7,000 groups). This marked decline is due in part to the fact that, historically, isolated peoples had minimal immunity to introduced diseases and little time to develop immunological defenses. Colonizers brought more than ideas, religion, and new economic ways of living. They brought a host of viruses and bacteria— measles, chicken pox, small pox, the common cold. These diseases swept through "new" worlds at epidemic levels and wiped out entire nations. Imperialist expansion and war further decimated original, or "indigenous," populations.

Today's cultural diversity is further threatened by the biodegenerative conditions of nature. Our biophysical world's deterioration is evidenced by growing deserts; decreasing forests; declining fisheries; poisoned food, water, and air; and climatic extremes and weather events such as floods, hurricanes, and droughts. These degenerative conditions challenge our survival skills, often rendering customary knowledge and traditions ineffective.

Cultural diversity is also threatened by unparalleled transformations in human relations. Isolation is no longer the norm. Small groups continually interact and are subsumed by larger cultural, political, and economic groups of national and global dimensions. The rapid pace of change in population, technology, and political economy leaves little time to develop sustainable responses and adjust to changing conditions.

Across the world cultural groups are struggling to maintain a sense of unique identity while interpreting and assimilating an overwhelming flow of new ideas, ways of living, economies, values, and languages. As suggested in some chapters in this series, cultural groups confront, embrace, adapt, and transform these external forces in ways that allow them to survive and thrive. However, in far too many cases, cultural groups lack the time and means to adjust and change. Rather, they struggle to retain the right to simply exist as other, more powerful peoples seize their land and resources and "cleanse" the countryside of their presence.

Efforts to gain control of land, labor, and resources of politically and/or geographically peripheral peoples are justified and legitimized by ethnocentric notions: the beliefs that the values, traditions, and behavior of your own cultural group are superior and that other groups are biologically, culturally, and socially inferior. These notions are produced and reproduced in conversation, curriculum, public speeches, articles, television coverage, and other communication forums. Ethnocentrism is reflected in a language of debasement that serves to dehumanize (the marginal peoples are considered sub-human: primitive, backward, ignorant people that "live like animals"). The pervasiveness of this discourse in the everyday language can eventually destroy the self-esteem and sense of worth of marginal groups and reduce their motivation to control their destiny.

Thus, vulnerability to threats from the biophysical and social realms is a factor of social relations. Human action and a history of social inequity leave some people more vulnerable than others. This vulnerability results in ethnocide (loss of a way of life), ecocide (destruction of the environment), and genocide (death of an entire group of people).

The Endangered Peoples of the World series samples cultural diversity in different regions of the world, examines the varied threats to cultural survival, and explores some of the ways people are adjusting and responding to threats of ethnocide, ecocide, and genocide. Each volume in the series covers the peoples, problems, and responses characteristic of a major region of the world: the Arctic, Europe, North America and the Caribbean, Latin America, Africa and the Middle East, Central and South Asia, Southeast and East Asia, and Oceania. Each volume includes an introductory essay authored by the volume editor and fifteen or so chapters, each featuring a different cultural group whose customs, problems, and responses represent a sampling of conditions typical of the region. Chapter content is organized into five sections: Cultural Overview (people, setting, traditional subsistence strategies, social and political organization, religion and world view), Threats to Survival (demographic trends, current events and conditions, environmental crisis, sociocultural crisis), Response: Struggles to Survive Culturally (indicating the variety of efforts to respond to threats), Food for Thought (a brief summary of the issues raised by the case and some provocative questions that can be used to structure class discussion or organize a research paper), and a Resource Guide (major accessible published sources, films and videos, Internet and WWW sites, and organizations). Many chapters are authored or coauthored by members of the featured group, and all chapters include liberal use of a "local voice" to present the group's own views on its history, current problems, strategies, and thoughts of the future.

Collectively, the series contains some 120 case-specific examples of cultural groups struggling to survive and thrive in a culturally diverse world. Many of the chapters in this global sampling depict the experiences of indigenous peoples and ethnic minorities who, until recently, sustained their customary way of life in the isolated regions of the world. Threats to survival are often linked to external efforts to develop the natural resources of the previously isolated region. The development context is often one of co-optation of traditionally held lands and resources with little or no recognition of resident peoples' rights and little or no compensation for their subsequent environmental health problems. New ideas, values, technologies, economies, and languages accompany the development process and, over time, may even replace traditional ways of being.

Cultural survival, however, is not solely a concern of indigenous peoples. Indeed, in many parts of the world the term "indigenous" has little relevance, as all peoples are native to the region. Thus, in this series, we define cultural groups in the broadest of terms. We examine threats to survival and the variety of responses of ethnic minorities, as well as national cultures, whose traditions are challenged and undermined by global transformations.

The dominant theme that emerges from this sampling is that humans struggle with serious and life-threatening problems tied to larger global forces, and yet, despite huge differences in power levels between local communities and global institutions and structures, people are crafting and developing new ways of being. This series demonstrates that culture is not a static set of meanings, values, and behaviors; it is a flexible, resilient tool that has historically provided humans with the means to adapt, adjust, survive, and, at times, thrive. Thus, we see "endangered" peoples confronting and responding to threats in ways that reshape and transform their values, relationships, and behavior.

Emerging from this transformative process are new forms of cultural identity, new strategies for living, and new means and opportunities to communicate. These changes represent new threats to cultural identity and autonomy but also new challenges to the forces that dominate and endanger lives.

ENDANGERED PEOPLES
of Southeast and East Asia

Chapter 1

Identities, Ecologies, Rights, and Futures: All Endangered

Leslie E. Sponsel

Southeast and East Asia cover vast, diverse, and complex regions. The purpose of this chapter is twofold: first, to outline the general characteristics of these two regions; and second, to place these regions in the more general context of biological and cultural diversity as endangered phenomena.

There are two major divisions of Southeast Asia: the mainland (continental) part includes Burma, Peninsular Malaysia, Thailand, Laos, Cambodia, and Vietnam; the insular (island) part includes Indonesia, Singapore, Brunei, the Philippines, and island parts of Malaysia. This region evokes a rich and complex diversity of images: tropical forests with orangutans, sea gypsies, prehistoric ruins of ancient kingdoms like Angkor Wat in Cambodia, water buffaloes in wet-rice paddies, Balinese art, puppet shadow plays, the explosions of the volcanoes Krakatoa in Indonesia and Pinatubo in the Philippines, opium warlords in the Golden Triangle, Buddhist monks, the Tasaday (purported "Stone Age" cave people), ancient rice terraces of the Ifugao in the Philippines, Penan hunters blockading logging roads in Sarawak, the Vietnam War with the My Lai massacre and Agent Orange, boat-people refugees, the killing fields of Cambodia under the Khmer Rouge, Burmese prodemocracy leader Aung San Suu Kyi, and the modern city-state of Singapore.

East Asia includes the countries of China, North Korea, South Korea, Taiwan, and Japan. Hong Kong became part of China in 1997, and Macau joined China in 1999. (See Tables 1-1 and 1-2 for country profiles of Southeast and East Asia). East Asia also has its well-known images: in China, the Peking Man (*Homo erectus*), the Yellow and Yangtze rivers, landscape paintings, Ming porcelain, the Silk Road, ancestor worship, Daoism, Confucianism, ideographs, kowtowing, foot binding of women, the Great Wall,

Table 1-1
Population, Dominant Culture, Economy, Polity, and Biodiversity Conservation of Southeast and East Asia

Country	Capital	Area (sq.mi.)	Population (millions)	Density (/sq.mi.)	Languages
Brunei	Bandar Seri Begawan	2,226	312,000	140	Malay
Cambodia	Phnom Penh	69,898	11.3	162	Khmer
Indonesia	Jakarta	752,410	211.3	281	Bahasa, Indonesian
Laos	Viangchan (Vientiane)	91,429	5.2	57	Lao
Malaysia	Kuala Lumpur	127,320	20.6	162	Malay
Burma	Yangoon (Rangoon)	261,228	47.2	181	Burmese
Philippines	Manila	115,831	77.1	665	English
Singapore	Singapore	246	3.5	14,203	Chinese
Thailand	Bangkok	198,115	59.8	302	Thai
Vietnam	Hanoi	127,428	75.7	594	Vietnamese
China	Beijing (Peking)	3,690,045	1,234.3	334	Chinese
Japan	Tokyo	145,850	125.8	863	Japanese
North Korea	Pyongyang	46,540	24.5	527	Korean
South Korea	Seoul	38,230	46.9	1,229	Korean
Taiwan	T'aipei	13,900	21.7	1,565	Chinese, Taiwanese
United States	Washington, D.C.	3,787,425	270.1	71	English

Main Ethnic Group (%)	Main Religion (%)	Gross National Product (billions U.S.$)	Annual Income per capita (U.S.$)	Exports	Government
Malay (64)	Muslim (67)	4.6	15,917	oil, oil products, natural gas	Monarchy
Khmer (90)	Buddhist (95)	7	654	rubber, soy beans, wood	Constitutional monarchy
Javanese (45)	Muslim (87)	710.9	3,612	oil, gas, wood, rubber	Republic
Lao (50)	Buddhist (60)	5.2	1,060	electricity, wood, tin	Socialist republic
Malay (58)	Muslim	193.6	9,709	electronics, oil, wood	Federal constitutional monarchy
Burman (68)	Buddhist (89)	47	1,033	beans, teak, rice, wood	Military
Malay (96)	Catholic (83)	179.7	2,426	electronics, textiles	Republic
Chinese (78)	Taoist, Buddhist	66.1	22,762	oil, rubber, electronics	Republic
Thai (75)	Buddhist (95)	416.7	6,873	machinery, manufactures, food, raw materials	Constitutional monarchy
Kinh (87)	Buddhist	97	1,304	farm and marine products, oil	Socialist republic
Han (92)	Taoist, Buddhist	3,500	2,895	textiles, clothing, machinery	Socialist republic
Japanese (99.4)	Buddhist and Shinto (84)	2,679.2	21,304	machinery, motor vehicles, consumer electronics	Constitutional monarchy
Korean (100)	Buddhist	21.5	907	minerals, metal products, farm and fishery products	Socialist republic
Korean (100)	Christian (49), Buddhist (47)	590.7	13,115	electronic and electrical equipment, machinery	Republic
Taiwanese (84)	Buddhist, Confucian, Taoist (93)	290.5	13,458	machinery, textiles, food, wood, electronics	Republic
European (83), African (12), Asian (3), Native (1)	Protestant (56), Catholic (28), Jewish (2)	7,247.7	27,336	machinery, autos, food, manufactured products	Federal republic

Country	Conflicts (Ongoing)	Deaths	Land Area Protected (%)	Mammalian Species Total Number	Mammalian Species Threatened Number (%)
Brunei	N/A	N/A	N/A	N/A	N/A
Cambodia	1975–	3 million	16.2	123	23 (18.7)
Indonesia	1975– East Timor	> 500,000	9.7	436	128 (29.4)
Laos	N/A	N/A	N/A	172	30 (17.4)
Malaysia	N/A	N/A	4.5	286	42 (14.7)
Burma	civil war	thousands	0.3	251	31 (12.4)
Philippines	Muslim secessionist movements	N/A	4.9	153	49 (32.0)
Singapore	N/A	N/A	4.4	45	6 (13.3)
Thailand	N/A	N/A	13.1	265	34 (12.8)
Vietnam	N/A	N/A	3.1	213	38 (17.8)
China	Tiananmen massacre and aftermath of abuses of civil and political rights	N/A	6.4	394	75 (19.0)
Japan	N/A	N/A	6.8	132	29 (22.0)
North Korea	N/A	N/A	6.9	49	6 (12.2)
South Korea	N/A	N/A	2.6	N/A	N/A
Taiwan	Independence from China in dispute	N/A	N/A	N/A	N/A
United States	Civil rights	N/A	13.4	428	35 (8.2)

Note: The United States is included for comparison. Where data are not listed, they were not available (N/A) from the sources.

Source: Data extracted from *World Facts and Maps* (Chicago: Rand McNally, 1999), and World Resources Institute, United Nations Environmental Programme, UN Development Programme, and World Bank, *World Resources, 1998–99* (New York: Oxford University Press, 1998), 321, 323.

Table 1-2
Human Rights

Country	Imprisonment without Trial or after Unfair Trial	Torture	Prisons Inhumane	Executions without Trial	Disappearances
Brunei*					
Cambodia	X	X	X	X	X
Indonesia	X	X	X	X	X
Laos	X	X	X		
Malaysia*					
Burma	X	X	X	X	X
Philippines	X	X	X	X	
Singapore*					
Thailand*					
Vietnam*					
China	X	X	X	X	X
Japan*					
North Korea	X	X	X	X	X
South Korea*					
Taiwan*					
United States			X		

*Data on specific human rights violations in these countries were not available from this source.

Note: *Cambodia*: The Khmer Rouge have attacked ethnic Vietnamese villages. *Indonesia*: Genocide and ethnocide continue in East Timor. *Laos*: Official government information, coverage by news media, and independent human-rights monitors are inadequate. *Malaysia*: Members of the Dayak Iban indigenous community have been detained and badly treated over protests for their land rights. *Burma*: Hundreds have been arrested and thousands remain in prison for political reasons, while ethnic minorities continue to have their human rights abused and to be forced into labor and forcibly relocated. *Philippines*: Human-rights violations against counterinsurgents have declined, but the latter are responsible for deliberate and arbitrary killings and taking hostages. *Singapore*: At least thirty-eight members of Jehovah's Witnesses who are conscientious objectors to military service are prisoners of conscience. *Thailand*: The new constitution has strong provisions for human rights, but more than 6,000 refugees from the Karen, Mon, and Pa'o ethnic groups have been forcibly repatriated, and Burmese asylum seekers and refugees continue to be arrested for "illegal immigration" and detained under harsh conditions. *Vietnam*: Dozens of prisoners of conscience are detained for their religious beliefs. *China*: Thousands of political prisoners remain in harsh conditions. There has been a crackdown on suspected Muslim nationalists, religious

Table 1.2 (continued)

"extremists," and alleged terrorists after ethnic protests associated with many civilian deaths and injuries. There is harassment of "unapproved" Christian groups. Severe violations of human rights continue in occupied Tibet. *Japan*: Official secrecy surrounds sudden unannounced executions of several prisoners, including foreign ones. *North Korea*: This country is closed to independent human-rights monitors. The government attempted unsuccessfully to withdraw from the International Covenant on Civil and Political Rights of the United Nations, the first country ever to try. After three consecutive years of severe food shortages, more than two million people have died, including thousands of malnourished children each month. People caught stealing food have been executed. *South Korea*: Hundreds of people are political prisoners. *Taiwan*: There have been numerous violations of the human rights of military conscripts.

Source: Information on violations of civil and political rights summarized from *Amnesty International Report 1998* (London: Amnesty International Publications), where much more detail can be found, including citations for special country and issue reports.

Shanghai, the Cultural Revolution, the invasion of Tibet, and the massacre of prodemocracy demonstrators at Tiananmen Square; in Japan, Samurai warriors, Buddhist temples and Shinto shrines, tea ceremonies, sacred Mount Fuji, Hiroshima and Nagasaki, and modern electronics and automobile factories; and in the Koreas, colorful dance costumes, the Korean War and the Demilitarized Zone, and, more recently, the starvation in North Korea.

These images, some of which are deceptive, of both Southeast and East Asia (a region sometimes referred to as the Orient or Far East) hint at the tremendous cultural diversity to be found there. Representations of this cultural diversity have been greatly influenced by colonial and recent history and by the way different ethnic groups have been treated by the state and classified and studied by social scientists. In China, for example, internal political changes, including the Cultural Revolution of 1966–76, strongly influenced the way the different ethnic groups were recognized and treated by the state. Foreign research was greatly restricted in China from the 1950s to the 1970s and is still restricted in many areas today. Foreign research was also restricted in Vietnam, Cambodia, and Laos during the Vietnam War, and currently national governments severely limit opportunities to study and work with ethnic groups in Burma, North Korea, and parts of Indonesia like East Timor and Irian Jaya. The colonial history of different countries has also influenced the character of research in them, including, for example, the training of local anthropologists. Fortunately, increasing numbers of scholars from each of the Asian countries are active in research in their homeland, as is illustrated by two chapters in this volume written by local authors Hsiang-mei Cheng and Masami Iwasaki-Goodman.

In light of the vastness, diversity, complexity, and dynamism of Southeast and East Asia, this single volume can at best offer only an introduction to particular cultures and a sampling of cultural diversity in the region. Generalizations are difficult, especially when they are complicated by the political forces that inhibit research. Even ascertaining accurate population figures is difficult, given the cultural and linguistic diversity of the peoples of Southeast and East Asia, political obstacles, and the different types of census mechanisms employed. However, although this small sample of cases is only somewhat representative, when viewed collectively, it will illustrate how the cultural diversity and the people involved are endangered through varying combinations of economic, political, and environmental threats, often linked to severe human-rights violations. These case studies are offered with the faith that knowledge leads to understanding, appreciation, and tolerance for human diversity and its value and thereby contributes to harmony and peace. The characteristics and linkages between cultural diversity and identities, ecologies, spiritualities, colonialisms, conflicts and wars, and human rights and wrongs in Southeast and East Asia are discussed in the following paragraphs.

DIVERSITIES

Diversity is fundamental to evolution and adaptation, whether at the biological or the cultural level. A major general trend (megatrend) in some four billion years of biological evolution on planet Earth has been increasing diversity of beings, including species and their environments (ecosystems). A megatrend in human evolution over the last four to six million years has been increasing diversity at the cultural level. Paleontologists and other scientists recognize about five to twenty species in human biological evolution, depending on their interpretations of the fossil record. They also reveal that since the evolution of our own species (*Homo sapiens*) around 130,000 years ago, there has not been any further biological speciation in the human line. Today, while all humans are members of the same single species, culturally, they are incredibly diverse—a product of their efforts to survive and thrive in all of the world's environments. This cultural diversity evolved over a long period of time. In Southeast Asia and East Asia, for example, the evolution of human culture extends back, respectively, 1 and 0.5 million years.

While increasing diversity is a megatrend over the past four billion years of biological evolution, it is becoming increasingly apparent that loss of diversity (biological and cultural) is the new megatrend. During the last five centuries, European colonization of the Americas, Australia, and other regions of the world may have brought many positive achievements, but in other ways the world has been greatly impoverished. Many species have become extinct through depletion of natural resources, through introduced exotic species that have out-competed established ones, and through degradation or destruction of their habitats, for example, by deforestation. Likewise, under colonialism many cultures have become extinct, often through genocide (mass killing of a human population), ethnocide (profound cultural change imposed by an external contact society), ecocide (environmental degradation and destruction), or all three acting together. This reversal of the megatrends of diversification in biological and cultural levels of evolution is by far the single greatest threat to the future of humanity and planet earth and may remain so in the years to come.

IDENTITIES

In Southeast and East Asia, individuals here, as everywhere, have multiple identities: kinship, age, gender, racial ethnic, linguistic, religious, geographic, ecological, economic, political, and historical. These categories are fluid, changing through time and space, and may be recognized or imposed by the individual, the individual's group, some outside individual or group, or some combination of these. Kinship refers to extended family relations by blood and marriage; ethnicity to one's cultural identity in a multicultural or plural society; linguistic to one's primary language; geographic to residence, neighborhood, and region; ecological to the distinctive association of plant and animal species together with the landscape that characterizes the environment; economic to occupation and class; political to membership in different interest groups struggling for power and to nationality; and historical to the era or period in history.

Each individual has a distinctive combination of identities that may change through time and space. For example, the ethnic identity of a Japanese American may be interpreted differently in Hawaii, the mainland United States, Japan, or Europe. People in different parts of China have different ideas about the characteristics of being Chinese. The Han, the dominant ethnic group in China, define their character by contrast to "the other" (non-Han groups). Ultimately identities are human creations or cultural constructions, but often they are considered to be part of the essence of an individual's personality, social role, and cultural heritage.

Culture is one kind of identity. Culture provides meaning; it defines how we relate to nature and the supernatural as well as to other humans within our group and beyond. Every culture is a unique lifestyle, a socially learned, shared, and patterned system of ideas, behaviors, and their material products (artifacts). Thus humans do not live in just one biophysical world; they live in many different cultural worlds—some 6,628 distinct cultures. However, for centuries, if not longer, cultures have increasingly been coming into contact and influencing one another. Thus to some degree some individuals may be not only bilingual or multilingual, but bicultural or even multicultural.

Increasingly, transcultural phenomena such as modernization and globalization introduce and superimpose cultural traits on preexisting cultures. Examples of transcultural phenomena are material culture and technology (like flashlights, transistor radios, and motorized transport), Western medicine and the World Health Organization, Christian missionization, mass media like Hollywood movies and CNN News, the United Nations and its many development programs, and multinational business and industrial corporations.

While any culture is dynamic and may change rapidly and profoundly, individuals within society may nevertheless retain their identity as members of a particular culture. Thus unless cultures are faced by overwhelming forces, they may persist as identities for centuries or even millennia. This is not a matter of either an enduring essence or of some ephemeral cultural construction, although both may be involved in varying degrees and ways in any particular situation. In the case of an ethnic group, members may share in common a name, history, territory, society, culture, religion, and language.

Linguistic and Ethnic Diversity

Taking linguistic identity as one example, the same language may be spoken by people from different ethnic groups, or people from the same ethnic group may speak different dialects or even separate languages. Bilingualism and even multilingualism are common. The same individual may use a different dialect or language in different contexts. For example, in the city of Chiang Mai in northern Thailand, depending on the situation, the same individual may speak Standard Thai or the local Chiang Mai dialect of Thai. Some can speak English to foreigners as well.

Southeast Asian languages fall into three families: Austronesian or Malayo-Polynesian in the insular subregion; Sino-Tibetan (including Tibeto-Burman, Tai, and Sinitic subfamilies) in the mainland subregion; and Austroasiatic, Mon-Khmer, or Munda. In East Asia, beyond Chinese languages that belong to the Sinitic subfamily, Korean is remotely related at best but closer to the Ural-Altaic language family, and the Japanese language is independent of these previously mentioned families of languages. Aboriginal Taiwanese languages are classified as Austronesian.

The largest ethnolinguistic group in the world is that of the more than one billion Han, the dominant and most affluent nationality in the People's Republic of China. Most Han live in the temperate lowlands below an altitude of about 3,000 feet. Most are concentrated along major waterways for agricultural irrigation and transport, though Han can be found in towns and cities throughout Southeast Asia, working as laborers and merchants. (For example, Han are the main group of Chinese living on the island of Taiwan and in the city-state of Singapore.) As an ethnic group, the Han are the end result of many centuries of interaction between a diversity of ethnic and linguistic groups, and although they speak a common language, they exhibit many regional variations in customs, economy, and ecology.

Beyond the Han, there are some 56 "national minorities" or ethnic groups and 142 distinct languages spoken in the People's Republic of China. The "national minorities" total some 6 percent of the population of China and occupy about 60 percent of its territory. Most live in higher elevations, often in mountainous areas, and some in high plateaus. In the southwestern province of Yunnan, an area of extreme landscapes including subtropical and mountainous regions, there are at least 26 distinct ethnic groups. Many other non-Han ethnic groups overlap the borders between China and adjacent or nearby countries of Southeast Asia (Vietnam, Laos, Thailand, and Burma). For example, the Dai of southwestern Yunnan are culturally and linguistically related to the Thai of the north of Thailand, and their system of writing is similar as well.

Ethnic diversity in Southeast Asia is similarly rich, as reflected in the number of distinct languages spoken in Indonesia (672), the Philippines (167), Malaysia (146), Burma (101), and Laos (90). Even in modern Japan, which is supposed to be one of the more homogeneous societies remaining in the world today, there is significant cultural diversity, with the indigenous Ainu in the northern islands, the Okinawans in the south, remnants of the former class system (the nobility of samurai warriors, commoners, and the outcast *Burakumin* or *Eta-Hinin*), and immigrants from other countries, especially Korea, Thailand, and the Philippines (see Chapter by James Roberson).

In many parts of Southeast and East Asia, there has been a revival of ethnic consciousness, often marked by distinctive costumes, crafts, foods, and festivals. Some of this has been stimulated by new economic opportunities provided by the development of national and international tourism. In turn, tourism has stimulated the search for and construction of "authentic" ethnicities. At the same time, "traditional" customs and rituals may be converted to forms of entertainment for tourists, as in Bali, and some see this as endangering traditions. However, sometimes ethnicity is expressed as a form of resistance in response to economic and political pressures from the dominant society or state. Separatist movements have also arisen, such as the Moro Liberation Front of the Muslims in the southern Philippines. In China, ethnicity is encouraged as long as it does not threaten to promote separatism; indeed, in general, the country takes pride in its ethnic diversity. However, some ethnic groups, including Muslims, are currently under suspicion and attack by the government (see Chapters 14 and 15 by Dru Gladney and Margaret Swain).

ECOLOGIES

Another aspect of the diversity of Southeast Asia is its location at the crossroads of South Asia, East Asia, and Oceania. This is a biological crossroads, as well as a historical, economic, cultural, and religious one. In Southeast Asia, the high diversity is related to its extensive areas of tropical rain forest, numerous islands, and the juncture between various biological and cultural realms. For example, Indonesia comprises 13,677 islands and the Philippines 7,100 islands. Geographical isolation, which occurs especially on islands, is an important factor contributing to the evolution of species. Thus Indonesia is the country with the highest biological diversity, with over 20,000 species of plants, 515 of mammals, 1,519 of birds, 270 of amphibians, and 600 of reptiles. A significant number of these species are endemic; that is, they are limited in distribution to parts of Indonesia and are not found elsewhere. There is also considerable biological diversity in East Asia. China encompasses an enormous area, a variety of environments extending from coastal regions to lowlands, loess (silty) plains, high plateaus, hills, and mountains, and climates ranging from subtropical to subarctic.

In Southeast and East Asia, cultural identity is usually closely related to a particular geographic place and one or more similar ecosystems. The environment and economy as components of culture are intimately interrelated. Accordingly, in Southeast Asia, four general types of culture are generally recognized in relation to the homeland and its particular geographic features: coastal fishers and traders, lowland and valley wet-rice agriculturists, hill and mountain foragers (hunter-gatherers), and swidden horticulturalists (small communities of gardeners who cut the natural vegetation, burn the slash, and then plant their gardens in the ashes). The fishers and traders live and work along the great rivers of mainland Southeast Asia—the Irrawaddy, Salween, Chao Phraya, Mekong, and Red rivers—and China—the Huang He (Yellow River), Huai, and Hai. The river, sea, and land routes have interconnected the different regions and societies within and between China and Southeast Asia through extensive trade networks.

Numerous groups of foragers are scattered throughout the tropical forests of many countries in Southeast Asia. (See Chapter 10 on the Kubu by Gerard Persoon, Chapter 6 on the Batak by James Eder, Chapter 7 on the Batek by Kirk Endicott, and Chapter 13 on the Semai by Robert Dentan). Some anthropologists have speculated that these hunting and gathering bands may be the contemporary descendants of the earliest human societies in Southeast Asia. These peoples may still emphasize foraging for subsistence, but many also include some fishing and swidden farming as part of their economy. Many are also traders of forest products to neighboring lowlanders in return for rice, tobacco, metal tools, and other goods. Such trade networks can be ancient, extending back centuries, if not millennia. Thus these foragers have not been isolated in static cultures. Some are even political refugees displaced deeper into the forest because of resource competition and/or earlier slave raids from neighboring peoples. Increasingly they are being integrated in various ways and degrees into the regional, national, and global economies through forces such as logging and tourism that are penetrating their homelands. (Also see Chapter 2 by Richard Siddle on the Ainu of Japan.)

Horticulture, the extensive farming system of land use based on human power, tools limited to an axe and a pointed stick (dibble), minimal weeding, little or no attempt at fertilizing crops, and watering by rain with little or no irrigation, is the main form of farming in the hills and mountains of most of Asia. Swiddeners are often blamed for deforestation and pressured or even relocated by governments, and they are often manipulated as scapegoats for economic and political purposes. To make matters worse, many swiddeners live in border regions, and in some countries they are not considered citizens with the corresponding rights. However, swiddening does not cause deforestation as long as the economy is chiefly focused on subsistence rather than market production, the population size and density are low, settlements are widely spaced, and forest reserves are abundant for future gardens and fallow land. When any of these factors change, swiddening can contribute to the degradation and even destruction of the forest (see Chapter 3 by Cornelia Ann Kammerer on the Akha and Chapter 9 by Yoko Hayami and Susan Darlington on the Karen).

Agriculture, with its intensive farming based on animal power like the water buffalo pulling a wooden or steel plow, on weeding, fertilizers, and irrigation, and on emphasizing one or a few crops (monocrop), is most developed in the floodplains of Southeast and East Asia, but is also practiced through terracing in some uplands. Rice is the major Asian crop, and wet-rice paddies are the typical rural landscape of much of the lowlands. This variety of agriculture may extend back 7,000 to 8,000 years in China and Southeast Asia.

In Asia, beyond domesticated species, wild plants and animals are used for a diversity of purposes. Some 6,500 species of medicinal plants have been identified in Southeast Asia, and the Hanunoo of the southern Philippines alone use over 1,000 different plant species. As another example, the Lua of the hills and mountains of northern Thailand have 75 food crops, 21 medicinal plants, 20 ceremonial plants, and 7 plants for weaving and dyes. Such diversity reflects in part the high biological diversity of tropical forests. However, even in temperate zones, such as in East Asia, a wide variety of wild plants and animals are used in local subsistence and market economies.

Other food-production systems include traditional and Westernized subsistence and commercial fishing, using ancient as well as modern aquaculture techniques such as fish farms. Fish is the main source of quality protein in coastal, riverine, and lake zones. Tonle Sap Lake in Cambodia is a famous fishing area. The majority of the area of Southeast Asia, especially the insular subregion, is sea rather than land. The so-called sea gypsies or sea nomads, such as the Moken in the Andaman Sea off the coasts of Burma and Thailand, live on boats most of the year and focus their economy on natural resources from the sea and coasts. In Japan, whole communities have developed an economy and culture that traditionally revolved around whaling (see Chapter 5 by Masami Iwasaki-Goodman).

Some ethnic groups have developed more specialized niches in local and regional economies. The Chinese work in plantations and tin mines, farm vegetables, and work as merchants. In particular, they have developed highly sophisticated, efficient, productive, and sustainable farming systems with intensive land use in a small space, integration of diverse crops and animals including chickens, ducks, pigs, fish ponds, and water plants, irrigation, fertilization, and waste recycling. In some societies, a certain class or caste occupies a special niche. For example, in Japan, the *eta* or *burakumin* were traditionally associated with polluting activities like burying the dead and were stigmatized accordingly. As another example, in Japan, many of the prostitutes are from Korea, the Philippines, and Thailand.

The different systems of food production are correlated with tremendously different levels of population density (number of persons per square mile): foraging (less than one), swidden horticulture (a few dozen to over a hundred or so), and wet-rice agriculture (hundreds to over two thousands). The highest population densities are associated with farming on the rich soils of volcanic islands like Java in Indonesia. In cities, the population density is even higher, for example, 14,203 sq. mi. in Singapore. The higher the population density, the greater the complexity of social organization, political institutions, and other aspects of culture. Warfare among foragers is rare or absent, among swiddeners more common but little developed, among wet-rice cultivators occasional and more complex, and in states more frequent and intensive. (See Chapter 13 on the nonviolent Semai by Robert Dentan.)

Different levels of population density reflect different thresholds of human environmental impact, and trends toward increase in population increase human impact on the environment. These demographic indicators also reflect different thresholds of resource consumption, waste, and pollution. (See Table 1-1 for two indicators of environmental health: the percentages of land area protected and threatened mammalian species.)

As local natural resources are depleted, societies must extend their reach to the natural resources of other areas through trade or conquest, and states do this more than other societies. The state, or civilization, is a variety of culture that includes some combination of a centralized government, bureaucratic administration, police and military, cities, monumental architecture, writing, craft and other specialists, and social stratification (different socioeconomic classes). The earliest states in Southeast Asia began around 500–1 B.C. However, only later, starting around the eleventh century A.D., did famous cities develop, such as Borobudor in Java, Angkor Wat in Cambodia, and Pagan in Burma. They were among the societies heavily influenced by the spread of Hinduism and other aspects of culture from India.

Throughout insular Southeast Asia, the most important form of political organization was often connected with controlling trade and commerce, and the independent harbor principalities headed by chiefs, rajas, or sultans with small territories focused on river estuaries or seaports along the coasts. International commerce developed in Southeast Asia by the beginning of the Christian era and flourished from the fifteenth century onward. China was the main market until European colonialism began to change the dynamics of the political economy in the sixteenth century. For millennia, sporadic wars were fought for the control of trade routes, such as the many conflicts between Burma and Thailand in recent centuries.

It is noteworthy that rapid population growth did not begin in Southeast and East Asia until the eighteenth century or even later. For example, although estimates vary widely, the population of China in 1400, 1850, and 1997 was about 65 million, 430 million, and 1.209 million, respectively. As another case, in Thailand as late as 1825, the population was less than 1 million, whereas by 1997 it reached over 60.6 million. Population growth in Asia is likely to continue well into the next century before it stabilizes, thus putting increasing pressure on the land and resource base, on the ability of the environment to absorb waste and pollution, and on economic, social, and political institutions. For example, in Thailand, the highlanders compose only about 1 percent of the population but occupy nearly 20 percent of the national territory. Accordingly, they are destined to be under increasing pressure from lowlanders and the state in the future.

SPIRITUALITIES

While so-called modernization has contributed to the secularization of many societies, religion remains important in the lives of most Asians. It is amazing that religions have persisted for millennia under very different circumstances, yet they have obviously provided meaning and guidance in the lives of many people to this day. Religions have endured even when they have been suppressed by the state, as in China during the Cultural Revolution (1966–76). In addition, new religions have developed, and old ones have been revived and revised. For instance, Cao Dai emerged in Vietnam in the early twentieth century as a mixture of Confucianism, Daoism, Buddhism, and Christianity. In part, it was a response to French colonialism and was outlawed, although now it is an officially accepted religion in Vietnam.

In Asia, it is common for a person to follow more than one religion. For example, a Han Chinese may follow beliefs and rituals of animism (in which nature is believed to be animated by all sorts of spirits), ancestor worship with family altars, Daoism, Mahayana Buddhism, and Confucianism. A Japanese may follow Mahayana Buddhism, Shintoism, and Confucianism. In both Southeast and East Asia, animism including spirit cults is common, especially among uplanders, and ancestor worship is frequent throughout East Asia.

Islam is the main religion of Indonesia and Malaysia. However, on the Indonesian island of Java, where most people are supposed to be Muslims, orthodox Islam is mainly practiced by the merchant class, while urban bureaucrats emphasize forms of Buddhism and/or Hinduism, and animism is common among farmers and others in rural areas. Furthermore, there are enclaves of Muslims in countries that are otherwise dominated by another religion, as is the case for the Malays in southern Thailand, Cham in Cambodia, and 10 of the official fifty-five ethnic minorities in China. There are up to 30 million Muslims in China alone (see Chapter 14 by Dru Gladney).

Christianity has not been as influential in Southeast and East Asia as elsewhere, for example, Latin America. Nevertheless, today there are millions of Christians in China, Korea, Vietnam, Indonesia, and especially the Philippines. The impact of European colonialism has been more economic and political than religious in Southeast and East Asia. Nevertheless, 80 percent of Filipinos are Catholic, and in China there are more than three million Catholics and five million Protestants.

Lowlanders usually follow one of the major or dominant religions, such as Islam in much of Indonesia, Catholicism in most of the Philippines, and Theravada Buddhism throughout mainland Southeast Asia. It is mainly in Bali that Hinduism has flourished, although Hindu elements remain in the religion of many in Java, southern Sumatra, Cambodia, southern Vietnam, and Thailand. Mahayana Buddhism prevails in East Asia. The expansion of state to control the economy of peripheral areas was often linked with the spread of a major religion, such as Buddhism in Thailand. To this day, lowlanders pressure highlanders, who are usually animists, to convert to the dominant religion of the state (see Chapter 3 by Cornelia Ann Kammerer and Chapter 9 by Yoko Hayami and Susan Darlington).

Religion can promote adaptation to the environment through the influence of its beliefs, attitudes, values, and rituals toward nature, including other species. For example, in many parts of Asia there are individual trees, groves, and forests that are considered to be sacred, and thus resource exploitation may be reduced or even eliminated from these sites. In effect, sacred places in nature may serve as conservation areas that protect some species and portions of landscapes. However, in many areas, Christian missionization has threatened or even destroyed sacred places in nature because they are deemed "pagan."

Most Asian religions like Buddhism, Hinduism, Daoism, and Shintoism are environmentally friendly in principle. However, in practice, throughout Asia there is natural-resource depletion and degradation or even destruction of the environment. This discrepancy between religious ideals and environmental actions is nothing new but has been greatly intensified in recent decades with the pressures of the growth in both population and economic development. Thus one of the greatest challenges in Asia today is for individuals, communities, and nations to rediscover their cultural and religious principles in developing more sustainable and greener societies that conserve, promote, and enhance biological diversity.

COLONIALISMS

Colonialisms, successive influences of Chinese, Indians, Arabs, Europeans, Americans, and Japanese, have contributed to shaping the mosaic of diversities that make up Southeast and East Asia today. Colonialism is another force that can endanger societies and their environments, including biodiversity. Colonialism did not begin only some five centuries ago with the European age of exploration and conquest. Centuries earlier, through sailors, traders, missionaries, and others, peoples of Southeast and East Asia were influenced in various ways and to various degrees by the economies, cultures, and religions of South and Southwest Asia, including Islam, Buddhism, and Hinduism.

Early on, China profoundly influenced the rest of East Asia. For instance, the Korean peninsula has been affected by China at least since the Bronze Age. Vietnam was dominated by the Chinese for nearly a thousand years. Likewise, Japan was affected by China, and Chinese characters are still used by the Japanese in some types of writing. In Taiwan, the aboriginal population was displaced by the invading Chinese (see Chapter 4 on the Amis by Hsiang-mei Cheng).

The Philippines was affected by at least four different varieties of colonialism. The Spanish colonized the Philippines in 1571, and the Americans, in 1898, and their missionaries introduced Catholicism and Protestantism, respectively. However, in the century before the Spanish arrived, parts of the southern islands of the Philippines (Mindanao, Sulu, and Palawan) were strongly influenced by Muslim traders. To this day, there are various political and military forces in the Muslim communities (Moros) who are trying to secede from the rest of the Philippines. Finally, during World War II, the Japanese invaded and occupied parts of the Philippines.

Elsewhere in Southeast Asia, the British colonized parts of Borneo as well as Singapore, Malaysia, and Burma; the French occupied Vietnam, Cambodia, and Laos; the Portuguese, Timor; and the Dutch, Indonesia. One of the earliest attractions for trade was the variety of spices that the Dutch sought in the islands of Indonesia starting around four centuries ago. Among the countries of Southeast Asia, only Thailand (then Siam) was never directly colonized, although it was subjected to strong commercial exploitation from England and France and subsequently to political and economic influences from the United States during the Vietnam War.

During the European colonial era, Taiwan was briefly held by the Dutch and later the British. The English also occupied Hong Kong. The Portuguese established a trading colony in Macau along the south coast of China near Hong Kong. However, the Europeans were not as successful in penetrating East Asia as Southeast Asia during the colonial period; China and Japan were most successful in resisting them.

Japan has had its share of being occupier and occupied. During World War II, and in some cases even earlier, Japan occupied portions of Korea, Taiwan, and Southeast Asia. After the defeat of Japan in the war, the Americans occupied the country and transformed many aspects of Japanese society, most of all the economy and the government. In recent decades, the Japanese have been a major force in logging and deforestation throughout Southeast Asia and beyond into the Pacific islands. The Japanese have also been a major player in the whaling industry (see Chapter 5 by Masami Iwasaki-Goodman).

Economic Impact

Western colonial powers changed farming economies in Asia in at least three ways: introducing new crops from elsewhere, new plantation systems, and new farming technology. Surprisingly, the European colonization of the Americas eventually impacted local farming economies in Southeast and East Asia through the introduction of New World crops. Among the more important crops were manioc (tapioca) from the Amazon, potatoes from the Andes, and corn from Central America.

Europeans also introduced plantation agriculture. Large monocrop fields for commercial export replaced more diversified traditional subsistence farming systems and even forests in many areas of Southeast Asia. For example, the British introduced rubber-tree seeds from the Amazon into Malaysia for large-scale production around the turn of the 20th century. Other plantation crops in Southeast Asia since the eighteenth century have been sugarcane, tobacco, rubber, and palm oil. The plantations were often worked by indentured labor from elsewhere, such as Indians in Malaysia, Chinese in Indonesia, Vietnam, and Malaysia, and Javanese in Sumatra. The British developed teak-logging operations in the forests of Malaysia, Burma, and later Thailand.

In the 1960s, through the so-called Green Revolution, Westerners again transformed many farming economics throughout Asia. They introduced new genetically engineered seeds of rice and other crops dependent on large inputs of chemical fertilizers and pesticides. This revolution also magnified economic disparities between people because those with more capital could better afford the miracle seeds and necessary chemical inputs and machinery.

The countries of Southeast and East Asia have become increasingly oriented toward the world market economy, the World Bank and other development agencies, and international political organizations like the United Nations and the Association of Southeast Asian Nations (ASEAN). Nevertheless, many indigenous societies and ethnic minorities remain fairly independent and relatively isolated in marginal or frontier areas, even if they have not escaped global economic forces such as logging and tourism and political forces such as militarization. The island of Borneo is a notable example of an area that remains fairly isolated, although far from untouched by the outside (see Chapter 12 by George Appell on the Rungus).

Neocolonialism or internal colonialism continues in countries like Indonesia, Burma, Thailand, China, and Taiwan with the economic and political domination and exploitation of indigenous peoples and ethnic minorities, some of who are increasingly endangered. In recent decades, the Indonesian state, like the previous Dutch colonial regime, has relocated people from the densely populated central islands like Java to the "underpopulated" outer islands like Sumatra. This transmigration scheme changed the culture of the migrants as they adapted to the new environment and economy. It also threatened the long-term residents of the area who were invaded by the transmigrants. In the process, deforestation has accelerated. (See Chapter 10 on the Kubu by Gerard Persoon.)

CONFLICTS AND WARS

Conflicts of interest between individuals within a group and between groups is an inevitable part of being human. However, these conflicts may be resolved through either violence or nonviolence; that is, resort to violence is not automatic. Nonviolent means of conflict resolution include negotiation, mediation, and arbitration.

Conflicts of interest often arise when societies with different cultures come into contact, and especially when different groups or societies wish to exploit the same natural resources or area. Sometimes societies in the same region develop distinctive niches, using different types of environments or resources, thus eliminating or at least significantly reducing any direct competition that might lead to conflict and even violence or warfare. In other cases, some societies compete for the same resources or environments, and this is often related to population growth, which places increasing pressure on resources and environments. Most if not all state societies develop by enlarging their territory and population through military conquest and sometimes the enslavement or exploitation of the defeated enemy. Scenarios of resource competition or partitioning (niche differentiation) have been played out repeatedly in the prehistory as well as the history of Southeast and East Asia. Resource depletion, environmental degradation, and conflict and violence have reached new levels with colonialism and especially in recent decades with so-called modernization through economic development.

Conflicts and wars may arise over factors other than resources, such as the ideological conflict of the United States in the Vietnam War (1955–1975), with North Vietnam as a surrogate for Communist China and the Soviet Union. Prior to that Vietnam experienced conflict and warfare with French colonials (1946–54). Indeed, Vietnam has suffered from intermittent warfare for many centuries. China, Korea, and Japan also have a long history of feudal states and warfare.

In Cambodia, the massive genocide under Pol Pot of the Khmer Rouge from 1975 to 1978 killed about half of the six million people. Today most households and communities have an abnormal age and gender composition; most of the population are women and children because so many men were killed in warfare. It is also common to see people with limbs lost or maimed from land mines. The cultural, economic, and political recovery of Cambodia may require decades. Cambodia can be considered an endangered society.

Ethnic resistance and rebellions against the encroachment of external kingdoms and states are nothing new. For example, during the Ming dynasty in China (1368–1644), there were more than 200 tribal revolts in the Guangxi region alone. More recently, conflicts have been fought for decades by ethnic minorities for self-determination, for example, by some of the so-called hill tribes like the Karen along the border between Burma and Thailand. The Karen struggle for independence since 1949 is one of the longest by any indigenous group in Asia and is likely to continue until there is a major change in the political system (see Chapter 9 by Yoko Hayami and Susan Darlington).

The militarization of areas for security purposes can have far-reaching economic, social, and political consequences and can also endanger peoples. For instance, during the Vietnam War, the Americans saw Thailand as an ally against communism and invested there in road construction and other infrastructural development for security and defensive purposes. Through new roads, many communities that had formerly been relatively isolated suddenly had access to the national and international economic market, and vice versa. The Vietnam War generated millions of refugees, many of whom sought political asylum and resettlement in the United States and other Western countries. With assimilation into other societies, refugees may change their culture rapidly and profoundly. Also, American military personnel who were occupying South Vietnam and who went on leave in Thailand produced thousands of Amerasian children who were left behind and became outcasts (see Chapter 11 on Okinawa by James Roberson).

Demilitarization also has consequences. For example, in the Demilitarized Zone between the two Koreas, most human pressure on the land has been relieved for decades, so nature has rebounded. Now the zone is of some importance for biodiversity conservation.

Throughout Southeast and East Asia, there are tension and conflict between the highlanders and lowlanders, the former marginalized in almost every way and the latter more powerful economically, politically, and militarily. Throughout Asia, with increasing population, the need for agricultural expansion, and national security concerns, the highlanders, who usually live in border areas between countries, are often victimized through military attacks, involuntary labor, and forced relocation, as in the case of the Karen along the border between Burma and Thailand. As another example, in contemporary Vietnam, economic development in the highlands is controlled by the lowlanders, often with negative impact on highland societies and their environments.

Unfortunately, conflict, violence, and war are common denominators throughout much of Southeast and East Asia, although they vary in frequency and severity in different countries and at different times. They are likely to endanger peoples and cultures in the twenty-first century as well.

RIGHTS AND WRONGS

All cultures have ideas about what is right and what is wrong, about what people should and should not do. Murder is universally condemned, even if most societies allow for exceptional circumstances such as self-defense, blood revenge, and warfare. While human rights is a relatively recent and initially European conception, ideas about what any human deserves and never deserves, simply by virtue of being human, are very ancient and mostly widespread if not universal.

Human rights, especially civil and political rights, are a serious problem throughout Southeast and East Asia (see Table 1-2). In most cases, inadequate recognition, protection, and advancement of human rights by state governments such as in China and North Korea and the international community are the common denominators underlying the variety of threats that endanger societies.

East Timor has one of the worst records on human rights (individual chapters in this volume deal with the specifics of several other cases). The people of East Timor, a former Portuguese colony, have resisted invasion and economic and political control by the Indonesian state and military since 1974. The East Timorese have been subjected to arbitrary imprisonment, torture, mass executions, and disappearances amounting to genocide, as well as other forms of colonial state terrorism. More than 500,000 East Timorese have been murdered. But Westerners have largely ignored this tragedy in comparison to recent events in the former Yugoslavia, implying a racial bias in their humanitarian concerns. Meanwhile, the British, Americans, and others have supported Indonesia with financial and technical assistance, including military equipment and supplies, suggesting that money remains more important than morality in foreign policy.

Many of the chapters in this volume provide evidence of conflict and violence directed against diversity, especially racial, ethnic, and/or religious diversity. These violations of human rights are often linked with natural-resource depletion and competition and/or with environmental degradation and destruction such as deforestation in the tropics. However, the case studies in this volume also illustrate that the interconnections between economic, social, and environmental justice are increasingly being appreciated by individuals and organizations of many kinds and at many levels, governmental and nongovernmental, secular and religious. Indeed, this convergence in thinking and the resulting action are some of the most promising developments in the contemporary world that may help reduce the phenomena of losses of diversity and promote the welfare of humans and other beings. Indigenous peoples, ethnic minorities, and other groups are becoming better informed about human rights and are increasingly organizing politically and otherwise to defend and promote their human rights themselves. Growing numbers of concerned individuals are becoming active members of human-rights advocacy organizations (see the General Bibliography at the end of the volume), reading reports, and writing letters of protest to the embassies and consulates in the United States, and expressing their concern to representatives in the U.S. Congress and to foreign government ministries. The environmental, peace, and human-rights movements complement and support one another in many ways (see, for example, the lists of advocacy organizations and Web sites in individual chapters).

ALTERNATIVE FUTURES

Neither cultural diversity nor the endangered status of some peoples will necessarily disappear; by now it should be clear that these phenomena have existed for many thousands of years. Whether our near and distant futures are better or worse, or whether we even have any future at all, of course, involves a complex and difficult series of questions, factors, and processes. However, one thing is obvious: megatrend reversals greatly diminish the possibilities for the future. Evolution and adaptation, both biological and cultural, have always depended on the advantages offered by diversity. Whether investing financially for family security, university education, retirement, or some other purposes, it is wise for anyone to diversify their investments. It just makes common sense to not stake everything on only one resource. For the future of humankind and the biosphere of planet Earth, it makes sense, logically and evolutionarily, to develop a greater knowledge, understanding, appreciation, and respect for diversity. This respect must be based on the recognition, protection, and advancement of human rights as well as genuine consideration and reconciliation for the wrongs of the past and present. Ultimately this is a matter of respect for the dignity of every human being and for her or his cultural creativity in a world of diversity. Hopefully this volume will make some contribution, however small, toward these ends.

NOTE

Series Editor Barbara Johnston, Acquisitions Editor Wendi Schnaufer, and others on the staff at Greenwood Publishing Group, as well as Elaine Nakahashi, Secretary of the Department of Anthropology, University of Hawaii, were all most helpful in completing this book. My deep gratitude goes to them and to the contributing authors, who are internationally recognized experts on the particular groups they describe. However, it should be noted that each contributor is solely responsible for the contents of his or her chapter.

Chapter 2

The Ainu of Japan
Richard Siddle

When fishing or hunting game, the Ainu never took everything; some would be left on the snow for the foxes or hung on the branches for the crows. As a result, when one day an Ainu who had left some of his kill for the crows was carried away by a sea-spirit, the crows came to rescue him. In this way we were taught that if we left food for the birds, good things would happen in return, and so we were continuously reminded of how to interact with nature.

—Shigeru Kayano, Ainu politician, 1989

We teach our children that human language is mightier than the sharpest sword or poison arrow. We are taught—I myself was so taught—to first try our hardest to talk things out before any fighting and killing.

—Shigeru Kayano

CULTURAL OVERVIEW

The People

The Ainu are an indigenous people who now live on the island of Hokkaido in Japan, with small communities in Tokyo and other major Japanese cities. In their language, the word "Ainu" means "human being." Before colonization, their homeland also extended to the southern half of the island of Sakhalin and the Kurile Islands, now part of the Russian Federation. Archaeologists date the emergence of a distinct Ainu culture to around the thirteenth century, but it is likely that the people themselves are descended from earlier inhabitants of the region about whom little is known. The Ainu have been the object of considerable scientific interest since the late

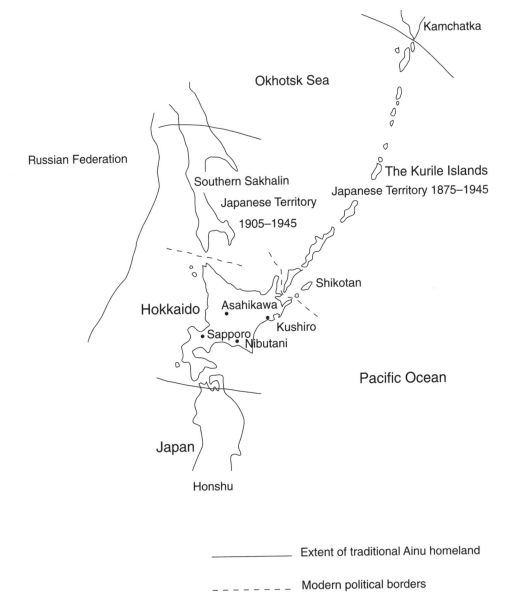

Kamchatka

Okhotsk Sea

Russian Federation

Southern Sakhalin

Japanese Territory

1905–1945

The Kurile Islands
Japanese Territory 1875–1945

Shikotan

Hokkaido   Asahikawa

Kushiro

Sapporo
Nibutani

Pacific Ocean

Japan

Honshu

_____ Extent of traditional Ainu homeland

– – – – – – – – Modern political borders

Map 2-1. Japan. Courtesy of Richard Siddle.

Figure 2-1. Souvenir postcard with stereo-
typical caption from Hokkaido, 1930s. The
Ainu elder is Benikara from the village of
Kussharo. Courtesy of Richard Siddle.

nineteenth century because although they have cultural similarities with
other hunting peoples of maritime Siberia, in physical appearance and language they differ sharply from all surrounding groups. Early scientists, ob-
sessed with classifying the "races" of the world, took the rounded eyes and
heavy beards of Ainu men as evidence of "a lost white race," and references
to "Caucasians" still appear in much present-day literature on the Ainu.
Such "scientific" classifications are now obsolete, and the origins of the
Ainu remain unclear. The activities of Western and Japanese anthropologists, however, have contributed toward stereotyped images of the Ainu as
a backward "vanishing race" (Figure 2-1) and have included the widespread desecration of Ainu ancestral gravesites in the name of science.

From the earliest times, the Ainu had trading links with both the Siberian
peoples to the north and the Japanese to the south, but it was contact with
Japanese traders and feudal officials that was to exert the major influence
on Ainu history. Traders were at the forefront of Japanese expansion into

the region and from the seventeenth century began to construct trading posts and fishing stations along the coasts, where many Ainu were drawn into an unequal relationship that, in the worst cases, bordered on slavery. Major armed conflicts occurred in 1457, 1669, and 1789. When Russia expanded into the region beginning in the late eighteenth century, the Ainu became pawns trapped between two imperial powers. A treaty between Japan and Russia in 1855 placed the Ainu homeland within Japanese borders, and colonization began in earnest after 1869. Ainu lifeways were destroyed as the game and fish they depended on were drastically depleted and land was parceled out as farms for immigrants. A policy of assimilation was pursued by the Japanese authorities, who enacted a Protection Act in 1899 and set up a system of "native education."

The Setting

Hokkaido and the other islands of maritime Siberia form a different climatic and ecological zone from the rest of Japan. Although winters are long and harsh, the area is well endowed with resources. Before colonization, Hokkaido possessed rich herring and salmon fisheries and plentiful herds of deer. With large-scale immigration, the forests have been cleared for agricultural use or have been heavily logged, while the herring fishery has been severely overexploited. Hokkaido is now an important agricultural region and tourist destination.

Traditional Subsistence Strategies

Salmon, deer, and edible plants were the staple foods of the Hokkaido Ainu, while the populations in Sakhalin and the Kuriles also hunted seals and other sea mammals. In isolated and self-sufficient Ainu communities, the year revolved around these different seasonal subsistence activities. Men speared salmon in the autumn and hunted for deer and other animals with poisoned bow traps, while women gathered, processed, and in later times cultivated plants. Bear hunting was an important ritual activity for men. (A bow trap was an important hunting tool consisting of a fixed crossbow with a trigger arrangement connected to a tripwire. Game comes along, hits the tripwire and is impaled by a poison-tipped arrow fired from the bow.) Care was taken not to deplete resources; salmon, for instance, were only taken in large numbers for preservation after they had spawned. Ainu women wove cloth from tree bark or nettle fibers and made it into clothing, while men carved hunting weapons or household utensils from wood. As trade increased, the Ainu diet became supplemented by rice, a major trade commodity, and iron implements were also obtained. In return, the Ainu expanded their hunting and fishing activities to provide a surplus for trade or later worked for rations under Japanese contractors at the fishing stations.

Social and Political Organization

Ainu communities underwent many changes as a result of contact with the Japanese. Japanese historical sources indicate that between the fifteenth and eighteenth centuries, powerful Ainu leaders were able to control communities across regions and engage in warfare among themselves and against the Japanese traders. Trade goods, in particular lacquered vessels and swords, became prized assets of wealth and status. Oral literature also hints at a stratified society. As Japanese power increased, however, these regional leaders were toppled, and Ainu society fragmented into small inland communities and those around the coastal fishing stations. The leader of each community was an elder respected for his authority and eloquence. Individual or intervillage disputes were settled by *charanke*, an often-lengthy process of discussion and debate in which the losers were usually required to offer compensation. With the transition to a modern industrialized society, Ainu social and political movements began to emerge in the 1920s. The first organization for all Ainu in Hokkaido was formed in 1930 and provided an important forum in which Ainu leaders from scattered communities could unite. Present-day Ainu have maintained their regional affiliations, while effective leadership is in the hands of the officials of the Hokkaido Utari Kyokai (the Ainu Association of Hokkaido), a quasi-governmental organization that oversees welfare policies while campaigning for human and cultural rights. In 1984, Ainu demands were formally spelled out when the association adopted a draft resolution for new legislation to replace the 1899 Protection Act. The so-called Ainu New Law called for basic human rights; the right to guaranteed political participation; rights to education and culture; economic measures to help Ainu farmers, fishermen, and small businessmen; a Fund for Self-Reliance to be administered by the Ainu themselves; and the establishment of consultative bodies at national and local levels. Despite the general consensus among Ainu over the aims of the New Law, the authority of the Ainu Association has occasionally been challenged by more radical activist groups uncomfortable with its links to the authorities.

Religion and World View

Religion entered into every aspect of the life of the Ainu people. Gods were believed to inhabit every living thing and inanimate object, even human-made utensils, so virtually every activity involved an interaction with the gods. Gods caused both good and evil happenings and had to be interceded with by individuals or communities. When Ainu men were hunting, for instance, they would recite prayers and conduct ceremonies to "send off" the spirits of animals just killed back to the land of the gods, where they would report on the courteous behavior of the Ainu and be eager to "visit" them again. This belief reached its ultimate expression in the *iyomante* or bear ceremony, in which the elders of a village "sent back" a specially reared bear cub along with much dancing and feasting. Men led the organized ceremonial activity, although there were some women who acted as healers. A rich oral literature grew up that took the adventures of gods as its theme, while other literary forms included long epic poems (*yukar*) with Ainu heroes and more everyday folktales (*wepeker*) that served to pass on the accumulated wisdom and world view of the elders. Oral epics and tales were recited by both men and women.

THREATS TO SURVIVAL

> The Ainu were robbed of their land, forests, and seas. Taking deer or salmon became poaching, and collecting firewood was deemed theft. On the other hand, Japanese immigrants flooded into the land, destructive development began, and the very survival of the Ainu people was threatened.
> —Ainu New Law, 1984

> The tendency to hide the fact that one is Ainu and try hard to assimilate to Japanese is certainly strong. But is it right that even while with our mouths we say that we have not experienced discrimination, we should spend our whole lives increasingly conscious of the Ainu blood that flows in our bodies? I know far too many examples around here of the dangers of trying to assimilate at any cost. There are women who think that as long as a man is from the mainland, anyone will do if only Ainu blood can be diluted, so they produce illegitimate offspring with the laborers who drift into Hokkaido.
> —Matsutaro Kaizawa, Ainu from Biratori, 1972

Demographic Trends

Although introduced diseases caused great tragedy in Ainu communities from the nineteenth century on, the Ainu population has remained around 15,000 to 25,000 for most of the time records have been available. Increasing intermarriage since 1945 has led many to assert (despite the racist social Darwinism implicit in such characterizations) that "pure Ainu" or "full-blooded Ainu" no longer exist. Such views provided a convenient justification for removing the Ainu from the agenda of social issues. On the other hand, the lack of a clear legal definition of Ainu status and social pressure to hide Ainu ancestry mean that the current Ainu population can only be estimated. Around 15,000 people belong to the Ainu Association. Informal criteria were used to include others to give an official figure for Hokkaido Ainu of 23,830 in 1993. Around 700 Ainu reside in metropolitan Tokyo, and there are others in surrounding areas and other major cities. Ainu activists, on the other hand, claim that there are many more "Ainu" hiding their ancestry out of fear of discrimination; figures of 50,000 to a wildly inflated 300,000 are often cited. But can people, regardless of ancestry, who refuse to identify as Ainu be counted as such? One fear is that if self-identification is made the legal basis for Ainu status, the Ainu population might actually fall sharply.

Current Events and Conditions

Although the situation of the Ainu people has improved considerably since the 1970s, they remain an impoverished and marginalized population within a highly affluent Japanese society. Surveys conducted in Hokkaido since the 1960s show that Ainu are generally poorer than their neighbors and are disproportionally concentrated in farming, fishing, and tourism. Levels of alcoholism and divorce, often exacerbated by economic stress, remain high. Their rate of educational advancement is lower (though it is improving), while reliance on welfare remains over double that of other Hokkaido residents.

The current situation of the Ainu people is a direct consequence of the colonization and settlement of their homeland by the Japanese state. Inaugurated with the establishment of the Kaitakushi (Colonization Commission) in 1869 and the nationalization of land in 1872, mass immigration and land clearance from the 1890s on turned Hokkaido into a major agricultural region of Japan by the early twentieth century while displacing its original inhabitants. The Ainu were overwhelmed; by the end of the nineteenth century they accounted for only 2 percent of the population of Hokkaido. The loss of their hunting and fishing territories and the game and fish themselves, which were severely overexploited by Japanese commercial interests, had drastic consequences for Ainu communities. Social disintegration and alcoholism became commonplace and led to a perception of an "Ainu problem." Although the Ainu were legally Japanese citizens after 1871, Japanese officials regarded them as a "savage" and "dying race," taking their cue from colonial ideas elsewhere. Even before the Protection Act of 1899, Ainu were relocated, sometimes forcibly, to reservationlike "native villages" where they were granted small plots of land. Most could not become farmers and drifted into vicious cycles of alcoholism and poverty.

Suffering from prejudice and discrimination and under pressure to assimilate, most Ainu adopted the Japanese language and customs. Assimilation was encouraged between 1899 and 1937 through a system of "native education" that aimed to turn the Ainu into loyal and useful subjects of the Japanese Empire. After Japan's defeat in 1945, survivors of the Sakhalin and Kurile Ainu were deported by the Russians to Hokkaido along with

Figure 2-2. Ainu from Shiraoi pose for the camera with a Japanese anthropologist during the making of a film on traditional cultures, 1960s. Courtesy of Richard Siddle.

Japanese settlers. With the rapid transformation of Japan into an industrialized economy after defeat in 1945, Ainu culture in its "traditional" form appeared to be almost extinguished by the 1960s and to be lingering on only in tourist attractions (Figure 2-2). But despite the eagerness of scholars and officials to pronounce it dead, Ainu culture is now experiencing a powerful regeneration and reinterpretation.

Nevertheless, the pressures to assimilate have meant that most Ainu in Hokkaido today live a daily life indistinguishable on the surface from that of their rural Japanese counterparts. The Ainu language is spoken now only on ceremonial occasions by some elders who themselves speak Japanese in everyday life. Others have migrated to the large cities in "mainland" Japan, where they find work as laborers. Until recently most Ainu have attempted to "pass" and live their lives as ordinary Japanese to avoid prejudice and discrimination at school, at work, and in marriage, although this has often not been possible in small rural communities where family ancestry is common knowledge. Generally speaking, any fraction of Ainu ancestry is enough for an individual to be labeled an "Ainu." On the other hand, common acceptance in wider society of the idea of Japan as a homogeneous society having "no racial minorities" (as Prime Minister Yasuhiro Nakasone put it in 1986) has made it difficult for Ainu to find a positive self-identification as members of an acknowledged and valued ethnic group.

Until 1991, in fact, the government did not even recognize the existence of the Ainu as a separate ethnic group. Despite the gains made in recent years, many nonactivist individuals prefer not to identify themselves as Ainu in everyday life and express little interest in Ainu culture. The increase in recent decades in social mobility and a lessening in overt discrimination have led to further intermarriage, so that even among those who identify as Ainu and are married, around 90 percent have a non-Ainu partner. As their children grow up and enjoy the increased opportunities for education and travel that were denied to older generations of Ainu, how they will identify themselves is of serious concern to those involved in the maintenance and transmission of Ainu culture and identity.

Sociocultural Crisis

The situation of the Ainu is not one of a "traditional" culture facing threats to extinction. There are no isolated or shrinking enclaves of Ainu stubbornly persisting in hunting and gathering. In fact, Ainu culture has never really existed in total isolation and has been influenced at various times by contacts with the Japanese. Modern Ainu share their ancestral homeland with around five million descendants of Japanese immigrants. The modernization and industrialization that have made Japan so successful have ensured that the "traditional" lifestyle of the Ainu has been destroyed as thoroughly as the "traditional" lifeways of their Japanese neighbors.

This does not mean, however, that Ainu culture is extinct. Despite the assimilation policy, many Ainu do not feel "Japanese" and seek the expression of their difference through a reinterpretation of their cultural heritage into a form suitable for the contemporary age. In fact, with the enactment in 1997 of the Ainu Cultural Promotion Law, Ainu culture is probably more vital now than at any time since the end of World War II. Now that the existence of Ainu culture has finally been recognized by the Japanese government and its survival in some form has been guaranteed in law, the main issue facing the Ainu people is just what form the Ainu culture of the twenty-first century will take. Will Ainu regain control over their material culture and ancestral remains that Japanese scholars have collected and stored in museums and laboratories? Will "Ainu culture" be limited to sterile reproductions of "traditional" dances, crafts, or ceremonies, divorced from their original contexts and with their creative spontaneity extinguished? What will happen when the elders of today, who provide an important continuity as they remember the "old ways" and speak the language, are no longer alive? Or can older forms and ceremonies be reinterpreted for the needs of the modern age to become occasions to celebrate identity and heritage?

To a certain extent, this redefinition of Ainu culture is already occurring

Figure 2-3. Ainu celebrate the Ceremony to Welcome the New Salmon in Sapporo, 1992. Courtesy of Richard Siddle.

through festivals like the annual Ceremony to Welcome the New Salmon (Figure 2-3), originally celebrated by every community but now held on the banks of the Toyohira River in Sapporo every autumn and attended by Ainu from all over Hokkaido. Many Ainu in local communities are also rediscovering their cultural roots in this way. Much work is also being done on the Ainu language and the transcription and translation into Japanese of the thousands of recorded hours of marvellous oral epics so that they can be enjoyed by modern Ainu or other readers. But the government funds now available for Ainu cultural promotion are in danger of falling under the control of certain powerful individuals who would then be in a position to dictate their agenda of "Ainu culture." Will such funds, for instance, be available for the successful Ainu ethnojazz band Moshiri or the creative efforts of the Yukara-za troupe that combines old Ainu tales and dances with influences from ballet, modern dance, and music? The debate on the future of Ainu culture has entered a new phase.

RESPONSE: STRUGGLES TO SURVIVE CULTURALLY

The yellow race, the white race, the black race, and the Ainu are all equal before God. We have no need to despise ourselves. Despising ourselves is taboo for us. Rather, we must come to have pride in ourselves as Ainu.
—Contributor to journal of the Ainu Association, 1930

We are now editing our history, claiming our rights, understanding our identity, beginning to walk for ourselves.
—Tokuhei Narita, Ainu activist, 1984

The current recognition of Ainu identity and culture is not the result of a natural tolerance in Japanese society. On the contrary, Ainu activists have been engaged since the 1960s in a struggle against society and the state for recognition and justice that is just now beginning to bear fruit.

Organized Ainu activity dates back to the 1920s. Under the patronage of a British missionary, John Batchelor, some young Ainu received a decent education and formed a small group dedicated to working toward the "improvement" of their people. Given their Christian beliefs and idealism, in practical terms this resulted in a movement that concentrated on "self-help" and the promotion of assimilation. Education, the adoption of the Japanese language and customs, and the eradication of alcoholism were seen as the keys to bettering the situation of the Ainu. The more they proved themselves loyal subjects of the emperor, they reasoned, the more discrimination would fade away and equality be achieved. This, of course, meant the abandonment of the Ainu language and culture, but the leaders of the movement saw this as the only practical way forward, especially after Japan moved toward militarism in the 1930s. However, they remained proud of their heritage. The Ainu Association was formed in 1930 with the assistance of the Social Welfare Section of the Hokkaido government to campaign for an end to "native education" and an improvement in the land situation (many Ainu had lost control of the land granted to them under the 1899 Protection Act). Despite these links to the authorities, the association played an important role in bringing together Ainu leaders from otherwise isolated rural communities.

This orientation toward assimilation continued after Japan's defeat in 1945 as the movement reorganized itself under the same leaders. But tensions began to grow in Ainu communities as Ainu remained stigmatized and despised however Japanized they appeared on the surface, and poverty increased as the rest of Japanese society enjoyed the benefits of high economic growth. In the 1960s, radical social movements in Japanese society influenced young Ainu activists to inaugurate a new kind of Ainu movement.

Initially fragmented into small groups and with a variety of ideologies borrowed from left-wing radicals, the new breed of Ainu activist took direct aim at the structures of state and society that contributed to their marginalization: the activities of scholars, popular stereotypes and prejudice, and the comfortable links of conservative Ainu to the authorities. Scholars were denounced, sued, and forced to apologize. The return of ancestral remains was demanded. Publishers and broadcasters who produced discriminatory material were forced to withdraw it and apologize. Tensions increased even further when a group of Japanese urban terrorists adopted the Ainu cause and set off bombs at a variety of targets between 1972 and 1976, causing destruction and deaths. The response of the state was to attempt to defuse Ainu anger by implementing a special welfare policy for the Ainu in 1974, administered through the Ainu Association of Hokkaido.

As the movement entered the 1980s, the initial anger was complemented by a wider consensus as to where the movement was heading. Political involvement had led many alienated young Ainu to go back to their cultural roots despite not having been brought up in Ainu ways. Younger Ainu began reviving ceremonies or creating new ones with help from the knowledge of sympathetic elders. Ainu intellectuals challenged the dominant views of the history of "development" in Hokkaido that had relegated them to a footnote. Contacts with indigenous peoples in North America, Alaska, and Australia had contributed to a growing awareness of the Ainu as an indigenous people and the worldwide movement for indigenous rights. The rhetoric of class struggle evident in the 1970s became more muted as Ainu united around their identity in what was now a clearly ethnic movement. The formerly assimilationist Ainu Association of Hokkaido, still the main channel for bargaining between Ainu and the state, adopted in 1984 a draft New Law for the Ainu People that demanded the abolition of "racial prejudice" and guaranteed "ethnic rights" to maintain and transmit Ainu language and culture. The adoption of this New Law became the main Ainu demand for the next decade. Activism was further stimulated by the remarks in 1986 of Prime Minister Nakasone, also widely publicized in the United States and elsewhere, to the effect that Japan was an educationally superior society due to the "absence of racial minorities."

The Ainu Association carried the campaign to the United Nations in 1987, participating in this and every subsequent year in the United Nations Working Group on Indigenous Populations. Having denied the existence of minorities in Japan in a report to the United Nations in 1980, the Japanese government finally admitted in December 1991 that the Ainu were a minority under the terms of Article 27 of the International Covenant of Civil and Political Rights, ratified by Japan in 1979. The government remained reluctant, however, to recognize the Ainu as an indigenous people. The authorities cited the lack of a clear legal definition of "indigenous peoples," but another reason was that this could weaken Japan's claim to certain northern islands taken by Russia in 1945.

With the realignment of Japanese politics in the early 1990s, further progress was made on consideration of the New Law after consultations had been stalled under the previous conservative administration. In early 1997, a court decision on a case involving two Ainu opposed to the construction of a dam on Ainu sacred sites stated for the first time in a legal context that the Ainu were an "indigenous people." It seemed as though the official recognition as an indigenous people that Ainu leaders had been campaigning for was finally about to be conceded. In this mood of optimism, the Ainu Association supported a government proposal to finally scrap the 1899 Protection Act—another key Ainu demand—and enact new legislation. But the Cultural Promotion Law of July 1997 was a great disappointment to many Ainu activists. Drafted by bureaucrats with no Ainu input, the legislation contains no reference to self-determination or any of the "indigenous rights" and "land rights" demanded by activists and instead only provides money for cultural activities. The special Ainu welfare policies are also being continued.

Although Ainu politics has perhaps missed an opportunity, in terms of cultural survival much has been gained. It is now up to the Ainu themselves to define the boundaries of their community—who is or is not an Ainu—and determine just what is to constitute Ainu culture in the postindustrial Japan of the twenty-first century.

FOOD FOR THOUGHT

Cultural survival perhaps has a different meaning for the Ainu than for more "traditional" peoples still fighting encroachment on their ancestral lands. The colonization process has already been completed, and the Ainu and their homeland have been incorporated into a modern industrialized economy. Recovery of an autonomous homeland is not a realistic option. A century of pressure to assimilate has ensured the loss of traditional Ainu culture and, perhaps soon, their language as a living medium of communication. But many Ainu have reacted to their continued marginalization and the refusal of the majority to accept them as fully "Japanese" by rediscovering and reinterpreting their culture as a means to express their difference and pride. Others, however, prefer to live and raise their children as Japanese.

Questions

1. Does the historical experience of the Ainu parallel that of other indigenous peoples?
2. Are the Ainu a "vanishing people," as an American anthropologist once described them?
3. How relevant is ancestry when determining Ainu identity?
4. Should modern Ainu be any more or less "traditional" than their Japanese neighbors?
5. Can Ainu culture adapt to conditions in postindustrial Japan in the twenty-first century and yet retain a distinctive identity?

RESOURCE GUIDE

Published Literature

Loos, Noel, and Takeshi Osanai, eds. *Indigenous Minorities and Education: Australian and Japanese Perspectives of Their Indigenous Peoples, the Ainu, Aborigines, and Torres Strait Islanders.* Tokyo: Sanyusha, 1993.

Siddle, Richard. *Race, Resistance, and the Ainu of Japan.* New York: Routledge, 1996.

Sjöberg, Katerina. *The Return of the Ainu: Cultural Mobilization and the Practice of Ethnicity in Japan.* Chur, Switzerland: Harwood Academic Publishers, 1993.

Takakura, Shinichiro. *The Ainu of Northern Japan: A Study in Conquest and Acculturation.* Trans. J. Harrison. Transactions of the American Philosophical Society, n.s. 50, pt. 4. Philadelphia: American Philosophical Society, 1960.

Watanabe, Hiroshi. *The Ainu Ecosystem.* Seattle: University of Washington Press, 1973.

Video

The Way Forward: The Ainu, Indigenous People of Japan. English-language video produced by the Hokkaido Utari Kyokai (Ainu Association of Hokkaido).

Organizations

The Ainu Association of Hokkaido

Kita 2, Nishi 7

Chuo-ku

Sapporo 060-0001, Japan

Ainu Culture Centre

Urban Square Yaesu 3F

Yaesu 2-4-13

Chuo-ku

Tokyo 104-0028, Japan

Hokkaido Ainu Culture Research Centre and

The Foundation for the Research and Promotion of Ainu Culture

Presto 1-7, Kita 1, Nishi 7

Chuo-ku

Sapporo 060-0001, Japan

Chapter 3

The Akha of the Southwest China Borderlands

Cornelia Ann Kammerer

Akha people carry Akha customs.

—Common Akha saying

CULTURAL OVERVIEW

The People

The Akha are an indigenous or tribal people of southwest China and mainland Southeast Asia.[1] They live in the contemporary nation-states of the People's Republic of China, Burma (officially known as Myanmar), Vietnam, Laos, and Thailand. Their northernmost home is China, which they and scholars believe to be their traditional homeland. Among Akha in Burma and Thailand, about whom the most scholarly research has been done, their oral tradition tells of crossing many rivers as they migrated southward from China. Akha arrived in what is now Thailand, their southernmost home, in the first decade of the twentieth century.

They call themselves *Akha za*, meaning "Akha people," and believe themselves to be the descendants of Sm-mi-o, the first man, who was himself the descendant of nine generations of spirits. Thus Akha believe that all members of their ethnic group are kin. When Akha meet for the first time, they inquire about one another's kinship group, asking, "What lineage are you?" Besides kinship, Akha traditionally define themselves as a people in terms of their allegiance to their customs.

The Akha language is tonal and belongs to the Tibeto-Burman language family. Although Akha did not develop a written language of their own, Christian missionaries and academic scholars have developed various meth-

37

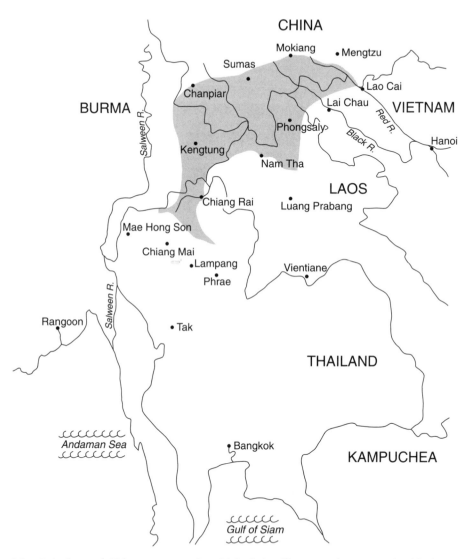

Map 3-1. Area of Akha occupancy in which their villages are interspersed with those of other hill people. Courtesy of Cornelia Ann Kammerer.

ods of writing their language during the second half of the twentieth century. These methods are based on either the Roman alphabet used in English or the Thai alphabet derived from Sanskrit of India. Both Catholic and Protestant missionaries in Burma and Thailand have printed books of Christian hymns and texts in the Akha language, including a translation of the Bible's New Testament.

In the various countries in which Akha live, their non-Akha neighbors have their own names for them. Speakers of Tai languages in China, Burma, Laos, and Thailand call them Ekaw (Ikaw), Kaw, and Kha ("slave"), all of which Akha consider insulting. In China, the Chinese officially classify Akha along with other related peoples as belonging to the Hani national minority.

Census data are few and unreliable, but experts estimate that there are between 400,000 and 500,000 Akha: 150,000 in China, 180,000 in Burma, 59,000 in Laos, 12,000 in Vietnam, and 33,000 in Thailand. While Akha traditionally live in the mountains, they have been migrating to lowland cities in search of wage labor and education in the national language since the 1950s. In the early 1990s, there were over 300 Akha living in Chiang Mai, the largest city in northern Thailand.

The Setting

The landscape of mainland Southeast Asia is dominated by mountains and large lowland river valleys or plains. Broadly speaking, the peoples of the region are categorized as either hill people, also known as hill tribes, who practice dry-rice farming dependent on rainfall, and valley or lowland people, who practice wet-rice farming dependent on irrigation. The valley people, such as Chinese, Burmese, Lao, Vietnamese, and Thai, are the region's national majorities, while the hill people, such as the Akha, are minorities in every nation in which they live.

Akha build their villages at an altitude of about 3,000 feet (Figure 3-1), neither at the tops of the hills, the preferred dwelling place of some other hill tribes such as the Hmong (called Meo or Miao by outsiders), nor in the small river valleys within the hills, where irrigated rice can be grown. Traditionally, their villages are interspersed with those of other ethnic groups. In the highlands, their neighbors are other hill-tribe minorities, while in the small river valleys below their villages, their neighbors are often Tai-speaking Buddhists.

Traditional Subsistence Strategies

In their dry-rice agriculture, Akha follow a method called slash-and-burn, or swidden, cultivation. Farmers cut down the forest, burn off the logs, and plant in the soil nourished by the ash from the burning. After planting

Figure 3-1. Akha village in the hills of northern Thailand, 1987. Courtesy of Cornelia Ann Kammerer.

a field for three to five years, they then abandon it and allow the forest to grow up again (this is called leaving the field fallow).

Rice is the key crop both economically and religiously. Akha do not ask "Have you eaten yet?" but "Have you eaten rice yet?" Rice is the centerpiece of every meal. Vegetables, including cucumbers, greens, and beans, are grown in the same field as rice, while corn, soybeans, and cotton are grown in separate fields. Corn is predominantly food for pigs and other livestock, while rice husks are fed to chickens. Meat is typically eaten at weddings and other feasts rather than daily.

Although their economy is traditionally focused on subsistence, Akha have long been involved in cash cropping and trade with hill people and lowlanders. For centuries, hill people have depended on trade with outsiders for the necessities of salt for their diet and iron for making tools. In the nineteenth century, opium and cotton were the main cash crops. In the twentieth century, Akha in Thailand have sold recently introduced crops such as cabbages and tomatoes. Today, as in the past, they also sell forest products such as charcoal. From the forest, Akha gather wild fruits, mushrooms, and other edible plants for food.

Hunting is traditionally an important male activity. Indeed, in rituals a man is symbolized by a miniature crossbow, while a spindle for making thread symbolized a woman. Nowadays guns have replaced crossbows for use in hunting, though not in ritual. Largely because of deforestation, wild pigs, deer, bamboo rats, and other game are not as plentiful as in the past. Akha fish using both traps and nets in the streams and rivers of the narrow valleys within the hills.

Social and Political Organization

Akha kinship follows the male line, with sons and daughters officially joining their father's lineage at a birth ritual. At marriage, a woman joins her husband at his father's household. Villages are founded and headed by a ritual and political leader who is responsible for initiating the first in the cycle of yearly rice rituals and heading the annual community ceremonies. He also has a judicial role, leading male household heads in reaching a decision in any court case, for example, about a charge of adultery. Other traditional leaders are the village blacksmith, who makes knives used to sacrifice animals in religious rites as well as farming tools, and the ritual specialist, who has memorized the many religious chants of Akha customs. These include the three nights of chants recited at the funeral of a respected elder survived by at least one son.

The kinship system serves a political function by uniting all Akha as descendants of the first man. There is, however, no traditional political organization above the level of the village. In the past, Akha villages were sometimes considered part of the region's traditional princely states such as the kingdom of Siam (now Thailand), and, in the present, they are part of modern nation-states. In each Akha village in Thailand, those who are citizens elect a headman who is part of the national governmental system.

Religion and World View

Akha traditionally define themselves as "carrying Akha customs," the religious and cultural traditions given to them "long ago by the Creator" and handed down from their ancestors generation by generation. Their customs are a set of rules for proper behavior and correct religious practices. Akha respect their customs but also lament that "they are many" and "difficult." Their customs are indeed intricate and demanding, stipulating such things as how to carry a dog (by the scruff of the neck), what time of year to marry (between December and April), and who can offer food to ancestors at annual offerings (any male in the household, however young, and old women, but only those few who have undergone an elaborate and expensive initiation ceremony celebrating their success in bearing at least one son).

Each ritually independent household has an altar at which numerous yearly ancestor offerings are performed. Interwoven in the annual ritual calendar are ancestor offerings, rice rituals, and community ceremonies such as the renewal of the village gates. Ancestor offerings and community rituals are associated with men, while rice rituals are associated with women, who have the honor of beginning to eat first at these feasts. The complementarity of men and women is central to the traditional Akha religious and cosmological system. The Akha year is divided into two gendered seasons: the dry season (September to April), linked to men and hunting, and the rainy season (May to August), linked to women and rice. The house also has two gendered sections: the room for men, where hunting rituals take place, and the room for women, where ancestor offerings, which are associated with rice and rice rituals, are performed. Since the 1920s, many Akha have converted to Christianity, abandoning their own ancestral and agricultural rites.

THREATS TO SURVIVAL

> Akha are not willing to accept development.
> —Thai government official, northern Thailand, 1986

> I have become stupid from the pesticide I sprayed on cabbages.
> —Former Akha farmer now working in Chiang Mai City, northern Thailand, 1987

> The people increase, but the land gets smaller.
> —Akha farmer, northern Thailand, 1993

Contemporary Context and Demographic Trends

Overall, the current situation of Akha depends heavily on the political-economic context in which they live. The governments of the People's Republic of China, the Lao People's Democratic Republic, and the Socialist Republic of Vietnam are Marxist in orientation. Since Lenin first formulated a minority policy in Russia, autonomous zones for minorities have been set up by socialist states. In the People's Republic of China, there are autonomous zones, yet the existence of such zones does not insulate Akha and other tribal peoples from prejudice and misunderstanding on the part of the dominant majority. In socialist Laos and Vietnam as well as in democratic Thailand, governments have at various times resettled highlanders to the lowlands, motivated in part by the aim of curbing slash-and-burn agriculture.

Historically, in southwest China and mainland Southeast Asia, Akha and other hill peoples have been in contact with lowland states for centuries. The nature and intensity of that contact, however, changed dramatically in the twentieth century. In the past, Akha and others were basically left to themselves, though they were occasionally called on to provide forest products or labor. Since the 1950s, state penetration has had a major impact on Akha and their lifeways in all the countries in which they live.

Until the 1990s, the overall Akha population was not threatened by decrease or extinction. From the mid-1960s to 1990, the number of Akha in Thailand doubled, but not all of this increase was due to natural population growth. Instead, some was accounted for by Akha who fled to Thailand from Burma, where they are threatened both physically and economically due to ongoing warfare and the near collapse of all but the black-market economy. In the 1990s in Thailand and elsewhere, the AIDS epidemic has threatened Akha, although the extent of this threat is not yet known. Some observers suggest that HIV/AIDS among Akha will eventually lead to a decrease in population.

Prejudice and Violence

The key to understanding the situation of Akha throughout the region is awareness of the prejudice that many members of national majorities feel toward them and other hill-tribe minorities. Tribal minorities, including the Akha, are seen as backward, in part because they live in remote areas considered unsafe and undesirable by many members of national majorities. Traditional Thai ethnic identity and traditional Akha ethnic identity are both framed in terms of religion: "To be Thai is to be Buddhist" and to be Akha is to "carry Akha customs." It is therefore ironic that many Thais look down on Akha and other hill tribes as "people who have no religion" because Thais do not consider the animism, ancestral, and agricultural rituals of Akha as true religion. Many Thais view Akha as the most "primitive" of the hill tribes. Why this is so is difficult to explain. It may be related to Thai perceptions of traditional Akha style of dress and their insularity from lowland society. Akha women's dress (Figure 3-2)—short skirts, small bodices, and sometimes bare breasts—is considered improper by contemporary Thai standards of decorum, despite the fact that many northern Thai women went bare breasted in the nineteenth century. Akha have historically withdrawn from contact with lowlanders and lowland states, preferring to follow their customs in their gated villages.

Given the existence of prejudice, government policies throughout the region are frequently not based on a correct and complete understanding of Akha customs and lifeways. Despite the fact that when dry-rice agriculture is practiced correctly, it does not destroy the environment—the forest is, after all, allowed to grow back after use—policymakers tend to see it as

Figure 3-2. Older relative helps a teenager
don a woman's belt for the first time, 1981.
Courtesy of Cornelia Ann Kammerer.

causing deforestation, soil erosion, and flooding. Akha and other hill tribes
have therefore been depicted in democratic Thailand as well as in socialist
Vietnam as destroyers of the natural environment.

Another common misconception among the region's national majorities
is that Akha and other hill tribes are "nomadic." While Akha and others
do move their villages and fields in response to calamities such as illnesses
and in search of new lands to farm, they are not nomadic: the first Akha
village founded in Thailand in approximately 1906 is still an Akha village
today. To view them as nomadic is to see them as not attached to their
villages, fields, and houses. Under this view, the social and cultural disrup-
tion caused by forced resettlement to the lowlands can be conveniently
ignored or underestimated.

In Burma, Akha and other hill-tribe minorities have been subjected to
various forms of violence by representatives of the military regime. (See
Chapter 9 on the Karen for additional details.) Human-rights violations
have been extensively documented, including compulsory relocation and

forced labor. Akha and other tribal women have been raped by members of the Burmese military, and men, women, and children have even been used as human mine sweeps to walk in front of military forces in areas thought to be mined. In 1987, the Thai government burned several Akha villages and transported the inhabitants to the Burma border in an apparent effort to stem the flow of Akha from Burma. The influence of the Thai majority's view of Akha as "primitive" and "nomadic" was evidenced when an army commander responsible for the operation was quoted in a Thai newspaper as saying that what were burned were "only huts." Whereas the government considers these Akha to be illegal immigrants, human-rights activists consider them to be refugees. Since the 1960s, the Thai government has explained the slow pace at which citizenship has been granted to Akha and other hill-tribe minorities as motivated by a desire not to encourage migration from neighboring countries.

Deforestation and Development

In Thailand and elsewhere, Akha and other tribal minorities are blamed for deforestation. Yet a Thai government official and scholar has demonstrated that the majority of deforestation in the mountains of northern Thailand is due to commercial logging, whether licensed or illegal. Road building is another contributor not only to deforestation but also to soil erosion. Since the 1960s, initially to protect national security in the context of the Vietnam War (the Second Indochina War) and more recently to advance development, the Thai government has done extensive road building in the northern hills.

Land traditionally farmed by Akha and other tribal farmers has been taken from them for roads, government development projects, and commercial enterprises such as resorts for tourists. In 1988 in one village, an Akha farmer complained bitterly that the government had planted tree saplings in his rice field. Akha and other tribal farmers do now contribute to environmental degradation, but not because dry-rice farming is intrinsically destructive to the environment or because they do not know any better. To feed their families, Akha and other hill-tribe farmers must work the little land they have left too many years in a row, thereby diminishing the soil's productivity and not allowing the forest to regenerate.

Thailand's development efforts in the hills began in the 1960s, inspired by security concerns. Border-patrol police established schools in some villages as part of their work to protect the nation's northern frontier. By the 1990s, government-sponsored village schools were common in the hill-tribe villages. Since the 1960s, a central concern of the government in its development efforts has been reducing opium production.

Historically, opium has served as a form of money in the hills. It has been the most dependable cash crop, easily transported and readily sold.

To suppress opium production, the government has used crop-substitution programs, replacing opium poppies with other cash crops such as cabbages and strawberries. Unlike opium, these cash crops do not have a dependable market and do not always fetch a good price. In a cycle of boom and bust, the first farmers to grow cabbages, strawberries, and other substitution crops often initially made good money only to have the market collapse later when prices fell due to the increased competition as greater numbers of farmers planted the new crop. Cabbages have been left to rot because the price they would bring at a lowland market would not cover the cost of transporting them there.

An additional problem with crop-substitution programs is that they are based on cash cropping rather than subsistence farming. Akha families depend on rice as their major food—their nutty-tasting ivory-colored rice is richer in protein and other nutrients than the white rice familiar to Americans—and in recent years their crop yields have fallen as the land available for farming has decreased. Many families no longer have enough rice to eat from one harvest to the next. Neither can they live on opium-substitution crops like cabbages and strawberries that, unlike rice, cannot be stored for months. So farmers have neither enough rice of their own to feed their families nor enough money from substitution crops to buy rice.

Since the 1960s, tourism has had a major impact on Thailand's northern hills. At first, trekkers arrived on foot, usually with a guide. Then, as road building increased access to remote villages, vans and buses filled with tourists began to arrive. Most recently, resorts have been built on land formerly farmed by Akha and other hill tribes; these often have shows in which local tribal people wearing their traditional clothes sing and dance for tourists. Another form of commercial development in the northern hills is monocrop plantations on which fruit trees or other crops are grown. While commercial development offers work for Akha and other highlanders as guides, singers, dancers, waiters, or field hands, it also takes land away that was traditionally available to them to farm.

Indeed, access to land and land rights are key issues for Akha and other tribal minorities throughout the region. Forced relocation of hill people to the lowlands has occurred at various times in recent years in all five countries in which Akha live. In China, Vietnam, and Laos, there has been collectivization of agriculture in minority areas. In the military despotism of Burma, the hills inhabited by Akha are part of a war zone, while in the democratic monarchy of Thailand, where most hill land technically belongs to the state, government and commercial interests have claimed land.

Lack of Education and Employment Options

Akha are traditionally educated in their own customs, but nowadays parents and grandparents recognize that children need to be educated in national languages and learn modern skills. With the collapse of their traditional subsistence farming, they realize that new ways to make a living must be found. Many Akha families in Thailand send their children to government-sponsored village schools. Unfortunately, only those students who have Thai citizenship can continue their education beyond elementary school. Apparently no high schools are located in hill villages. All continuing students must move to a town or city in lowland Thailand and have enough money for room, board, and school uniforms and fees.

Despair and Drug Addiction

Many Akha feel a growing sense of despair due to the political, economic, and cultural threats to their survival. As the forests and the game in them have disappeared, men have been increasingly unable to fulfill their role as hunters. This assault on the traditional concept of manhood seems to be related to the rise in drug addiction among Akha men.

Opium has long been a medicine in the hills, smoked to soothe pain, coughs, and diarrhea. Some old people, especially men, became addicted through either medicinal or recreational use. Addiction among young people was rare, however, until the 1980s, when it began to grow among young men and, to a lesser extent, young women. Drug addiction among Akha and other tribal minorities must be seen, at least in part, as a response to despair. Partly because government suppression efforts made transporting opium increasingly dangerous, more and more of it was refined into heroin in the hills. This contributed to a rise in injecting drug use in the hill villages, as did heroin tourists—Thais and foreigners who come to the hills to obtain cheaper drugs closer to the source. The number of Akha heroin addicts skyrocketed, with one village having eighty known addicts, mostly men, by 1998.

AIDS, Malnutrition, and Other Health Threats

With injecting drug use comes AIDS. Thailand has been hard hit by AIDS, with the northern region, where Akha and other tribal minorities live, having the highest rates of infection with HIV, the virus that causes AIDS. In Thailand—and indeed around the world—most HIV transmission occurs through heterosexual intercourse with an infected partner. Thailand's epidemic is fueled by the country's sex industry. Akha not only in Thailand but throughout mainland Southeast Asia and southwest China are threatened by HIV infection through both contaminated needles and sexual contact, including contact within the commercial sex industry, whether as prostitutes or clients.

Akha girls and women from China, Burma, Thailand, Laos, and perhaps also Vietnam have been tricked, kidnapped, or sold into Thailand's massive

Figure 3-3. Malnourished Akha children begging in a Thai town, 1987. Courtesy of Cornelia Ann Kammerer.

and pervasive sex industry. Pushed by poverty, young women have left hill villages for what they thought was to be a job as a waitress or maid in lowland Thailand only to find themselves in a brothel, sometimes in chains. In Burma and Thailand, impoverished and drug-addicted fathers, stepfathers, and brothers have sold their daughters or sisters into the commercial sex industry. In so doing, they are following a pattern common in some northern Thai villages, from which for decades families have sent young women into prostitution. A few young Akha women in Thailand, faced with poverty in the hills, have even "chosen" to become prostitutes in the lowlands.

Yet AIDS is not the only significant health threat that Akha face. Thai government researchers have documented the growth of malnutrition among Akha and other tribal minorities. Children are significantly affected (Figure 3-3). As deforestation and development pollute previously pure mountain streams, waterborne parasites and infectious diseases have increased. Dirty water leads to diarrheal diseases that are more life-threatening to undernourished children. Malnutrition magnifies the health threat of infectious diseases, such as tuberculosis and measles, and mosquito-borne diseases, such as malaria and dengue fever. In Thailand, government medical workers visit hill villages to vaccinate children, but the same is not true in Burma. Without childhood vaccination, measles can kill, especially malnourished children who are more vulnerable to bronchitis and meningitis, which can follow measles.

On cabbages and other new cash crops farmers use pesticides, sometimes highly toxic ones banned in the United States and other Western countries. Frequently these farmers, who are typically not able to read instructions and warnings, spray dangerous chemicals without proper protective gear. Some, like the brain-damaged young man quoted, are told to do so by the owner or manager of the plantation where they are working.

RESPONSE: STRUGGLES TO SURVIVE CULTURALLY

I am sending my grandchild to the city to study.
—Akha blacksmith and elder, northern Thailand, 1981

My children are hungry.
—Akha mother begging on the street in Chiang Mai City,
northern Thailand, 1988

I am writing down Akha chants.
—Akha political and cultural activist, northern Thailand,
1998

Adopting New Agricultural Practices

Struggles to sustain economic survival often take precedence over struggles to sustain cultural survival. In response to the deteriorating economic situation in the hills, Akha have adopted new crops and agricultural practices. Unfortunately, none of the recently introduced cash crops are very profitable. New agricultural practices include use of chemical fertilizers and pesticides that are expensive. However, as Akha themselves realize, they cannot rely completely on farming in the future because of the decrease in their land base.

Changing Customs

Increasing poverty makes it difficult to follow Akha customs properly. Many traditional ceremonies require pigs and chickens for sacrifice. Some Akha have tried to reduce the requirements, offering, for example, a duck rather than a pig. Others have abandoned their traditional religion in favor of either Protestant or Catholic Christianity, which are perceived as being less expensive customs. A few Akha have abandoned their own customs but have not adopted anything new to replace them. Such economically and culturally impoverished Akha, including beggars on the streets of Thai towns and cities, were described by an Akha elder sadly as "like bats," neither this nor that. His reaction reflects the traditional Akha view that customs make identity.

Marketing Culture

Akha have adapted to tourism by charging trekkers money to stay in their houses or in specially constructed guesthouses. One Akha Christian community in Thailand attracts tourists with an outdoor museum containing a traditional village gateway, a swing like that used in the annual women's New Year's ceremony, and other cultural artifacts. Some young Akha men have become guides for tourists. As noted, both men and women have gotten jobs singing, dancing, and playing traditional instruments for Thai and foreign tourists at resorts in the hills. Others do the same at restaurants and "cultural centers" in the lowlands. Such culture for display is a far cry from the lived culture of a traditional Akha village, in which the rules and rituals of customs create identity and establish daily and annual rhythms.

Tourists buy bags, belts, and jackets decorated with the traditional embroidery and appliqué done by Akha women as well as baskets made by Akha men. Clothing and other handicrafts are produced specifically for the tourist trade. Yet impoverished Akha have also sold their heirloom silver jewelry and even the clothes off their backs to make money. Often it is not Akha but middlemen and lowland store owners who make the most profit from such handicrafts. Akha women's beautiful silver-studded headdresses and embroidered clothing have even made their way to fancy stores in Tokyo and New York.

Seeking Jobs and Education

As agricultural yields have fallen, Akha have turned increasingly to wage labor. As early as the 1970s, they sometimes worked for wages—often in the form of opium—in the fields of other hill tribes whose villages are located at the higher altitudes where opium poppies grow successfully. They began migrating in significant numbers to lowland cities in search of paid work in the 1980s. Unfortunately, without schooling in the Thai language and the skills needed for well-paying jobs, Akha usually earn low wages. Both refugees to Thailand from Burma and many Thai-born Akha lack national identity papers. Without such papers, they are illegal workers who cannot turn to the law to protest dangerous working conditions or pay that is below the legal minimum wage.

In the late 1970s and early 1980s, Akha families began to send their children, especially their sons, to the lowlands to continue their Thai education, hoping that they would eventually be able to earn enough money to help the entire family back in the hills. But sons who left could not help in the family fields, and schooling cost money, so few families succeeded in educating their children through high school, much less beyond. Moreover, those children who lacked citizenship papers could not continue on to high school. As of the early 1990s, only two Akha, both men, had completed any college. Thus education has not yet proved an easy avenue for advancement for Akha.

Preserving Customs

Recognizing that young people are no longer apprenticing with ritual specialists, Akha are now writing down the chants of their oral tradition in their own language so they will not be lost to future generations. In this effort, they have received help from a Dutch anthropologist, Leo Alting von Geusau, who has worked with Akha in Thailand since the late 1970s. At a hostel for Akha students in the lowland city of Chiang Rai, ritual specialists come to teach about customs. Protestant Akha, who no longer practice traditional rituals, emphasize the importance of preserving traditional Akha clothing, which is worn on holidays such as Christmas.

Forming Linkages and Alliances

Akha activists have made links with environmental activists in Thailand and beyond. In 1987, Survival International, a London-based organization "dedicated to campaigning for tribal peoples," protested the burning of Akha villages and initiated an international letter-writing campaign to the Thai government. Locally in Thailand, Akha living in Chiang Mai City have formed a mutual-aid association that joins together those who follow their traditional customs, Protestants, and Catholics. In collaboration with scholars, Akha from Thailand and China have visited each other to learn about their respective worlds. The First International Conference on Hani/Akha Culture was held in southwest China (Yunnan Province) in 1993 and the Second in northern Thailand in 1996.

FOOD FOR THOUGHT

Whether Akha live in China, Burma, Vietnam, Laos, or Thailand, they are a minority facing misunderstanding and prejudice. Land they formerly farmed has been taken from them through government-sponsored and commercial development. Unable to feed their families and carry their customs as they traditionally did, Akha now seek modern education and wage labor, often migrating from their hill villages to lowland cities. HIV/AIDS is a major threat to them throughout the region.

Questions

1. Does cultural survival mean that a culture does not change? Can Akha maintain their ethnic identity while also changing their customs?
2. For Akha, how are economic and cultural survival related?
3. In what ways is the current economic situation faced by Akha shaped by political forces?
4. If you were an Akha, how would you respond to the threats to your economic and cultural survival?
5. How would you go about designing an effective AIDS-prevention campaign for Akha? What would the campaign include? Try to think not only in terms of AIDS education and condom availability but also in terms of changing the structural conditions (political, economic, and cultural) that create vulnerability to HIV infection.
6. What can you do that might help improve the lives of Akha and other hill tribes in mainland Southeast Asia and southwest China?

NOTE

1. The terms "indigenous" and "tribal" are not always synonymous. Akha are an indigenous people in China, their homeland, but not in Thailand, which they reached around 1900. Anthropologists and others have correctly criticized the term "tribe" because it carries misconceptions. Contrary to these common misconceptions, tribal people are not primitive, unchanging, or isolated; neither do they necessarily inhabit a discrete tribal territory. Akha are scattered among various ethnic groups over a broad geographical area. Despite the problems with the terms "tribe" and "tribal," I use them because it is as tribal or semitribal peoples that Akha and other hill tribes have rights under international law.

RESOURCE GUIDE

Published Literature

Alting von Geusau, Leo. "Dialectics of Akhazan: The Interiorizations of a Perennial Minority Group." In *Highlanders of Thailand*, ed. John McKinnon and Wanat Bhruksasri, 243–277. Kuala Lumpur, Malaysia: Oxford University Press, 1983.

Gray, Jennifer. "Operating Needle Exchange Programs in the Hills of Thailand." *AIDS Care* 7, no. 4 (1995): 489–499.

Grunfeld, Frederic V. *Wayfarers of the Thai Forest: The Akha*, Peoples of the Wild Series. Amsterdam, The Netherlands: Time-Life Books, 1982.

Hanks, Jane Richardson. "The Power of Akha Women." In *Gender, Power, and* the Construction of the Moral Order: Studies from the Thai Periphery, ed. Nancy Eberhardt, 13–31. Monograph 4. Madison: University of Wisconsin, Center for Southeast Asian Studies, 1988.

Kammerer, Cornelia Ann. "Customs and Christian Conversion among Akha Highlanders of Thailand." American Ethnologist 17, no. 2 (1990): 277–291.

———. "Of Labels and Laws: Thailand's Resettlement and Repatriation Policies." Cultural Survival Quarterly 12, no. 4 (1988): 7–12.

———. "Territorial Imperatives: Akha Ethnic Identity and Thailand's National Integration." In Ethnicities and Nations: Processes of Inter-ethnic Relations in Latin America, Southeast Asia, and the Pacific, ed. Remo Guidieri, Francesco Pellizzi, and S. J. Tambiah, 259–292. Houston: Rothko Chapel (distributed by the University of Texas Press, Austin), 1988.

Kammerer, Cornelia Ann, Otome Klein Hutheesing, Ralana Maneeprasert, and Patricia V. Symonds. "Vulnerability to HIV Infection among Three Hilltribes in Northern Thailand." In Culture and Sexual Risk: Anthropological Perspectives on AIDS, ed. Han ten Brummelhuis and Gilbert Herdt, 53–75. Amsterdam, The Netherlands: Gordon and Breach, 1995.

Lewis, Paul, and Elaine Lewis. Peoples of the Golden Triangle: Six Tribes in Thailand. London: Thames and Hudson, 1984.

Tooker, Deborah. "Identity Systems of Highland Burma." Man 27, no. 4 (1992): 799–819.

Films and Videos

Dying for Sex, a British Broadcasting Company (BBC) production, focuses on the local sex trade in Thailand, especially Thai men's demands for "younger girls in the mistaken belief that they are less likely to be infected with HIV."

Other People's Children examines child prostitution in Thailand, with a focus on the sector catering to British and other Western men. It opens with the story of an Akha girl rescued from a brothel and the Akha headman, an antiprostitution activist with a price on his head, who escorted her home to the hills. Included is a scene from the New Life Center, identified as "a Baptist children's home." A production of Granada Television of Britain, the video is available from Evolutions, 17 Nassau Street, London W1N 7RE, London, United Kingdom; phone: 44-171-580-3333.

Sacrifice (1998), an award-winning documentary produced and directed by Ellen Bruno, presents four case studies that movingly illuminate "the social, cultural, and economic forces at work in the trafficking" of tribal girls from Burma into prostitution in Thailand. Available from Film Library, 22-D Hollywood Avenue, Ho-Ho-Kus, New Jersey 07423; phone: 800-343-5540; fax: 201-652-1973.

Organizations

Association for Akha Education and Culture in Thailand

370 Moo 4

T. Rimkok, Chiang Rai

Thailand 57000

Phone/Fax: 66-53-714250

A spin-off from Mountain People's Culture and Development Education Foundation, AFECT is a hostel in the lowland city of Chiang Rai for Akha students who want to study their own customs at the same time that they pursue a modern education in the Thai national language.

Mountain People's Culture and Development Education Foundation

137/1 Nantharam Road

Chiang Mai

Thailand 50100

Phone: 66-53-276194

Fax: 66-53-274947

Founded by Leo Alting von Geusau, a Western scholar and activist, and Deuleu Choopoh, his Akha wife, MPCDE is devoted to documenting traditional Akha culture, including knowledge of the medicinal properties of forest plants, promoting sustainable economic development, and marketing Akha art and handicrafts.

New Life Center

Information can be obtained through:

International Ministries

American Baptist Churches

PO Box 851

Valley Forge, PA 19482

Phone: 1-800-ABC-3USA (ask for the International Ministries)

Located in Chiang Mai City, the New Life Center was founded and is run by American Baptist missionaries. It offers a refuge for tribal girls and young women who have been in Thailand's commercial sex industry and is open to Christians and non-Christians alike. Akha, Lahu, Karen, and other hill-tribe girls and young women live together under the supervision of a housemother. They are given access to medical care, including HIV testing, and opportunities to study and learn skills such as making handicrafts.

Project Majé

0104 S.W. Lane

Portland, OR 97201

E-mail: maje@hevanet.com

Founded by Edith Mirante, a human-rights activist, Project Majé is an independent information project about the political situation in Burma, particularly human-rights, narcotics, and environmental issues. Its reports document human-rights violations by the Burmese military against Akha and other ethnic minorities.

Chapter 4

The Amis of Taiwan
Hsiang-mei Cheng

CULTURAL OVERVIEW

The Amis,[1] one of nine indigenous cultures in Taiwan, have changed as a result of various colonial influences as well as recent economic development pressures, but many still retain their ethnic identity. This chapter provides a historical and anthropological perspective on changes in Amis culture.

Taiwan was for many years known as Formosa, a name used by Portuguese explorers, which means "beautiful island." Today Taiwan is one of the most economically developed areas in Asia. Although the Taiwanese are often regarded as homogeneous, among the 21 million people in the 1995 census were 358,000 indigenous persons composing 1.7 percent of the national population. The Amis are one of the nine principal indigenous groups which also include Atayal, Bunun, Paiwan, Puyuma, Rukai, Saisiat, Tsou, and Yami (Table 4-1). All of these indigenous groups speak distinct languages that are related to Austronesian rather than Chinese languages. Frequent contact with the outside world since the 1960s has accelerated the integration of the Amis' economic system into Taiwan's.

THREATS TO SURVIVAL

Demographic Trends

The nine indigenous groups presently live in an area of 6,100 square miles, or 44 percent of Taiwan's land area. The Amis and Puyuma have lived in the east coastal plains for generations; the Yami live on the offshore Orchid Island of Taidong; and the other six ethnic groups are settled in

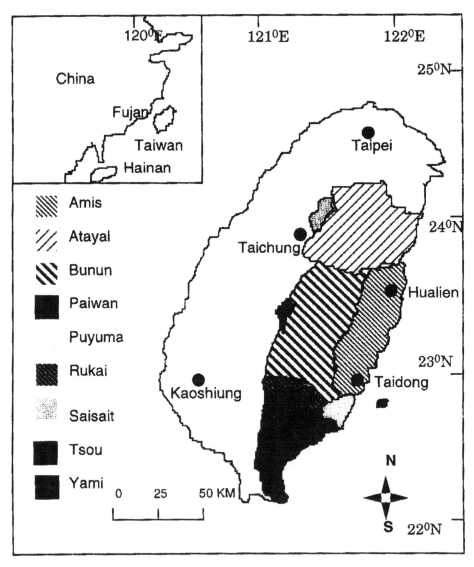

Map 4-1. Settlement areas of the indigenous peoples in Taiwan. Courtesy of Hsiang-mei Cheng.

Table 4-1
Population Distribution of Taiwanese Indigenous Peoples in 1995

Ethnic Groups	Population
Amis	132,649
Atayal	84,910
Bunun	40,112
Paiwan	64,797
Puyuma	9,742
Rukai	10,118
Saisiat	5,474
Tsou	6,640
Yami	3,863
Total	358,305

Source: 1995 Taiwan indigenous-population statistics, Taiwan Provincial Government.

mountain areas of central Taiwan that the government has reserved for them. Lack of reserve land has accelerated the disintegration of the social organizations of the Amis and Puyuma. The Amis and Puyuma are free to sell their ancestral lands to outsiders in the eastern coastal areas of Taiwan, and many have sold. Consequently, the size of the Amis- and Puyuma-speaking population has decreased due to frequent contact with the Han Chinese.[2] Many Amis and Puyuma are fluent in Mandarin and Min-Nan dialect or Taiwanese languages. In other words, they have become more 0integrated with the Han Chinese than have other groups.

The territory of the Amis has shrunk through various eras of Taiwan's history. The period of Portuguese colonization began in the sixteenth century. In 1622, the Dutch started to occupy the island after the Portuguese. Meanwhile, the Spanish army occupied a portion of northern Taiwan and ruled there for sixteen years. The Dutch drove the Spaniards out of Taiwan in 1642. Subsequently, the Dutch colonized Taiwan and remained until Koxinga drove them out of Taiwan in 1662.

The Chinese colonization of Taiwan began in earnest shortly after Koxinga drove the Dutch out. Koxinga retreated from the Fukien Province with 25,000 men during a revolt against the Manchurians who had established the Ch'ing dynasty. He established his own regime of the Southern Ming in Taiwan. He recognized that the task of restoring the Ming throne could not be fulfilled within a short period of time, so he made his soldiers become both fighters and farmers.

Table 4-2
Taiwan Population from 1895 to 1995

Year	Population (in millions)
1895	3.0
1910	3.2
1920	3.5
1930	4.5
1944	6.3
1956	9.3
1966	12
1976	16.5
1985	19.2
1989	20
1995	21

Source: Taiwan Provincial Government, 1995.

By 1683, the Ch'ing troops took over Taiwan. However, Taiwan was not established as a whole province until 1875, when Pao-cheng Shen, a Han Chinese general governor, proposed that the Ch'ing court extend the boundary of China to include the whole island of Taiwan. His proposal was accepted, and Taiwan became a province of China. The expansion of the Han Chinese was slowed by the prevalence of malaria.

During the pre-Japanese period, the Amis had not been passive victims. At the end of the nineteenth century, the Amis fought the Hans but seldom succeeded due to their shortage of weapons. After being defeated by the Han Chinese several times, the Amis altered their strategies of survival. In response to various threats of different historical regimes, a strategy based on maintaining their collective identity became acceptable.

In 1895, at the end of the Sino-Japanese War, Taiwan was ceded to the Japanese. Taiwan became a base for southward expansion and a bastion for the Co-prosperity Sphere.[3] As part of its policy, the Japanese colonial government tried to strictly control the Han Chinese migration because of the Japanese immigration. Nevertheless, the Taiwan population has continually grown through natural increase since 1895 (Table 4-2).

The population of the indigenous peoples has increased in recent decades, but its proportion of Taiwan's total population has gradually decreased. As noted, by 1995, the population of the nine ethnic groups was 1.7 percent of Taiwan's total population. The Taiwanese indigenous peoples, including the Amis, thus fit the criterion of a minority as being a small population or ethnic group. The Amis are the largest group among the Taiwanese indigenous peoples, but they have become a real minority in the sense that they have been subordinated culturally, socially, politically, and economically.

Disappearing Traditional Amis Social Organizations

The distinctive features of the Amis culture traditionally were expressed in two important elements: the matriclan (kin traced from the female) system and men's age-grade system. The social order in a village was maintained by intensifying the links of households, lineages, and the age-grade system through traditional ritual activities. The roles of Amis women in the household and Amis men in political organization were complementary. For instance, rituals dealing with fishing and hunting were arranged by the male village heads, and rituals that dealt with agricultural activities were arranged by the female head of the individual household.

Kinship System: From Matrilineage to Patrilineage

Amis women used to have an important position in property holding and the household economy in the matriclan system. Succession and inheritance were transmitted through the female line. The eldest daughter had the right to succeed as the family head and inherited the household (*ruma'*), which was the primary social unit.

The eldest female of each household controlled the household property, which consisted of the house, the garden, and tools and other implements. The communal property included the village ground, roads, fields, and fallow land, as well as the hunting and fishing areas. Members of different age groups who were given fishing rights for a certain section within the fishing territory carried out the farming around the village. Individual property included men's weapons, women's looms, and the clothing and ornaments of both genders. A man passed on his personal possessions to his own sons or his sister's sons if he had no sons, while a woman passed hers on to her own daughters or her sister's daughters.

The basic characteristic of the Amis' kinship terms is that they do not distinguish between maternal and paternal relatives nor a speaker's gender. For example, *kaka'* refers to both male and female older siblings of maternal and paternal relatives. *Vavahi a kaka'* is used for older sisters, while *vavainai a kaka'* is used for older brothers. Further, the kinship terms are distinguished by generation and are further divided into terms for consanguineal (relatives related by biological descent only, such as parental ties and/or sibling ties) and affinal kin (relatives related by marriage; for example, a husband is related in this way to his wife and her consanguineals).

The maternal side was always stressed in Amis society. The term *ina'* (mother), for example, is the most important in the Amis' elementary terminologies since any kind of kinship group starts from the mother. A mother is in charge of all household affairs. In contrast, *ama'* (father) is never regarded as an important person in his wife's family. In case of divorce, a husband returns to his mother's house, and his relationship with his children continues, although the mother has custody.

The mother's brother, or *vaki* (*mama'* among the southern Amis), is the most important male relative, and the eldest one has special authority in any important decisions and practices of his sisters' families. This was possible for the Amis when they practiced local endogamy, in which one may choose his or her marriage partner from the same ethnic group or the same village. Brothers and sisters lived in the same village. Nevertheless, today it is not uncommon for Amis siblings to live in different cities or counties in Taiwan.

In terms of residence rules, the Amis were matrilocal, that is, a man was usually married in his wife's household or built a new house near the house of his wife's parents. The rate of matrilocality declined from 54 percent in the 1950s to 24 percent in the 1970s, whereas the percentage of patrilocal residence (the couple live with or near the groom's family) increased from 41 percent to 71 percent in the same period of time; the percentage of extended families dropped from 94 percent in 1950 to 44 percent in 1978 as the frequency of single family households increased.

The distribution of property favors particular rules of residence, and residence influences marriage patterns. As mentioned, women as individuals possessed more property than men; thus women were more likely to be localized in traditional Amis society. In contrast, a man married into his wife's family, but his membership in his kin group remained permanent and his position as guardian of his sister's family was maintained just as before his marriage. Nowadays, men feel embarrassed to move in with their wives' families. More and more Amis couples live with the husbands' families because these husbands are educated in the Han Chinese and the Christian marriage patterns, which regard a father as the head of the household. Besides, a father's surname is legally used by children. Thus patrilineage (a relationship reckoned to a known male ancestor) and patrilocality have become predominant among the young generation in contemporary Amis society.

Disintegrating Age-Grade System

The political organization of the people was based on the age-grade system. The position of a man in the political organization was based on his status in the age-grade system, not in the kinship system. In the age-grade system, the Amis men may be classified into three groups: uninitiated boys (*wawa*), the young men (*kapah*, seventeen or eighteen to forty years old), and the old men (*matuasai*, forty-one to eighty-two years old). Boys of the age of seventeen or eighteen had to pass a series of tests to become members of a new grade. Old men had many privileges but few duties, while the youth were asked to be absolutely obedient to the members of higher grades at all times. A village chief was chosen from the elders.

Subsistence System: From Swiddening to Wet-Rice Cultivation

In the slash-and-burn (swiddening) cultivation period (up to the late nineteenth century), the agricultural activities were primarily concerned with the production of food for local consumption. All of the swidden work, such as felling trees, cutting away the underbrush or forest lands, and burning the dried plant growth, was collectively done by the members of the lower class of the age-grade system under the guidance of the upper class. This system of work was supported by various social sanctions. For instance, to obey the orders of the elders and to work diligently were the most important virtues in traditional Amis society. Young men were willing to obey the elders and join in the tasks requiring great strength and energy like transporting crops. Today, the elders are losing their authority over young people. The youth are not willing to unconditionally obey the elders.

Amis women and men generally had their sex- and age-specific duties. Women uprooted and cut away the thick carpet of weeds that covered the farm. Men built a hut (talu'an) on a central and elevated site. They built a strong palisade of stakes and set traps on level ground on the borders of the farm to catch animals like pigs and deer. Men accompanied by dogs regularly patrolled their farms at night with a bush knife, while women guarded their farms during the daytime. Young men assisted in harvesting and carried back the crops in a basket. The task of storage could be done by either male or female household members. The ritual of the storage of the millet was performed by the eldest man or woman in the household.

It is not clear when the communal landholding in each Amis village ended. The enactment of the Land-to-the-Tiller Programs (1949–58) apparently had profound influences on the land-usage system of the Amis. Its main purpose was to equally distribute the arable land in Taiwan by converting the land-tenancy system into one relying on owner-cultivators. However, the older Amis who received Japanese education had difficulties with the enactment of the program because of their lack of literacy and speaking ability in Mandarin.

The Amis learned wet-rice cultivation from either the Han Chinese or the Calaiwan (one of the ethnic groups of the Pingpu) in the late nineteenth century. With the introduction of the plow and the use of water buffaloes for tillage in wet-rice cultivation, wet rice gradually replaced millet in the Amis economy. Consequently, the division of labor of the Amis was changed; although women still played an essential role in production, men spent much more time on wet-rice farming than slash-and-burn cultivation. Men now participated in tasks such as farm plowing and training water buffaloes.

Religious Life

The center of the Amis religious beliefs was *kawas* (the collective name for gods, goddesses, and any kind of spirit). The Amis traditionally believed in the existence of spirits, both good and evil. They ascribed all misfortunes and sickness to punishment from these spirits. They also believed that a shaman (*tsikawasai*), one who could be possessed by spirits, had the power not only to heal sickness but also to maintain the security and order of their communities.

Malatao was the most important god and was intimately connected with the daily life of the Amis. Malatao was not only the leader of the gods but also a benevolent divinity. For instance, when a man had difficulties in hunting or fishing, he would ask Malatao for help. However, it was taboo to invoke Malatao in any household rituals, which were connected with ancestral spirits only. Confusion of spirits in household rituals would result in hardships at home.

The traditional rituals of the Amis generally could be classified into individual rituals (*lisin nu tsatsai a tamdao*), household rituals (*lisin nu ruma'h*), and collective rituals (*lisin nu niaro'*). The individual rituals consisted of black magic (*milati*) and the individual hunting ritual (*milelek*). An Amis woman used to perform *mivetik* (a ceremony in which one sprinkles rice wine on the earth for ancestral spirits [Figure 4-1]) and then crossed two sticks in the entrance to her garden. If someone entered the garden without her permission, the intruder would become ill. *Milelek* was a ritual in which a hunter would perform *mivetik* and call the spirits of hunters in his hunting hut after placing traps in the forest. Both rituals were managed by individuals without the assistance of the shaman and were not based on the ritual calendar.

The household rituals, including the rituals for sowing, birth, naming, and the marriage ceremony, were performed by either male or female shamans. These rituals were more concerned with offering food to ancestral spirits. The Amis believed that ancestral spirits had the capacity to help living descendants with advice offered in dreams or to punish their descendants if they were neglected. They also believed that if one fulfilled one's obligation to the *kawas* and treated others kindly, then she or he would go to heaven and become an ancestral spirit (*kawas nu matuasai*). One who had committed crimes or died unnaturally would become a spirit on the earth and then become a wild animal, for example, a bear or a snake.

Most of the collective rituals were performed either by village chiefs who were men or by both male and female shamans. These rituals consisted of weeding, appeals for sun or rain, communal hunting or fishing, and the Harvest Festival, which took place on a calendrical basis. During the period of each ritual performance, there were taboos on vegetable eating, fish eating, and sexual intercourse. Additionally, *mivetik* and *pakelang* (*malialats*

Figure 4-1. Amis elders performing *mivetik*, a ceremony in which one sprinkles rice wine on the earth for ancestral spirits. Courtesy of Hsian-mei Cheng.

among the northern Amis) were two essential observances in the performance of each ritual. *Pakelang* was a fishing expedition that marked the completion of each ritual. It removed all previous taboos and brought the community from the ritual state to the state of normal everyday life. The age-grade system played an essential role in the collective rituals. For example, the *pakelang* or *malialats* (fishing) on the last day of each ritual was entirely male dominated.

Before the coming of the nation-state system and particularly its educational system, the men's house (*talu'an*) served as a sort of combined dormitory, military barracks, school, and clubhouse for men. It was not only the center for ritual performances but also a place for cooperative groups: men who would help each other in hunting, farming, and building houses.

During 1895–1945, the Japanese attempted to assimilate the Taiwanese indigenous peoples. The power of the colonial government has gradually infiltrated eastern Taiwan since the 1910s. Some traditional rituals of the Amis were forbidden because they were regarded as superstitious by the Japanese. Furthermore, hunting was forbidden in the 1920s. The rituals of hunting (*misalivong*), sun asking (*pakatsidal*), and rain asking (*pakaurad*) were prohibited under the assimilation policy of the government in 1930.

During the Japanese regime, the colonists not only built Shinto temples in villages but also popularized compulsory education. The Amis were requested to practice Shintoism and receive Japanese education. By the 1950s, the Amis faced more disintegration of their social organization due to the coming of Christianity.

The Coming of Christianity

Christianity was another force that changed Amis society. The North Presbyterians set up a mission to evangelize the Taiwanese indigenous peoples in 1909. However, the Japanese did not allow the missionaries to enter the territories of the indigenous peoples. Instead, the Japanese tried but failed to convert the peoples to Shintoism or a mixture of nature worship, hero worship, and shamanism.

In 1945, Taiwan was ceded to the Republic of China. The Kao Ming Tang government did not hinder religious freedom but discouraged people from believing in Shintoism. Both Protestants and Roman Catholics established their churches in Amis villages in the mid-1950s. Many villagers converted to either Presbyterianism or Catholicism by the 1960s. A great number of the Presbyterians converted to Roman Catholicism because Protestantism identified the Amis traditional practices, including the Harvest Festival, as evil and abolished them entirely. It was forbidden for the Amis Presbyterians to attend traditional rituals. In contrast, the Roman Catholic Church did not forbid its indigenous converts from participating in their traditional activities.

Today, the men's house has disappeared in Amis villages, and the age-grade system does not have the functions it possessed in the past. Since 1945, most of the young Amis under forty-five years old, particularly those who live in the cities, do not even know which grades they belong to. Furthermore, the former cooperative groups no longer exist, and instead, members of the same church help each other in farming, fishing, and building houses. In Makutaai, for instance, the Catholic Church has replaced the men's house (talu'an) as the center of the village. A single village is now divided into several Christian denominations, each with its own form of worship.

The spread of Christianity has changed many Amis social and cultural practices. For example, people used to marry within the local group, but outside of their own lineage. With Christian influences, many individuals felt that it was more important to marry within the same religion even if that required ignoring the traditional taboo on marrying within one's lineage. Likewise, many traditional rituals are no longer practiced.

Taiwan Development

After World War II, Taiwan's economy was still predominantly agricultural. Agricultural products accounted for 46 percent of Taiwan's exported goods. From the mid-1950s on, the "industrialization-first" strategy of the Taiwan government discriminated against agriculture and the rural sector. Therefore, the role of agriculture in Taiwan's economic development appeared in the 1970s to be switching from that of a supporting sector providing important resources to the rest of the economy to that of a dependent and protected sector.

The Accelerated Rural Development Program of 1973, however, influenced Taiwan's rural development. Under this program, all similar farms in a locality were urged to form a specialized agricultural production area such as rice production. Further, the Six-Year Plan (1976–81), which enabled Taiwan to become more developed, promoted mechanization, developed higher-value crops for exports, improved the marketing system for greater efficiency, and improved farm housing, country roads, and environmental sanitation. The share of agricultural exports in total exports, however, declined dramatically to 17 percent in 1973 (Thorbecke 1979, 133–141). Work opportunities expanded outside agriculture. The "industrialization-first" strategy provided a productive way to absorb rural labor. A growing number of former members of the agricultural population became commuters to the cities, seasonal workers, and long-term employees.

By the early 1980s, 25 percent of the total indigenous population of Taiwan lived in urban areas, most in Taipei and Kaoshung. The vast majority of these people were Amis. The rural to urban migration continues, so the percentage is now much higher. Many young men have moved to the cities in search of careers. Because of their lower level of education and technical skills, approximately half of them work in construction, coal mining, transportation, and public services.

As a result, there is a lack of young Amis men in villages, and the foundation of the gender division of labor in farming based on the age-grade system is fading away. The authority of the women as household heads has also been weakened by the modern individual wage work of men. Amis men nowadays seem to make more money and contribute to the households' economic needs more than women.

RESPONSE: STRUGGLES TO SURVIVE CULTURALLY

Fundamental Amis social organizations, including the matriclan system and the age-grade system, are disintegrating because of the confrontation with the Japanese and Han Chinese cultures, which are patrilineal and male dominated. The disintegration is linked to political and social phenomena, including the transformations of the economy and religion.

Since the religious beliefs and social organizations of the Amis are closely interrelated, the coming of Christianity has accelerated the disintegration of Amis cultural traits, such as female dominance in the household and male dominance in the age-grade system. Today, most of the Amis are either Roman Catholics or Protestants.

Throughout Taiwan's history, the Amis have struggled with the policy objectives of assimilation and integration. Under the "development-first" strategy of the Taiwan government, the Amis became economically marginalized. Rapid economic growth in the process of industrialization provides an environment that improves the material life of the Amis, but it creates difficulties for adaptation. The Accelerated Rural Development Program and the Six-Year Plan improved rural Taiwan's development, for example, in mechanization and the marketing system, but the social status of the Amis has not improved much. The household income of the Amis ranks far below the average for Taiwan's total population. The average household income of lowland aborigines, including the Amis, was 114,475 N.T.D. (New Taiwan Dollars), while that of Taiwan farm families was 282,919 N.T.D. by 1978 (Bureau of Civil Affairs of the Taiwan Provincial Government 1980).

Today the Amis are facing far more complex problems than in the past. Alienation from their original villages and traditional ways of life accelerates the assimilation of the young Amis within the dominant society. There is a general feeling among the older Amis of loss of control over lands, their lifeways, and their destiny. As a village chief said, "The Amis society is not like the one when I was young. Social organizations have either disappeared or are fading away. For example, the function of the age-grade system is deteriorating. The young people who work in the cities do not obey the older generation when they come back to the village" (personal communication).

Like many other indigenous peoples, the Amis traditionally had a special relationship with their land, which was the basis of their economy and identity. Land as the cultural basis of the Amis has been gradually lost as a result of alienation from traditional ways of life. The younger generation assimilates to the dominant culture and ignores the value of land. Thus losing land is a threat to the Amis lifestyle. Members of the younger generation drift to the cities for a better life since they are unable to make a decent living in their original villages. Some urban Amis sold their lands, which were not reserve land, before they moved to the cities. They expected to have better jobs in the cities, but most of them are engaged in low-paying jobs due to their low educational attainment.

Politically, the Amis are disfranchised because of their small population proportion. The indigenous representatives are not numerous enough to sway important votes at all levels of the Taiwan government. It is difficult for the Amis to seek legal recognition of their problems and of their existence. Under this situation, the political, economic, and social status of the Amis is not likely to genuinely improve. A deeper understanding of Amis culture and other indigenous cultures is essential. The Amis age-grade system, for instance, is one of the indigenous cultural elements worth mentioning in school textbooks and mass media. This may correct some misconceptions about Amis culture. Not until the dominant society returns dignity to the Amis people will the Amis be able to exercise more self-determination for their future.

FOOD FOR THOUGHT

In summary, the Amis and other indigenous groups in Taiwan have been profoundly changed throughout the island's history by a succession of different external powers—Portuguese, Dutch, Spanish, Chinese, Japanese, and American. These colonial forces have variously changed Amis patterns of settlement, land, and resource use as well as material, social, political, and religious aspects of their culture. Although subjected to tremendous pressures from these forces, the Amis have not been merely passive recipients of change, but have responded by adjusting, and sometimes sacrificing, some of their customs while adding new ones. Overall many of their traditions have been lost and those that remain are increasingly endangered. Nevertheless, many Amis have retained their ethnic identity, and this may be strengthened in the future by their growing consciousness of their history, culture, and human rights, including self-determination.

Questions

1. How has modernization in Taiwan influenced the disintegration of traditional Amis social organizations?

2. What are the effects of the nation-state system on the functions of men's houses?

3. How have the pressures of economic development affected culturally important virtues of the Amis, such as respect for elders?

4. Does the decrease of the Amis-speaking population caused by a lack of reserve lands and expanded contact with the outside world imply that the Amis are becoming more integrated with the dominant society?

5. How have the Amis responded to events in the history of Taiwan?

NOTES

1. The Amis call themselves "Pangtsah" or "Amis." "Pangtsah" means "humanity" and refers to the people of the whole coastal valley region from Hualien to Taidong. "Amis" means "north" and has been given to the inhabitants of the northern coastal valley by people from the southern section of the same region. Although "Ami" has been used in official documents since the Japanese era (1895–

1945), "Amis" is in fact the correct pronunciation in the Pangtsah language. "Amis" instead of "Ami" or "Pangtsah" is used in this chapter.

2. The Hans or Han-chu are the main core of the Chinese people, but they are not homogeneous in any sense. Even the Taiwanese are not a special ethnic group since they are from neither a single locality nor a single dialect area.

3. The Co-prosperity Sphere was a Japanese policy to extend its territory from East Asia to Southeast Asia during World War II. Many male Amis above the age of seventy now, who were sixteen or seventeen then, have experiences participating in World War II for the Japanese government in Southeast Asia. Consequently, the Amis villages lacked young men during the war.

RESOURCE GUIDE

Published Literature

Cohen, Marc J. *Taiwan at the Crossroads: Human Rights, Political Development, and Social Change on the Beautiful Island.* Washington, D.C.: Asia Resource Center, 1988.

Galenson, W., ed. *Economic Growth and Structural Change in Taiwan.* Ithaca, NY: Cornell University Press, 1979.

Shepard, John Robert. *Statecraft and Political Economy on the Taiwan Frontier 1600–1800.* Stanford, CA: Stanford University Press, 1993.

Thorbecke, Erik. "Agricultural Development." In *Economic Growth and Structural Change in Taiwan*, ed. W. Galenson, 132–205. Ithaca, NY: Cornell University Press, 1979.

Chapter 5

The Ayukawa-hama Community of Japan

Masami Iwasaki-Goodman

In 1988, a substantial part of small-type coastal whaling (STCW)[1] operation was banned in Ayukawa-hama[2] as a result of implementation of the International Whaling Commission's moratorium on commercial whaling.[3] The whaling ban has caused devastating impacts on this community, creating a situation in which the local people are unable to ensure the survival of Ayukawa-hama as a viable community. While the moratorium has been generally viewed as a resource-conservation measure outside of Japan, the people in Ayukawa-hama who traditionally have utilized the whale as a resource for human consumption regard it as a form of cultural imperialism in which a foreign ideology that discourages the killing of whales is forced upon them. This aspect of cultural confrontation becomes more evident as scientific research reveals that some whale stocks have recovered enough to sustain a regulated whaling operation. The people in Ayukawa-hama, while making various adjustments to the new circumstances, are persistent in their efforts to normalize their STCW operations, hoping to return to the situation that existed before the 1988 whaling ban came into effect. ("Hama" refers to a shore community.)

CULTURAL OVERVIEW

The Setting

Ayukawa-hama is located in the southeastern portion of Oshika (Ojika) peninsula, facing the Pacific Ocean (see Map 5-2). It is one of the sixteen subdistricts within the municipality of Oshika, which had a total population of 6,700 as of 1993.

69

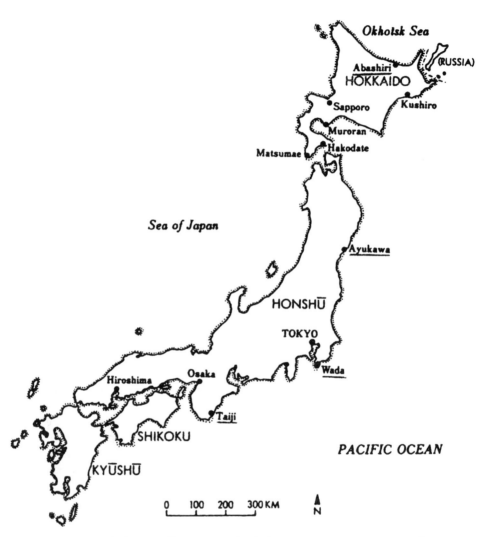

Map 5-1. Japan with four small-type coastal whaling communities. Courtesy of Masami Iwasaki-Goodman.

Map 5-2. Ayukawa-hama. Courtesy of Masami Iwasaki-Goodman.

Figure 5-1. Overview of Ayukawa-hama. Courtesy of Masami Iwasaki-Goodman.

The climate of Ayukawa-hama is mild throughout the year. The people enjoy mild winters and cool summers, with the mean temperature of the last thirty-seven years being 54. The average temperature of the coldest month in the year is 36.5 in February. The seasonal wind is frequently strong in Ayukawa-hama, causing rough conditions on the ocean. The wind and the fog in June and July create weather conditions that hinder the regular operation of a ferry that connects Ayukawa-hama with two nearby islands (Figures 5-1 and 5-2).

The distance between Ayukawa-hama and the closest major city, Sendai, is about 53 miles. The winding mountain road that connects the two locations slows down traffic significantly, so that the trip to Sendai from Ayukawa-hama by car often takes two to two and a half hours. Major public transportation between Sendai and Ayukawa-hama is by train and bus, by which means traveling time is doubled.

Prewhaling Period

The earliest proven evidence of settlers in this region are some twenty monuments dated around the fourteenth and fifteenth centuries. These are the *kuyo-hi* (memorial towers), which were built to house the souls of the ancestors of certain families in the Kannon-ji and Yakushi-do temples. The people who settled and built these *kuyo-hi* are not known, but it is evident

Figure 5-2. Gate to ferry port connecting Ayukawa-hama and Kinkasan. Courtesy of Masami Iwasaki-Goodman.

that religious practices were carried out among the early settlers of Ayukawa-hama. Around 1644, the Sendai feudal domain recognized the need for guarding the coastal area along the Pacific Ocean from the invasion of foreign vessels. Ayukawa-hama was chosen as one of five sites for building an observation tower for that purpose.

The Ayukawa-hama area later served as an important gateway to Koganeyama Shrine on Kinkasan Island, which received numbers of pilgrims. However, significant expansion of the settlement did not occur until the late Meiji era, when large-type coastal whaling (LTCW) operations were established in Ayukawa-hama.

The Whaling Era in Ayukawa-hama

The Japanese whaling tradition was established toward the end of the seventeenth century when organized net-whaling operations were developed in the southern coastal communities. Whaling played a significant social, cultural, and economic role in the coastal communities in areas such as the northern part of Kyushu, Shikoku Island, and Wakayama Prefecture during the net-whaling periods. The common expression that describes the historical importance of whaling is "Kujira itto de shichiura uruou" ("One whale enriches seven bays"). Since the net-whaling period, whales have been an important source of human food in Japan. Such long traditions inevitably involve integration with religious beliefs and ceremonial activities.

The rich whale resources offshore of Kinkasan had been known as early as the nineteenth century. Several attempts using various methods were made to catch large whales in the Kinkasan whaling ground during the pre-Meiji period. In the Meiji era (1868–1912), small-scale whaling companies were established in the Ayukawa-hama area. It was around this time that the American whaling method was adopted and the Japanese whalers began whaling with a fleet consisting of a 350-ton mother ship and several catcher boats engaged in whaling, using hand harpoons. This was followed by the success of whaling operations by a fishery company that had adopted the newly introduced Norwegian whaling methods. The use of cannons to shoot harpoons in the Norwegian whaling methods made it possible to catch fast-moving whales and generated interest by other major whaling companies. Although there were concerns among the fishermen who harvested small fish and seaweeds in the coastal water that flensing operations (stripping whales of blubber, meat, and skin) at the shore station might pollute the area, village leaders such as the mayor of Ayukawa-mura (Ayukawa village), the executive of the Ayukawa Fisheries Cooperative Association, and the village councils made an extensive effort so that the importance of whaling for the development of Ayukawa-hama would be understood by the local people.

Within a few years, several whaling companies built their whaling bases in Ayukawa-hama. A small hamlet of some 50 households of fishermen made historic progress as a result of the diffusion of whaling culture into these regions. The population survey of 1888 indicates that there were 67 households in Ayukawa-hama, a size similar to those of the other hama (shore) communities in the Oshika peninsula. It was the establishment of these whaling bases that generated the population growth as well as the economic growth of Ayukawa-hama. In Meiji 41 (1911), only five years after the whaling operation started, the population of Ayukawa-hama had more than doubled to 149 households. The pattern of population increase at this time is significant in that a substantial portion of the population were immigrants from distant communities.

The establishment of these bases led to the opening of whaling-related industries such as whale-products processing, craft making, and transportation in Oshika and the surrounding area. The economy of the town prospered because of financial benefits from the ample whaling activities. More important, there was a massive migration of people who consequently served as agents for the diffusion of the whaling culture. By this process, technology, social dynamics, religious observances, and other social and cultural practices concerning whaling were introduced to Ayukawa-hama.

One of the most important whaling-related industries that took firm root in Ayukawa-hama was fertilizer production. A local entrepreneur pursued a plan to develop the community by producing a stable supply of necessary fertilizer to the local and neighboring communities. This also provided a solution to the problem of pollution in Ayukawa-hama coastal waters. By 1919, twenty-eight fertilizer producers were in operation in Ayukawa-hama and the neighboring community. Ayukawa-hama gradually created an economic foundation based almost solely upon whaling and whaling-related businesses.

In 1925 (Taisho 14), the Ayukawa Whaling Corporation was established by a local entrepreneur in Ayukawa-hama. The main interest was to develop a reliable source of sperm-whale products to meet the demands of local fertilizer and oil processors.

Whaling companies that operated out of Ayukawa-hama paid a special prefectural tax and a surtax during the Taisho and Showa eras until Showa 25 (1950). Revenues from whaling companies enriched the financial capacity of the municipalities, which resulted in reduction of municipal taxes and improvement of public facilities.

Development of Small-Type Coastal Whaling in Ayukawa-hama

Small-type coastal whaling boats are known as *minku sen* (minke boat) from their target whale species (minke whales), which the LTCW boats based in Ayukawa-hama did not harvest. The origin of STCW is quite distinct from LTCW, which was operated by nonlocal investors. The first person to attempt minke-whaling operations was Hasegawa Kumazo, who was originally from Taiji and moved to Ayukawa-hama. Hasegawa, who had earlier experienced LTCW as a boat captain, brought the small boat named *No. 1 Yuko-maru* from Taiji, one of the traditional whaling communities in Honshu. Equipped with a 20-mm five-barreled gun, which was originally invented for pilot whaling in Taiji, and a 26-mm harpoon cannon, which was imported from Norway, this first STCW boat started its test operation in the coastal waters of Ayukawa-hama in Showa 8 (1933).

The catch of the first whaling season was some ten minke whales, which did not have much commercial value because minke-whale meat and blubber were less appreciated than those of other larger whales at that time. The year 1933 thus marked the beginning of locally originated small-scale whaling. In the following year, *No. 1 Yuko-maru* was sold to a local entrepreneur in Ayukawa-hama, and *No. 2 Yuko-maru*, a new boat designed exclusively for minke whaling, was launched.

No. 2 Yuko-maru continued to harvest minke whales for several years until World War II broke out in Japan in 1941. While LTCW boats were sent to different theaters of war, STCW boats began to play a greater role as food suppliers to the local people. In Ayukawa-hama, three STCW boats were in operation around this time. In 1944, when the war intensified, the government introduced emergency measures to permit STCW boats to harvest sperm whales in order to increase food production. Under this special permission, STCW boats had to operate under the Fishery Control Company, which was established under government control. In addition to the original three STCW boats, more boats were brought into operation, totaling thirteen nationally. At that time, approximately one-third of the STCW boats were based in Ayukawa-hama.

After World War II ended, severe food shortages struck the people of Japan, and the need for efficient production of food became urgent. While LTCW boats were sent in for repairs of the damage caused by their participation in the war effort, STCW boats continued and expanded their operations until the number of STCW boats increased to approximately seventy nationally. There were five STCW boats based in Ayukawa-hama; they harvested minke whales from February to June and sperm whales and pilot whales for the rest of the season.

In 1947, the government of Japan introduced a licensing system in an attempt to regulate STCW both for the sound development of the industry and for resource-conservation purposes. A ministerial ordinance restricted the tonnage of boats to under thirty tons and restricted the target species as well as introducing the requirement of an annual renewal of the ministerial license. STCW boats were no longer allowed to harvest sperm whales under the newly introduced restrictions.

The records indicating the number of whales landed in Ayukawa-hama since 1924 show that the whaling industry in Ayukawa-hama had a fairly stable production. The local people recall the stability of whaling since its establishment in Ayukawa-hama.

STCW in Japan is strictly controlled by domestic regulation (Figure 5-3). These regulations limit the taking of whale species under national authority (including Baird's beaked whales, pilot whales, dolphins, and porpoises) and implement quotas and other regulations concerning whaling operations passed by the International Whaling Commission at its annual meetings for species under its jurisdiction (minke whales).

Social and Political Organization

The local people in Ayukawa-hama refer to their community as "hogei no machi" ("a whaling town"), indicating a commonly recognized intricate relationship between their everyday life and local whaling operations. The historical development of Ayukawa-hama is distinct from that of the other hama communities in the region in that the establishment of a whaling base in Meiji 37 (1906) drastically altered the demography of the community. The population growth in the short time following the establishment of the whaling operations, as a result of a major migration of newcomers to Ayukawa-hama, affected various social and cultural aspects of the com-

76

Fig. 5-3. Small-type coastal whaling boat in search of a minke whale. Courtesy of Masami Iwasaki-Goodman.

munity. The traditional social structure in Ayukawa-hama as a fishing community was reformed to a great extent after the introduction of whaling since various aspects of whaling activities are highly specialized and distinct from other types of fishing. These have become deeply integrated into the economic, social, and cultural lives of the people.

Development of STCW in Ayukawa-hama was crucial to the establishment of the present local whaling culture. While only the production phase of whaling activities was locally concentrated in the case of LTCW, in the case of STCW operations, all three phases of whaling and whaling-related activities—the production, distribution, and consumption of whale products—were locally concentrated. The STCW operation thus is community-based whaling that has economically, socially, and culturally influenced the development of Ayukawa-hama. It is these social and cultural aspects of the people's lives in Ayukawa-hama that constituted the local whaling culture and gave rise to the creation of community identity. One of the whalers in Ayukawa-hama said that the "image that the local people have in this town is firstly [of] minke whale. Rather than having to use money to eat whale, having to buy and eat it, the history for the people here is to be given a share of whale by whaling-station workers, whaling crew, or relatives of the boat owners."

Some social networks in Ayukawa-hama have been established around various activities related to STCW production and the distribution and consumption of products. The smallest unit of these social networks is found among those directly involved in the whaling operations. One of the most overt characteristics of STCW in the production phase is its small-scale nature and the consequent intimacy among the people who are involved in STCW production. Five to eight people comprise an STCW crew and operate a boat that is owned by local individuals in Ayukawa-hama. The crews, flensers, and other workers in the flensing station are locally recruited through personal networks, including kin-based relationships. Therefore, complex ties that connect the people involved in STCW are inevitably very personal. The work conditions of the crews as well as the flensers reinforce such intimacy in that they form a cohesive working group in which they maintain their membership over many years. They often refer to the process of establishing the work relationship as "ketsuen wo tsu-kuru" ("create kin relationship"). Thus the kinship and the quasi-kinship form one of the binding forces that characterize the production phase of STCW.

The interaction among the crew, flensers, and boat owners is most intense during the whaling season, yet during the off-whaling season a close relationship is maintained by occasional visits to each other, by attending common social functions, and through their gifting network. The whaling crews, flensers, and boat owners and their family members form an identifiable social group within the local community.

The social network surrounding the STCW operations in Ayukawa-hama extends further through gift giving in which whale meat and blubber are distributed among the local people. Gifting of both a formal and a casual nature is an important social institution typically observable in Japanese society. In Ayukawa-hama, whale meat and blubber have high social and symbolic value as gift items and thus play a dominant role in sustaining the gifting institution. One elderly whaler emphasized one importance of gifting: "When you think of local specialty here, whale come[s] to . . . mind. . . . We try to give away even a slice to the people we know." At a gifting to celebrate the first catch of the season, the people in Ayukawa-hama take bottles of saki and whisky or crates of beer and Coca-Cola to the whaling-boat owners. The boat owners, in return, distribute blocks of whale meat to each gift sender. A wife of a boat owner said, "I had to deliver lots of whale throughout the town, a bucketful of whale." In addition, it is common for people to take gifts of whale meat to temples and shrines. Through such communitywide reciprocal gifting, the people in Ayukawa-hama reinforce their social ties among the people within the community and also with their ancestors who founded whaling in the community. This is also an occasion for a communitywide celebration in which the whale symbolizes wealth and prosperity.

Once the whale is brought into the flensing station, the flensers and the helpers engage in flensing operations while the local people gather to watch them. The whale meat and blubber are processed for commercial distribution, which is managed by the local Fishery Cooperative Association. At the same time, varying portions of the flensed whale are distributed as gifts through the social network.

Complex reciprocal rules govern the specifics of giving, such as the appropriate partners, the time, the manner and degree of formality, and the quality of the gift item. Such whale-based gift giving is practiced year-round, including during the off-whaling season.

In Ayukawa-hama, whale-based gift giving is carried out extensively throughout the community. Whale meat and blubber are given to the crew members, the flensing team, and relatives and neighbors of the crew members. Whale-meat gifts also reach public institutions such as the community center, the fire station, temples and shrines, the children's association, and old people's clubs. Such communitywide gift exchanges using whale meat and blubber have been so intensive that for the local people, "kujira wa moraumono" ("whale is something to be given") rather than "something to buy."

It is important to note that despite the economic importance of whale catching and product processing and distribution in the subdistrict of Ayukawa-hama and indeed in Oshika-cho township as a whole, this commercial distribution of STCW products also contributes significantly to fulfilling varied cultural and social needs of the local people. For example, the whale meat sold at the stores is often used for gifts or for private consumption, which consequently helps to maintain the whale-based food culture that has been developed over the years. Communitywide social networks are further reinforced through the maintenance of the local whale-based cuisine.

The Local Whale-Based Cuisine

The consumption phase of the STCW operation is extremely significant because it closely relates to the local dietary patterns of Ayukawa-hama. The importance of whale meat and blubber in the local food culture is best expressed in the recurring statement by the local people that "it is not Ayukawa if we don't have whale meat to eat." A housewife in Ayukawa-hama said, "For us, meat means whale since we were small. We eat whale on happy occasions and sad occasions. Whale is indispensable at every important occasion in our life."

In all whaling districts throughout Japan, it is common to find differences in regional preferences of whale cuisine involving varied cooking methods and the preferred species and selected parts of the whale. The favored whale species in Ayukawa-hama is minke whale, which is eaten as sashimi (thinly sliced raw meat and blubber). An elderly man in Ayukawa-hama described how his children like whale sashimi: "When tuna, minke whale, then other, let's say three other kinds are served . . . I watch them. The first thing that their hand[s] reach for is whale. . . . It is delicious, honestly." Minke sashimi is eaten year-round. During the whaling season, it is eaten fresh mainly as a part of everyday meals. Fresh minke-whale meat is also used for ceremonial purposes during the whaling season. During the remainder of the year, when fresh minke-whale meat is not available, whale meat is used as a part of everyday meals much less frequently. It has also been served by public institutions such as schools and hospitals. Ceremonial consumption of minke sashimi also occurs during the off-whaling season, using blocks of minke-whale meat that are kept frozen.

The whale and whaling are closely connected with the historical development of the community and symbolize local prosperity. Whale meat and blubber are considered the nutritionally and culturally superior food in Ayukawa-hama and have formed an important aspect of the local whaling culture.

Religion and World View

Celebration and religious rites are important aspects of culture and are manifested in a series of localized ritual events associated with production, distribution, and consumption of whale products that occur within the whaling community. An intricate merging of two main religious belief systems, Buddhism and Shintoism, is a common phenomenon in Japanese society. This merging, or syncretism, produces the core of Japanese religious life, which focuses on values that emphasize filial piety, reciprocity, and cooperation. It also involves purely localized religious traditions since community people are more committed to the continuous observance of those rites that memorialize ancestors or celebrate the local mode of subsistence.

In rural Japanese communities, whatever a family's or community's mode of subsistence may be, its perpetuation is regarded as a sacred religious duty. In Ayukawa-hama, whaling has been a historically significant subsistence activity that remains well integrated into the economic, social, and cultural domain of the people's life today. Naturally, religious rites that these people practice have been closely linked to whaling and whaling-related activities.

Another important aspect in the local religious observances relates to the perceived relationship between animals, namely whales in Ayukawa-Hama, and humans. The Japanese perceive an interdependent world between animals and humans and reciprocal relations between these realms. Such interdependence and an appropriate reciprocal relationship between whales and humans are influenced by the religious acts on the part of humans, who achieve the required goal through the appropriate observance of religious rites. There are three Shinto shrines and one Buddhist temple in Ayukawa-hama, all of which serve as the sites for such religious observances. Shinto gods (*kami*), who reside in nature and govern the spiritual interaction between the natural world and humans, become the subjects of religious rites through which humans seek their reward, such as a good catch and safety. A sound relationship with the souls of whales as well as those whalers who died at sea is achieved through various religious practices that are held often at Buddhist temples. Such religious rites are carried out individually and collectively, as shown in Table 5-1.

The people in Ayukawa-hama engage in numerous whale-related religious practices. These rites also occur at dedicated shrines outside of the community itself (e.g., the Kinkasan shrine). Other rites are practiced at home, on whaling boats, and in public places such as Buddhist temples and Shinto shrines. Furthermore, these religious practices are observed daily, seasonally, and annually, requiring extremely frequent individual and collective participation.

THREATS TO SURVIVAL

In 1972, a resolution was adopted at the United Nations Conference on the Human Environment calling for a ban on commercial hunting of whales. Ten years later, at its 1982 meeting, the International Whaling Commission (IWC) set zero-catch limits for commercial whaling of all species of whales under its management authority beginning with the 1985–86 open ocean and 1986 coastal seasons. It is important to note that the Scientific Committee of the IWC did not support such a drastic measure and regarded the moratorium as unnecessary.

The decline of Ayukawa-based whaling became evident when the annual IWC quota utilized by the LTCW operations began to decrease. The concern about the eventual ban on commercial whaling led to a series of actions to protest the direction the IWC was taking. The leaders of Oshika-cho, led by the mayor, periodically went to Tokyo to present their view to the government officials in the Ministry of Foreign Affairs and the Ministry of Agriculture, Forestry, and Fisheries. Around 1980, the decline of the whaling industry gradually began to affect the community.

The proper conservation of whale resources is generally considered to involve protection of depleted whale stocks and implementation of management measures to ensure that nondepleted stocks are sustainably utilized. However, the decision to implement an extreme and unnecessary protectionist measure such as the moratorium was inevitably influenced by the existing public views of whales as a special class of animal threatened with extinction and of whaling as being cruel and rapacious, which originated in urban Western Europe, North America, Australia, and New Zealand. Such views have been effectively promoted by the antiwhaling lobby groups and were an important driving force behind the eventual adoption of the moratorium.

Table 5-1
Whale-Related Religious Practices and Associated Phenomena

Domestic rites
Daily prayers at Shinto altar for whaler's safety.

Domestic memorial rites for deceased whalers on a daily, annual, and periodic basis at Buddhist altar.

Rites on board whaling ships
Installation of soul of the boat, talismans under the bow.

Observance of taboos regarding sea deities.

Purification of boats and crew by Shinto priest before first sailing of season.

Shinto shrine placed in steering house of ship.

Celebration of catch of first whale of season; prayers for safety of crew and for souls of whales to be caught.

Flensing station contains small Shinto shrine at which to pray for safety of crew and a large catch.

On the first day of the whaling season, whalers sail close to island shrine, offer sea water to deity, and pray for safety.

Rites at Shinto Shrines
Laypersons' and Shinto priests' prayers to ensure whalers' safety at sea (daily, seasonal, annual).

Rites for atonement for accidental violation of taboos on board whaling ships.

Dedication of votive plaques.

Pilgrimages to pray at distant shrines for whalers' safety at sea.

Annual festival dramatizing whaling techniques and giving thanks for annual fishing/whaling harvest.

Erection of whale jawbones as sacred gates for Shinto shrines.

Whaling companies and whalers' associations dedicate a variety of items to shrines in gratitude for divine protection.

Whalers offer whale meat to shrine deities as "first fruits."

Whaling drums, whaling festivals.

Miniature shrines offered for thanksgiving.

Votive plaques for lost harpoons and knives offered to shrine deities.

Whale models are used as targets at archery festival, and later, good-luck charms are brought to boats for successful whaling.

Rites at Buddhist Temples
Construction of whale graves and "whale mounds."

Construction of whale memorial pillars within temple grounds and elsewhere.

Laypersons' prayers for whalers' safety at sea.

Table 5-1 (continued)

Priests' annual and equinoctial prayers for pacifying the souls of whales, fish, and whalers lost at sea.

Composition of posthumous names for deceased whales.

Compilation of death registers for whale spirits.

Temple visits to offer thanks for the season's catch.

Whaling companies, whalers, whalers' associations, and temple parishioners sponsor memorial services for whales and commission memorial tablets for whales and whalers lost at sea.

Lanterns for whale spirits are sent out to sea at *bon* (Buddhist All Souls Day).

The moratorium also has revealed itself as a human issue, particularly after the impact of the cessation of commercial whaling has been repeatedly reported at the IWC meetings. The STCW communities in Japan are examples of the social, cultural, and economic impacts of the moratorium threatening the survival of communities. The moratorium also contradicts the universally accepted basic human right of access to culturally significant food and diet as prescribed in numerous international covenants and agreements, including the Universal Declaration of Human Rights (Article 25), the International Covenant of Economic, Social, and Cultural Rights (Article 11), the International Covenant of Civil and Political Rights (Article 1), and the International Covenant of Economic, Social, and Cultural Rights (Article 1).

Data from 1985 show that about half of the total labor force of about 1,596 in Oshika-cho were engaged in fisheries. This number is further increased when people employed in fishery-related occupations are added. Among about thirty types of fisheries based in Oshika-cho, whaling has been the most stable and prominent industry since the town was founded in 1906, with considerably more than half of the gross fishery sales at the Oshika-cho wholesale market generated from STCW operations. Recent sales data are shown in Table 5-2.

Both LTCW and STCW boats continued their operations until the end of the 1987 whaling season after the government of Japan had negotiated that date in order to allow time to phase out LTCW operations and to reduce STCW operations in an orderly fashion. LTCW boats operated by the Tokyo-based companies ended their whaling operations at the end of the 1987 whaling season, at which time government compensation was given to cover the economic losses created by the closure of their whaling operations. However, STCW companies, which have been operated by local entrepreneurs, decided to wait for the normalization of their operations and to refuse to surrender their STCW licenses, issued annually by the government. The consequence of this decision was that the STCW opera-

Table 5-2
Gross Fishery Sales at Oshika-cho Maritime Wholesale Market, 1984–1987 (in Japanese Yen)

	Whale Products	Other Fishery	Total Sales	Whale-Products Sales as Percentage of Total Sales
1984	348,967	190,407	539,374	64.70%
1985	292,677	253,709	546,386	53.57%
1986	417,253	272,339	689,592	60.51%
1987	723,538	193,177	916,715	78.93%
Average	445,609	227,408	673,017	66.21%

Source: Ted Bester, 1989, "Socio-Economic Implications of a Zero Catch Limit on Distribution Channels and Related Activities in Hokkaido and Miyagi Prefecture, Japan." International Whaling Commission/42/SE1 1989, Table 5.

tors did not receive any government compensation for the loss of minke whaling, which composed the most substantial part of their operations.

The reduction of the population in Oshika-cho began around 1965 and has continued to the present. One woman (fifty years old) who has been living in Ayukawa-hama all her life said, "What has changed the most since the moratorium is that many friends and neighbors left the town. We used to have 800 children going to our elementary school. But now we only have 150." The population of Oshika-cho was 5,891 in 1995, showing a steady decline from 13,753 in 1955. There is a high ratio of elderly people in the population. Table 5-3 shows the population decline of Oshika-cho from 1955 to 1995.

After the 1988 whaling season, the STCW operators, having abided by the IWC's decision, stopped their minke whale harvest and rationalized their whaling operations by forming partnerships in order to reduce the number of boats in operation and the size of the work force. Without minke whaling, the nationally regulated hunts for Baird's beaked whales and pilot whales became the basis of their operations. Only about half of the whalers continued to work as whalers. Their salaries were reduced by 50 to 90 percent of their previous year's salary. They also received only a small customary share of the whale meat. Some laid-off whalers left Ayukawa-hama and moved to larger cities to find better job prospects. Many wives of whalers had to take part-time jobs. These changes caused various profound interpersonal and emotional stresses, including the loss of self-esteem, in these families. A number of stress-related health problems are reported among former whalers and their families. A fourteen-year-old junior-high-school student expressed her sadness: "I hear that whaling has

Table 5-3
Population in Oshika-cho, 1955–1995

Year	Population
1955	13,753
1960	13,405
1965	11,974
1970	10,581
1975	9,535
1980	8,450
1985	7,814
1990	6,773
1995	5,891

Source: Population Statistics from Oshika-cho Township Records.

to be finished now. All of the people in Ayukawa are very worried, because the whaling moratorium with long and dark shadows is approaching with a threat to our livelihood. To my granddad, whose whole life has been dedicated to whaling, it is a turmoil and his words express his sorrow and agony."

Economic decline in Ayukawa-hama is apparent throughout whaling-related business and thus affects the township as a whole. The continued existence of whaling-related businesses such as whale-meat processors and small-scale distributors is threatened. This has inevitably affected local tourism in Ayukawa-hama, since whale meat and blubber served as local specialty foods that attracted tourists from distant communities.

In the fall of 1990, Oshika-cho completed construction of its new museum, Whale Land. This was an attempt to help promote tourism, which the township hoped would compensate for the loss of whaling. Oshika township officials are fully aware that the new museum will not in itself be enough to cause any increase in the number of tourists visiting the township. However, they are expecting that the new museum will provide enough interest to the visitors to the Kinkasan shrine that they will spend more hours in Oshika-cho, thus benefiting the restaurants, stores, and hotels in Ayukawa-hama.

The loss of whale meat in the diet has caused concerns over the health of the local people. Since the reduction of whale-meat gifting, the people in Ayukawa-hama have begun to purchase substitute meat at the stores. Whale meat is apparently a superior source of animal protein to agriculturally produced meat; thus the substitution of store-bought meat for whale meat caused health officials to be concerned when obesity, high blood pressure, and elevated cholesterol levels began to appear among elderly people in Ayukawa-hama.

RESPONSE: STRUGGLES TO SURVIVE CULTURALLY

Throughout the debates related to the STCW issues, the people in Ayukawa-hama have not merely been passive victims affected by the IWC's decisions. Rather, they have been making conscious decisions based on their observations of the given situation and their judgment concerning alternative courses of action. The people in Ayukawa-hama are very knowledgeable about the state of the STCW issues and have become informed about the nature of the IWC and its decision-making process.

Since 1989, community representatives have been attending the IWC meetings, participating and observing as part of the Japanese delegation and as nongovernmental observers. They are fully aware of the commission's decision to accommodate the social and cultural needs of the aboriginal/subsistence whalers and communities by exempting this form of whaling from the moratorium.[4] They are also aware of the fact that in the case of Alaskan Eskimo whaling, in the past, special consideration for humane reasons was given to this group of people despite the threat continued whaling appeared to have on the seriously depleted whale stock that they have been harvesting. Moreover, the Ayukawa-hama representatives are aware of a discrepancy between the recommendations of the Scientific Committee of the IWC and the outcome of the commission's discussions that relate directly to their livelihood, including the moratorium decision itself, which was passed by the commission despite the lack of any recommendation from the Scientific Committee in support of such action. Furthermore, the Ayukawa-hama representatives have noted the commission's vote against the Japanese request for fifty minke whales as an emergency relief allocation, despite the agreement of the Scientific Committee that this number could be taken without any threat to the stock in question.

The persistent effort by the people in Ayukawa-hama to continue to seek an understanding of the social, cultural, and economic need for the normalization of their STCW operations is firmly based on their conviction that the IWC's decision to ban minke whaling in their coastal waters is unwarranted. An elderly man said, "We hope that whaling will resume. There is a problem if the moratorium continues, because whales are a part of our environment and our life. Of course we could eat pork or beef, but I do not think I would have much zest for living, or could work hard without whale meat."

The moratorium has adversely affected the strategy through which the local people have developed their community of Ayukawa-hama, through utilizing local whale resources. It is the local people's conviction that the deterioration of the social, cultural, and economic systems of Ayukawa-hama can be remedied only by normalizing STCW operations.

FOOD FOR THOUGHT

Diffusion of the centuries-old whaling tradition in Japan resulted in the emergence of the Ayukawa-hama whaling community at the beginning of the twentieth century in Miyagi Prefecture in the northeastern part of Honshu. STCW operations continue to meet important contemporary needs associated with the high symbolic value of whales and whaling, the high dietary value placed on whale products, and the high value of whale meat in gift exchanges and for various other ceremonial purposes. The recent development of the international debate about whaling and STCW, in particular, has demonstrated that the basis of the current prohibition on commercial whaling lies in a value conflict between the whaling cultural tradition in which whales are viewed as a renewable resource for human consumption and the protectionist and animal rights view that demands a nonuse principle with respect to whales.

Questions

1. Describe the two distinct views toward whales and whaling underlying the STCW debate and the fundamental conflict that prevents the pro-whaling and anti-whaling groups from reaching compromise.

2. Would you support a closely regulated take of nonendangered species of whales for food by people for whom whaling is socially and culturally important? Why or why not?

3. Are there rational reasons for the people in Ayukawa-hama to have to give up whaling?

4. In what ways might the people in Ayukawa-hama resolve the problems they face?

5. Has the involvement of animal-protectionist and animal-rights groups in issues related to the conservation of other species such as seals and elephants caused conflicts similar to that of the whaling issue and the problems in Ayukawa-hama?

NOTES

1. Small-type coastal whaling is one of the three types of whaling operations conducted in Japan, along with large-type coastal whaling and open ocean whaling. Small-type coastal whaling is a significantly smaller-scale operation than the other two types and harvests minke whales and other small-type whales, while large-type whaling is usually conducted by large fishery corporations and harvests larger spe-

cies of whales. In open ocean whaling, a fleet of catcher boats with a mother ship travels to the Antarctic for whaling operations.

2. Ayukawa-hama is one of the four small-type whaling communities in Japan, along with Abashiri in Hokkaido Prefecture, Wada-ura in Chiba Prefecture, and Taiji in Wakayama Prefecture.

3. The objectives of the International Whaling Commission are expressed in the International Convention for the Regulation of Whaling. It aims to provide for the proper conservation of whale stocks and to make possible the orderly development of the whaling industry.

4. Aboriginal/subsistence whaling is one of the management categories that the IWC has established under which it grants a special quota of whales to the aboriginal groups that have demonstrated the traditional cultural and nutritional needs for whales. Presently, the Alaskan Eskimo, the Inuit in Greenland, and the aboriginal peoples in Russia and in St. Vincent and the Grenadines are granted such quotas.

RESOURCE GUIDE

Published Literature

Akimichi, T., P. J. Asquith, H. Befu, T. C. Bestor, S. R. Braund, M. M. R. Freeman, H. Hardacre, M. Iwasaki, A. Kalland, L. Manderson, B. D. Moeran, and J. Takahashi. *Small-Type Coastal Whaling in Japan: Report of an International Workshop.* Boreal Institute for Northern Studies, Occasional Publication no. 27. Edmonton. Also, Report IWC/40/23. International Whaling Commission, Cambridge, 1988.

Iwasaki, Masami. "Cultural Significance of Whaling in a Whaling Community in Abashiri." M. A. thesis, Department of Anthropology, University of Alberta, Edmonton, 1988.

Iwasaki-Goodman, Masami. "An Analysis of Social and Cultural Change in Ayukawa-hama (Ayukawa Shore Community)." Ph.D. dissertation, Department of Anthropology, University of Alberta, Edmonton, 1994.

Iwasaki-Goodman, M., and M. M. R. Freeman. "Social and Cultural Significance of Whaling in Contemporary Japan: A Case Study of Small-Type Coastal Whaling." In *Key Issues in Hunter-Gatherer Research*, ed. E. S. Burch, Jr., and L. J. Ellanna, 377–400. Oxford: Berg, 1994.

Japan Fisheries Agency. Papers on JSTCW Submitted to the IWC, 1986–1996, 1997.

Kalland, Arne, and Brian Moeran. *Japanese Whaling: End of an Era?* London: Curzon Press, 1992.

Film

Whalers and the Sea. Directed by Toshiaki Umekawa, distributed by Siglo, 5-24-16-210 Nakano, Nakano-ku, Tokyo, Japan 164-0001.

Organizations

The High North Alliance
PO Box 123, N-8390
Reine i Lofoten, Norway
http://www.highnorth.no

The Institute of Cetacean Research
Tokyo Suisan Bldg.
4-18 Toyomi-cho, Chuo-ku
Tokyo 104, Japan
http://www.jp.whale.sci.org

Japan Small-Type Whaling Association
4-5-10-506 Honcho, Nakano-ku
Tokyo 164-0012, Japan

Japan Whaling Association
2-8-3, Higashi-nihonbashi, Chuo-ku
Tokyo 103-0004, Japan
http://www.jp-whaling-assn.com

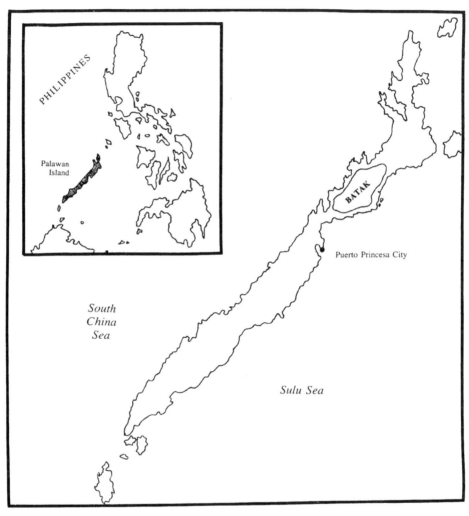

Map 6-1. Location of Batak on Palawan Island, Philippines. Courtesy of James F. Eder.

Chapter 6

The Batak of the Philippines
James F. Eder

Batak have lived here on the Tanabag River for as long as anyone can remember, and there were a lot more of us before than now. And yet the forest
is still here. If [lowland] Filipinos had been living here, the forest would be
gone.

—Udoy, of Calabayog

Even if the Batak became rich, and my house was made from cement and
my floor from stone, I'd still be a Batak—I'd still hunt pigs, collect honey,
and camp in the forest.

—Timbay, of Calabayog

CULTURAL OVERVIEW

The People

The Batak inhabit the forested interior valleys of the east coast of north
central Palawan Island. They are one of about twenty different groups of
indigenous foraging peoples in the Philippines. The Batak speak a language
related to the central Visayan group of Philippine languages, and they share
some important cultural similarities with the other indigenous peoples of
Palawan. However, the Batak are distinguished by their short stature and
dark skin color, physical attributes that long led outsiders to label them as
"Negritos." They are also distinctive in their extensive reliance on hunting
and gathering of forest and riverine resources as well as their use of the
bow and arrow.

For centuries the Batak have had important trading links with seagoing
peoples of the Sulu Sea region, exchanging forest products for manufac-

tured goods and other needs. The Spanish encountered Palawan in 1521 when the survivors of Ferdinand Magellan's expedition stopped there to seek provisions during their search for the Spice Islands, but Palawan was a largely unexplored and unsettled part of the Philippines throughout the Spanish colonial period and well into the American period, and the Batak remained relatively isolated and undisturbed until the 1920s.

The Setting

A chain of mountains runs the length of Palawan Island. The island experiences a June-to-December rainy season and a January-to-May dry season; the latter is particularly pronounced on the eastern coast, which receives about 63 inches of rain a year and is one of the driest areas of the Philippines. The interior regions presently inhabited by the Batak receive greater rainfall but are nonetheless home to relatively dry, monsoonal forests. While such forests lack the height, density, and species richness of evergreen rain forests, they provide a variety of accessible trees, shrubs, and vines producing carbohydrate-rich seeds, fruits, and tubers.

Traditional Subsistence Strategies

The Batak combine forest foraging, collection and sale of forest products, shifting cultivation (slash-and-burn), and wage labor for lowland Filipino farmers. The principal forest foods collected include wild pigs, gliding squirrels, jungle fowl, wild honey, wild yams, wild fruits and greens, fish, mollusks, and crustaceans. Most forest food collecting is done by solitary individuals or small task groups operating from local group settlements or from temporary forest camps (Figure 6-1); in the past, pig hunting and fish stunning were sometimes large-group activities. Pigs are taken with the spear and hunting dogs or from blinds with the bow and arrow or homemade guns. A variety of traps and snares are also used.

Commercially valuable forest products exchanged with outside peoples include honey, rattan, and Manila copal. The latter is a resin produced by the *almaciga* tree used in the manufacture of paint varnish and other industrial products. Exchange of forest products is the principal means by which the Batak acquire rice, clothing, and other consumer wants.

The Batak have also long produced some rice by shifting cultivation, together with smaller amounts of corn, cassavas, and sweet potatoes, but they emphasize farming far less than their lowland neighbors. Groups of Batak also hire out for several days at a time to help lowland farmers clear or weed fields, to harvest rice, or to pick coconuts or coffee. Guiding tourists has also become an occasional source of cash income.

Figure 6-1. A Batak mother and child in a leaf shelter at a forest camp. Courtesy of James F. Eder.

Social and Political Organization

The Batak trace descent through both sides of the family, and their kin terms resemble those of other peoples in the Philippines. Batak are prohibited, however, from using the birth names of their in-laws, and naming practices are elaborated accordingly. Marriage is monogamous, although a few cases of polyandry have been recorded. Divorce and remarriage were common in the past; a *surugiden*, or gathering of the elders, heard and resolved marital disputes. A newly married couple customarily lives near the wife's parents during the early years of a marriage; in later years a husband hopes to rejoin his own kin.

Nuclear-family households are the basic unit of production and consumption. Small groups of households often pool their labor resources, and there is considerable sharing of food, but households are expected to be autonomous and self-reliant. Within households, husbands and wives both enjoy considerable freedom of action. Batak have few children, and mean household size is only about 3.5 persons.

The Batak are strongly egalitarian and independent. Certain older men, by virtue of their kinship ties and personal attributes, emerge as natural leaders and become the focus of day-to-day residential clusters. The opinions of such individuals are respected and influential, but not binding.

Religion and World View

The Batak live in a world inhabited by a variety of nature spirits and supernatural beings, most falling into two broad classes: malevolent *panya'en* and capricious but potentially benevolent *diwata*. Visible only to shamans (part-time religious specialists), these spirit beings inhabit specific trees, thickets, rocks, and streams and are humanlike in their actions and desires. Nature spirits, particularly the *panya'en*, stand in a jealous protective relationship to the various forest and riverine resources utilized by the Batak. By ancestral agreement, Batak may exploit these resources to meet legitimate subsistence needs, but any wasteful or excessive use, intended or not, or even displays of disrespect toward forest animals, may so antagonize a caretaker *panya'en* that it punishes the offending individual with illness or even death.

Mediating Batak relationships with supernatural beings are mediums capable of entering trance states through song or dance in order to appeal to their *diwata* familiars to intercede on behalf of some human enterprise or misfortune, typically illness. Two group rituals occur when the natural equilibrium between humans, forest resources, and guardian spirits is disturbed. Should a honey collector accidentally drop a hive to the ground and waste the contents of it, the caretaker *panya'en* Ungaw may become so angered that he sends the bees away, and the entire local group is unable to collect any honey at all. Such circumstances call for a fifteen-day period of song, dance, and collective good behavior. Similarly, should an entire local group have trouble hunting pigs, it may appeal for relief to the caretaker *diwata* of wild pigs by performing a trance-inducing group dance.

THREATS TO SURVIVAL

Demographic Trends

At the close of the nineteenth century, before Palawan was extensively settled by migrant lowland Filipinos, the Batak numbered 800 to 1,000 persons. Today they number only about 300 persons, including the offspring of increasingly frequent marriages with outsiders. This abrupt population decline reflects the complex interactions of many factors, including high mortality at all age levels, low fertility, difficulties obtaining adequate nutrition, and vulnerability to such epidemic diseases as measles and such chronic diseases as tuberculosis.

These various factors underlying twentieth-century Batak population decline ultimately reflect the role that Palawan has played as one of the Philippines' principal remaining land frontiers. Since 1900, immigration by land-seeking lowland settlers has incrementally alienated Batak land and other ancestral resources. During the 1930s, the government established a series of reservations for the Batak situated along the coastal plain portion of their ancestral domain. The Batak abandoned these reservations after they were overrun by lowland settlers during the 1950s during a large surge of immigration to Palawan after World War II. Since the 1950s, the Batak have slowly retreated to the interior of the island, keeping their own settlements just ahead of those of advancing lowland farmers.

Today, the Batak are distributed in a series of eight local groups, each identified with a particular river and its watershed. Local groups range in size from three to twenty-four households, and each group has a fixed settlement site located about two to six miles upstream from a coastal lowland Filipino community. However, such settlements are not permanently occupied, as hunting and gathering trips to the forested interior, visits downstream to lowland employers, and the annual cycle of upland rice cultivation take small groups of individuals and households away from the settlement for days or weeks at a time.

Economic Problems

The importance of forest-products exchange and wage labor to Batak subsistence has made patron-client ties linking an individual Batak to an individual lowlander in sometimes-exploitative and debilitating relations of credit and debt a prominent feature of the Batak economy. Market wants are growing, but opportunities to earn cash are few, and how to obtain cash is a constant preoccupation.

Increasing competition from outsiders for Batak land and other resources has made this situation worse. Much ancestral territory has been lost in the twentieth century to lowland settlement as land-hungry migrants have permanently converted forest land to various upland agricultural uses. Even the still-forested portions of Batak territory have been extensively interpenetrated by Tagbanua (a neighboring indigenous people) and lowland migrants. Many of these people also collect copal and rattan; some even live and marry among the Batak.

Environmental Problems

The large numbers of people presently exploiting forest products and their often-unsustainable collection practices have created serious natural-resource-management problems within the still-forested portions of Batak territory. A significant fraction of the copal-bearing *almaciga* trees (*Agathis dammara*) are dead or diseased due to excessive tapping, and many stands of rattan have been seriously depleted by overcollecting. Some biodiversity has also been lost due to excessive collection and sale of jungle orchids and parrots. Where the forest cover has been removed, the agricultural practices of lowland migrants have sometimes contributed to soil depletion and to ecologically undesirable forms of land cover.

Political Subordination

Each Batak settlement today is politically subordinate to a downstream, lowland Filipino community (*barangay*) of which it is nominally a part. The elective leader of such communities, called the *barangay kapitan*, is the lowest-level administrative official in the Philippine government. Each Batak settlement today also has a *kapitan* of its own, popularly chosen to represent the group to the outside world and to be responsive to various government agencies. This position may originally have evolved in response to attempts to organize the copal and rattan trades. In any case, the lowland *barangay kapitan* is in charge, and some have used their positions to intimidate the Batak for their own economic gain. The Batak find lowlanders in general intimidating due to their greater numbers, formal schooling, and more aggressive behavioral styles, factors that over the years have made the Batak vulnerable to local political control by outsiders of all sorts.

Sociocultural Problems

The Batak have suffered extensive deculturation in the twentieth century: they have lost, without replacement by functional equivalents, many traditional cultural beliefs, practices, and institutions. One example of this is the decline and disappearance during the 1950s of the *umbay* ceremony, a unique puberty ceremony or rite of passage that initiated adolescents into a status whose behavioral expectations helped prepare them for adulthood and marriage. After initiation, for example, male and female *umbays* were expected to begin doing the food-getting activities appropriate to their gender in the company of siblings or age-mates, rather than in the company of their parents, as they had done before the ceremony. But the demographic changes that resulted from more extensive contact with lowland Philippine society after World War II—sedentarization, local group fragmentation, and continued population decline—made it more and more difficult to line up the unrelated opposite-sex partners needed to initiate a new *umbay*. In consequence, during the postwar years, more and more Batak adolescents began to "miss their turn," growing up to marry without ever becoming *umbays*, and the ceremony soon disappeared altogether.

Similar deculturation has occurred in the realm of curing ceremonies. Few spirit mediums or curers remain today to dance or sing in the traditional fashion to enlist supernatural assistance to effect a cure, and some Batak local groups no longer hold curing ceremonies at all.

Deculturation of these sorts has been costly to the Batak because it has reduced their capacity to cope with the physiological, psychological, and social exigencies—that is, the adaptive demands—of everyday life. Curing ceremonies, for example, do not just seek supernatural assistance on behalf of an ill person. Such ceremonies also mobilize social support, visible in the active participation of all local group members, and an individual's perception that he or she is socially supported by others is widely recognized to play a major role in his or her ability to recover from illness.

More generally, deculturation has eroded the Batak's sense of ethnic identity and the associated, culturally constituted patterns of motivation that such a sense of identity helps foster. This sense of identity, no less than control over land and adequate resources, may be critical to helping indigenous peoples such as the Batak resist marginalization to wider social systems.

RESPONSE: STRUGGLES TO SURVIVE CULTURALLY

The traditional Batak response to the economic, political, and sociocultural threats caused by growing contact with lowland settlers and the Philippine state was to minimize such contact by retreating farther into the island's interior. Today, a government ban on further cutting of primary forest and the Batak's own desires for greater access to the material benefits of participation in wider Philippine society have led them to make a stand in their present locations. The Batak are aided in this effort by two nongovernmental organizations (NGOs), supported in part by international funding, that currently work with them to develop their capacities to sustainably use and manage their natural resources and to secure their remaining ancestral domain against further encroachment by lowland migrants. One is the United Tribes of Palawan (NATRIPAL), a confederation of about fifty local indigenous-peoples groups formed by the Tribal Filipino Apostolate of the Catholic Church and supported in part by funding from the World Wildlife Fund; the other is Haribon Palawan, the regional chapter of a sometimes-controversial national environmentalist group supported in part by funding from the World Conservation Union.

Both organizations aim to help the Batak to become more self-sufficient economically and more independent socially and politically. To do so, they have been proceeding, in close consultation with the Batak themselves, on a number of fronts. First and most difficult has been the effort to secure the Batak's remaining ancestral domain. The problem has not been just competition from more numerous and more aggressive lowland settlers, but the fact that the Philippine government has traditionally regarded all forest land as "public" land and all occupants of such land as "squatters," regardless of length of occupancy. In short, in the eyes of the government, the Batak never "owned" their land to begin with. In recent decades, greater political recognition of the economic problems and human rights of the nation's indigenous peoples has led the Philippine government to develop social forestry and other programs that, if implemented, promise to improve the well-being of peoples like the Batak. Under recent legislation aimed at the ancestral-lands issue, for example, NATRIPAL and Haribon Palawan are working to empower the Batak to secure certificates of ancestral domain claim from the Department of Environment and Natural Resources. Two such applications have already been approved, and others are being sought.

The Batak have learned, however, that it is not enough just to have nominal control over their own land. They also need to control exploitation of the resources on their land: in particular, the forest cover itself (which they hope to preserve) and the various nontimber forest products—rattan, honey, and tree resin—that are one cornerstone of Batak livelihood. Hence on a second front and again with the assistance of NATRIPAL and Haribon Palawan, the Batak are seeking cancellation of the nontimber forest-products concessions held by outsiders, concessions that have enabled wealthy outsiders to exploit Batak resources and secure much of the profits for themselves. These efforts have enjoyed some success, but they face formidable obstacles, including opposition from entrenched lowland economic interests and the difficulty of instituting a natural-resource-management program that limits access by outside peoples.

On a third front, and with the recognition that the Batak now require cash incomes beyond what they can secure at present from the collection and sale of forest products, NATRIPAL, Haribon Palawan, and several local government agencies are encouraging the Batak to grow bananas and tree crops—cashew nuts, for example—in their upland rice fields after the harvest. Such "agroforestry" programs, as they are called, promise to diversify subsistence food sources, add new sources of cash income (cashew nuts command a good price in the regional market), and stabilize upland agricultural systems by enhancing biodiversity and minimizing erosion. Obstacles to success in this area include the poverty of the Batak, which makes them reluctant to invest effort in planting trees that may not bear edible or saleable fruit for several years, and lack of knowledge about what sorts of tree crops or other new agricultural activities would in fact be most appropriate to the Batak's environmental and economic circumstances.

Beyond these specific initiatives, Batak desires to preserve their ethnic identity are receiving significant support from local NGOs and the indigenous-peoples movement in the Philippines generally. Batak representatives, for example, are periodically invited to participate in conferences in Puerto Princesa City (the capital city of Palawan) and elsewhere in the Philippines to discuss the problems of indigenous peoples and to plan political strategies.

FOOD FOR THOUGHT

A hundred years ago, the Batak were a culturally distinct, relatively isolated, and largely self-sufficient group of forest food collectors. Today, engulfed by lowland Filipino homesteaders who have journeyed to Palawan in search of agricultural land, the Batak have become enmeshed in the economic, social, and cultural fabric of wider Philippine society. For this the Batak have paid dearly: they are declining in number, and those who remain are in ill health and have lost many elements of their traditional culture.

Questions

1. What political strategies should the Batak employ to best achieve their ends? Should they align themselves with other indigenous peoples on Palawan, for example, or should they "go it alone"?

2. What do the Batak really want in life? Can they really enjoy the material benefits of lowland Philippine life while simultaneously preserving their ethnic identity?

3. How should the Philippine government deal with the issue of lowland migration onto Batak lands and lowland settler competition for Batak natural resources?

4. The Batak say that they would like their children to attend school. What sort of educational system would best serve Batak needs: one that prepares Batak children to join mainstream lowland society, or one that is more specifically designed for the Batak own present lifeway?

5. What sorts of improved livelihood strategies would be most appropriate to implement among the Batak? The Batak desperately need both more food and more money, but are agroforestry programs and other efforts to improve their farming abilities the best way to meet these needs, or are there other, still-unexplored ways they might better be able to make a living?

RESOURCE GUIDE

Published Literature

Eder, James F. "Batak Resource Management: Belief, Knowledge, and Practice." *Issues in Forest Conservation*. Gland, Switzerland: International Union for the Conservation of Nature and Natural Resources and World Wide Fund for Nature, 1997.

———. *On the Road to Tribal Extinction: Depopulation, Deculturation, and*

Adaptive Well-being among the Batak of the Philippines. Berkeley: University of California Press, 1987.

――――. "State-sponsored 'Participatory Development' and Tribal Filipino Ethnic Identity." *Social Analysis* 35 (1994): 28–38.

Venturello, Manuel H. "Manners and Customs of the Tagbanous and Other Tribes of the Island of Palawan, Philippines." Trans. Mrs. Edward Y. Miller. *Smithsonian Miscellaneous Collections* 48 (1907): 514–558.

Warren, Charles P. *The Batak of Palawan: A Culture in Transition.* Research Series no. 3. Chicago: Philippine Studies Program, University of Chicago, 1964.

Films and Videos

The Batak: A Forgotten People. 1981. John Feretti.

Organizations

Haribon Palawan

Puerto Princesa City 5300

Philippines

NATRIPAL

Puerto Princesa City 5300

Philippines

Chapter 7

The Batek of Malaysia

Kirk Endicott

We Batek are rich if we have a cooking pot, digging stick, bush knife, lighter, tobacco, salt, and a fishing pole. Also, a man is sad if he doesn't have a blowpipe. When we live in the forest, we don't need lots of possessions. We can dig tubers. If someone doesn't have food, others give it.

—A Kelantan Man, Post Lebir, 1990

CULTURAL OVERVIEW

The People

The Batek De' of Peninsular Malaysia are one of the few peoples in the world still living to a substantial degree by hunting and gathering wild resources, rather than getting their food from farming or animal husbandry. Most of the approximately 800 Batek De' live in and around Taman Negara, Peninsular Malaysia's national park, which straddles the borders between Pahang, Kelantan, and Trengganu states. The Batek De' are one of several groups of Malayan aborigines (Orang Asli) who have traditionally lived by hunting and gathering (the groups called "Semang" or "Negritos" in the literature) and are the largest group of those still following that way of life. (In this chapter the term "Batek" refers to the Batek De' unless one of the other Batek groups is specified.)

The Batek are cultural and probably biological descendants of the earliest well-documented human population of the Malay Peninsula, the so-called Hoabinhians. Archaeological findings dating from about 11,000 B.C. show that Hoabinhians lived throughout the peninsula, from the coasts to the interior mountains, exploiting a wide range of wild plants and animals.

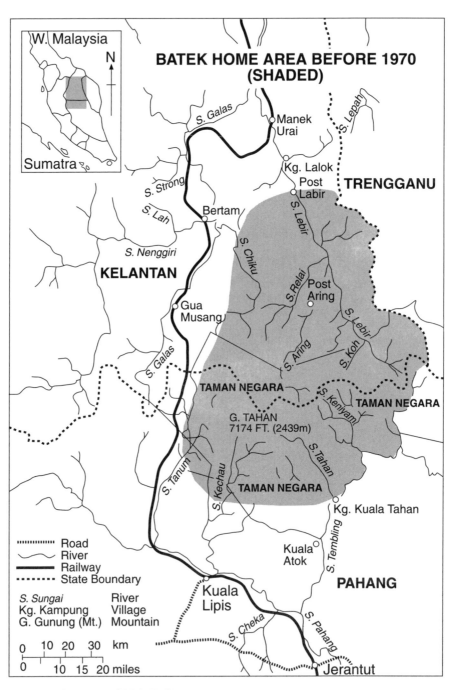

Map 7-1. Courtesy of Kirk Endicott.

About 2,000 B.C., immigrants from the north (present-day Thailand) brought horticulture, new technology (e.g., pottery), and Mon-Khmer languages into the peninsula. Some Hoabinhians mixed with the immigrants and became swidden (slash-and-burn) farmers. Others continued the foraging (hunting and gathering) tradition, but augmented it by trading forest products to farmers for food and craft items, which benefited both groups. The ancestors of the Semang apparently adopted Mon-Khmer languages from their trading partners. This suggests that the foraging and farming descendants of the Hoabinhians have maintained close and amicable relations for a long time.

The persistence of foraging peoples into the late twentieth century can be explained by the advantages of that way of life and their hostile relations with immigrant Malays who pushed into the interior from the coasts during the last millennium. Batek and other Orang Asli retreated into the depths of the rain forest to avoid Malay slave raiding, which peaked in the late nineteenth century. Until recently, the Batek preserved their culture by staying in the forest and limiting their contact with outsiders.

The Setting

The Batek call themselves *batek hep*, "forest people." Until about 1970, they lived in a vast expanse of lowland tropical rain forest extending from the lower Lebir River in Kelantan on the north to the Tembling River in Pahang on the south, and from the Chiku and Tanum rivers on the west to just over the Trengganu border on the east. The terrain is mostly rolling hills carved up by an intricate network of rivers and streams. Highlands that include the peninsula's tallest mountain, Gunung Tahan, rise in the southern part of the Batek territory, but Batek normally do not live there because the mountain forests contain little food. Since 1970, most of the land outside the national park has been selectively logged or clear-cut and replaced by oil-palm and rubber plantations. Batek wanting to continue their traditional way of life have retreated into the national park and the few remaining patches of partially logged forest nearby.

The lowland rain forest of Peninsular Malaysia, protected by year-round heat and high humidity and watered by about one hundred inches of rain each year, harbors the greatest number of plant and animal species of any forest in the world. It is dominated by huge trees, 100 to 250 feet tall, with smooth bark and flangelike buttresses at their bases. They overlap at their tops, forming a continuous "canopy" of limbs and leaves. Each tree is an ecosystem in itself, being festooned with vines, ferns, orchids, and other epiphytes (plants that grow on top of other plants) and providing homes for thousands of insects, birds, bats, and small reptiles and mammals, like squirrels and monkeys. The floor of the forest is covered with tree seedlings and stemless palms but is relatively open except along major rivers and where tree falls have opened up the canopy, allowing all manner of trees and bushes to fight for a share of the light. The rain forest provides food for humans in the form of tubers (mostly wild yams); nuts; vegetables like palm, fern, and bamboo shoots; seasonal fruits and honey; small tree-dwelling and burrowing game; and fish. Large ground-dwelling animals, like deer and pigs, are scarce due to the paucity of food for them at ground level.

Traditional Subsistence Strategies

Vegetables, especially wild yams, form the year-round staples of the foraging diet. Typically, parties of women and children leave camp in the morning to search for yams, sometimes heading for places where immature vines were seen before. When they spot the telltale leaves or vines, they dig up the starch-storing tubers, using digging sticks tipped with metal blades. The tubers may wind sinuously for several feet underground. Sometimes a woman will disappear into the hole as she pursues a tuber to its end. On the journeys to and from the tuber sites, the women gather any other wild vegetables and catch any small game they encounter. They return to camp when they have filled their pandanus-leaf back-baskets with food or have given up the search.

Wild fruits and honey are important seasonal food sources. In April and May, honeybees gather pollen and nectar from the rain forest's many flowering trees. They construct nests that hang underneath limbs of the tallest trees. Daring men climb to the nests after dark, when the bees are quiet, and smoke out the bees with leaf torches. The climbers then lower the nests, which contain honey, wax, and larvae, to the ground in bark baskets. After the honey season, numerous species of wild fruits ripen in succession, the last in November. Parties of mixed ages and both genders go out in search of fruit. Usually young men climb the trees and cut down the fruit-laden branches, but women may do so if there are no men available. People on the ground eat their fill and put the remainder in containers to take back to camp.

Small game and fish provide the meat in the Batek diet. Men (and occasionally women) hunt arboreal game—including monkeys, gibbons, squirrels, and birds—using bamboo blowpipes and darts poisoned with the sap of a rain-forest tree. Hunters usually go out alone or in small groups. As they walk, they scan the treetops, listen, look for scraps dropped by feeding animals, and sniff the bushes for the odor of animal urine. When they spot an animal, they creep to the base of the tree it is in and shoot as many darts as possible into it. Small animals die quickly because the poison stops their hearts, but a mature monkey may take half an hour. Hunters of both sexes also take any opportunity to track burrowing animals, like bamboo rats, porcupines, and scaly anteaters. They dig, chop, or smoke

Figure 7-1. Daun, a Kelantan Batek man (on left), joking with a Malay *gaharu* wood trader in a camp on the upper Lebir River, 1981. Courtesy of Kirk Endicott.

them out of their holes in trees or in the ground and kill them with blows from their machetes. Batek catch river fish by hook and line, spear-guns, nets, and vegetable poisons. People of all ages and both genders enjoy fishing, usually going out in groups in the afternoon. They also capture any frogs, crustaceans, turtles, and tortoises they find on their fishing trips.

Batek still supplement their foraging by trading forest products, though the buyers now are commercial traders, not subsistence farmers. The products most in demand in recent years have been rattan—the stems of climbing palms used to make furniture, baskets, and fish traps—and *gaharu*, resinous wood used in incense and perfume (Figure 7-1). Collectors enter into short-term agreements with traders to supply certain quantities of forest products at a certain time for a certain price. Men, women, and children participate in collecting and transporting the materials, with men generally doing the most difficult climbing. Once they find rattans, workers must pull or cut the plants down from their supporting trees, cut the stems to standard lengths, and carry or drag them to collection points. Resinous *gaharu* veins are not found in every tree of the proper species. Collectors usually have to chop down and split apart numerous trees to find even small amounts of the valuable wood. Batek trade these items for money, food, such as rice, sugar, and flour, tobacco, and manufactured goods, like metal tools, cloth, and cassette recorders. The proportion of traded food in their diet varies widely from season to season and year to year. Generally speaking, Batek depend more on wild foods during the rainy season, when travel by traders is difficult, and during the fruit season, when fruits dominate the diet, but nowadays they always try to have some rice on hand, if only to add variety to a predominantly wild-food diet.

The success of the Batek's foraging and trading economy depends on two basic Batek practices: mobility and food sharing. Batek normally live in temporary camps containing five to twenty lean-to shelters covered with palm-leaf thatch or, more recently, sheets of plastic. Each shelter houses a nuclear family, an unmarried adult, or a group of adolescents. The membership of the camp population changes almost daily as some families leave and others move in, and the entire group moves every few weeks or so. Because people can easily set up a new camp in hours, they do not hesitate to move when they want a change of company, have used up the resources in the immediate vicinity, or have heard of a new opportunity somewhere else. Making camp near the resources to be harvested minimizes the amount of time they must spend each day traveling back and forth between the camp and the work site. Batek enjoy moving, as it brings the excitement of exploring a new place and of meeting friends and relatives they may not have seen for a while.

Food sharing also contributes to the efficiency of their economy by freeing people from the burden of finding food every day. In a normal-sized camp, successful hunters routinely distribute shares of meat to every family, and families without enough carbohydrates need only ask to be given some tubers or rice. They share food without calculation (what anthropologists call "generalized reciprocity"), assuming that over the long term they will get as much as they give. This allows people to concentrate on activities that do not immediately yield food, like collecting forest products, or that have a high risk of failure, like blowpipe hunting, without fear that they may go hungry. Batek view food sharing as a major moral obligation, knowing that it is crucial to the success of their foraging economy. As one man said, "When we live in the forest. . . . We can dig tubers. If someone doesn't have food, others give it."

Social and Political Organization

The building block of Batek society is the nuclear family—the married couple and their immature children. Nuclear families occupy separate lean-to shelters, cook and eat together, take primary responsibility for their own welfare, and act as a child-rearing unit. Married couples decide independently where to live, when and where to move, and what kind of work to do. However, the nuclear families are bound together into a larger society by a number of flexible ties. Batek reckon kinship ties bilaterally, through both parents, and have a strong obligation to help close kin on both sides. Siblings and cousins, who are called by the same terms, form mutual support groups. Marriage creates complementary obligations to the spouses' relatives (in-laws) that continue even if the couple divorces, as often happens. Thus most Batek children have numerous older relatives (parents, stepparents, real and stepgrandparents, older siblings) who look out for them. Finally, the camp as a whole, despite its constantly changing membership, forms a community united by the obligation to share food.

Batek highly value personal autonomy. No one has a right to coerce any other adult, and even the authority of parents over young children is weak. Children usually ignore their parents' admonitions, and parents merely shrug and say, "What can you do? They're still kids." Males and females have the same rights and freedoms. Both men and women choose their own marriage partners and can initiate a divorce if they become dissatisfied. Husbands and wives have equal voices in family matters, and both genders can influence camp affairs.

Batek do not have institutionalized leadership positions except those imposed by the Malaysian Department of Indigenous People's Affairs (JHEOA). Few activities require coordination by a leader. In some group activities, like poisoning fish, people voluntarily follow the lead of whoever is most expert at it, but that leadership does not carry over to other activities. Some "natural leaders," both males and females, are so respected that others seek them out for advice and guidance, but they have no way of imposing their will on others. People may try to persuade others, but they cannot coerce them, and physical aggression is considered absolutely unacceptable. Batek say that they would abandon anyone who was persistently aggressive. Since the 1950s, the JHEOA has appointed headmen (*penghulu* or *batin*) who act as liaisons between the government and the Batek, but these people have no authority within Batek society.

Religion and World View

The Batek believe that immortal superhuman beings (*hala' 'asal*) created the earth and everything in it. After some superhumans made the first people, others created the plants and animals of the forest to serve as food, building materials, and body decorations for the people. Today the superhuman beings continue to maintain important "natural" processes, like the seasonal cycles of fruit and honey, and to preserve the separation of the sky, the earth, and the underground sea. The Batek must also play a role in preserving cosmic order. They must "guard the forest" (*jaga' hep*) by living in the rain forest and following the foraging way of life that the superhumans laid out for them. They must also observe an elaborate set of prohibitions on actions that confuse natural distinctions, like cooking different categories of foods over the same fire, or that insult the creator beings, for example, mocking apparently noxious creatures like leeches. They also have to maintain communication with the superhumans, which they do mainly by holding singing sessions in which shamans may fall into a trance and send their shadow-souls to visit the superhumans above and below the earth. They hold singing sessions when people are seriously ill, to get healing powers and knowledge, and before and during the fruit season, first to ask for abundant fruit and later to show their appreciation and happiness. If people break prohibitions, the thunder god sends a violent thunderstorm to topple a tree on the offender, and the earth deity, which lies in the underground sea supporting the earth on its back, shifts position, causing a flood to well up from the underground sea and dissolve the earth beneath the offender's camp. Batek can point out places where landslides or subsidences swallowed up camps. People counter the threat by burning incense and appealing to the deities or by offering a blood sacrifice. In the blood sacrifice, offenders lightly cut the skin on one shin, mix the blood obtained with some water, and throw the mixture to the sky and earth while calling to the deities to stop the storm.

Batek believe that the superhuman beings intended for them to live in the rain forest and look after it. Only in the forest can people maintain the communication with the superhuman beings that is necessary for the continued existence of the world. If the forest were entirely logged off or if the Batek were removed from the forest, the superhumans would be so angry that they would destroy the world by dissolving the earth in the underground sea.

THREATS TO SURVIVAL

We're against becoming Muslims. We can't live without eating monkeys, pigs, frogs. We don't want to pray. If the Department [JHEOA] tries to force us to become Malays, we will move into the forest.
—A Kelantan man, Lebir River, 1976

We can't just forget our *hala'* [superhuman beings].
—A Kelantan man, Post Lebir, 1990

Environmental Crisis

One major threat to Batek survival is loss of their land and forest resources. The Malaysian government's goal is to make Malaysia a fully industrialized country by the year 2020. Planners see development of primary industries, including logging, mining, and plantation agriculture, as a logical intermediate step. These would generate wealth that could be used to improve the infrastructure and provide capital for manufacturing and information-based industries. By 1970, much of the remaining undeveloped land and unlogged rain forest lay in traditional Orang Asli areas, but according to Malaysian land laws, inherited from the British colonial rulers, all land not held by individual title deeds belongs to the states. Legally, Orang Asli like the Batek are mere squatters on land where they have lived for generations. State governments can remove them at will, even from areas designated as Orang Asli areas or reserves. The only part of the Batek De' territory that is protected from logging and development is Taman Negara, a national park administered by the federal government.

About 1970, the Kelantan state government began dividing the Batek's homeland in the Lebir River valley into logging concessions and granting them to various state and federal land-development agencies and to influential individuals, including members of the royal family. The concession owners contracted with logging companies, which began bulldozing logging roads up the Lebir and removing the timber. In the early 1980s, hundreds of logging trucks each day barreled down the road past the JHEOA settlement at Post Lebir. Today almost the entire Lebir River watershed has been logged off up to the border of the national park (and in some places into the park).

Logging companies were required, after taking out all the commercially valuable hardwood timber, to cut and burn off all remaining vegetation, thus turning over bare land to the concession holders. Development agencies and private companies then terraced the land and planted plantation crops, mostly oil palms and some rubber trees. Now all but the fringe around the national park is covered by plantations at various stages of maturation.

In Pahang, the Batek homeland to the south and west of Taman Negara was also parceled out as timber concessions. There the owners selectively logged the forest and then left it to regrow, rather than replacing it with plantations. Nevertheless, the selective logging destroyed about 70 percent of the forest canopy, and the logging roads and skid tracks caused enormous erosion.

None of the parties logging off and developing the Batek homeland consulted the Batek or considered their needs. Loggers paid no compensation for destroying the Batek resource base except, occasionally, when they cut down certain species of fruit trees. The plantations made no provisions for the Batek, who did not want to work on them anyway. Some government development agencies turned over the land in their plantations to poor Malay settlers. Commercial plantations employed mostly immigrant laborers from Indonesia, Thailand, and Bangladesh.

At first the logging did not worry the Kelantan Batek, and some individuals even took jobs as timber cruisers and laborers. By the 1990s, however, they had become angry that outsiders had ravaged the forest and worried that the superhuman beings would respond by destroying the world. The Kelantan Batek were forced either to retreat into the national park and the few remaining patches of undeveloped (but already selectively logged) forest or to move to Post Lebir, the JHEOA-sponsored settlement on the lower Lebir. In Pahang, Batek were able to continue living both in the national park and in the adjacent, selectively logged forest. Selective logging seriously degraded the rain forest, but did not entirely destroy the resources the Batek depended upon for food and trade. In fact, by opening up the forest canopy, it may even have benefited some of the food plants that require lots of sunlight. The overall effect of logging and plantation development, however, has been to deprive the Batek of about two-thirds of the land and resources they had before.

The national park has remained available to its original occupants and has become a refuge area for other Batek driven out of their home areas. Federal and state governments recognize the right of Batek to live in the park, which is entirely within their traditional home area, but the relationship between the Batek and the park authorities is uneasy. The Department of Wildlife and National Parks, being concerned with maintaining the rain forest as a scientific research resource and a tourist attraction, only allows Batek to stay in the park if they live by foraging, using only traditional equipment and techniques, and wage earning, for example as tourist guides. Park authorities forbid them to establish permanent settlements, clear the forest and plant crops, and extract forest products to sell. Officials believe that as "pure" foragers the Batek do little harm to the environment, and tourist businesses promote the image of the "primitive" Batek as if they were another species of exotic wildlife. The Batek, for their part, greatly resent being forbidden to collect and sell rattan and *gaharu* on land that their ancestors occupied long before the park was established. Trading forest products has long been part of their economy, and the regulations have seriously hindered their ability to make a living. In addition, Batek fear, with good reason, that the Department of Wildlife and National Parks will eventually try to remove them from the park altogether.

Sociocultural Crisis

One socially disruptive effect of losing vast amounts of land and resources has been to force Batek to live closer together than they ever did before, both at Post Lebir and in Taman Negara. This has caused social tensions, especially between longtime residents of Taman Negara and Kelantan Batek migrating into the park. Even groups from adjacent river valleys have found it hard to maintain amicable relations when they are thrown together in close proximity. Traditionally, the basic remedy for such conflict was for disputants to move apart, but that is no longer feasible.

Even greater threats to Batek social harmony and cultural survival are deliberate government efforts to destroy their culture and way of life. The federal government's overall goal is to integrate all Orang Asli into the "mainstream" of Malaysian society by assimilating them into the Malay ethnic group, specifically as members of the rural Malay peasant population. The ostensible reason is that this would be the best way for Orang Asli to share in the prosperity of modern Malaysia, a dubious proposition given that rural peasants are among the poorest segments of the population. An unstated reason is that it would eliminate a category of people whose very existence undermines the Malays' claim to being the indigenous people of the Malay Peninsula, a claim the government uses as a basis for giving Malays special rights and privileges, like high quotas in university admissions. In addition, it would remove the embarrassment some officials feel at having "primitive people" as fellow citizens.

How would assimilation work? According to the Malaysian Constitution, a Malay is anyone who speaks the Malay language, follows Malay customs, and is a Muslim. The category "Malay" includes people of widely varying origins, from the descendants of Arab and Muslim Indian traders to recent immigrants from Indonesia, and some Malays are descendants of Orang Asli who adopted Islam centuries ago. Because the criteria of Malay identity are cultural, the idea of Orang Asli "becoming" Malays is not as bizarre as it may first seem. Most Orang Asli today already speak colloquial Malay. All that is needed, then, is for them to adopt a recognizably Malay way of life and to become Muslims. The Malaysian Constitution guarantees the right of all citizens to follow the religion of their choice and to maintain practices (such as languages) that are distinctive of their ethnic groups. But the government's desire to assimilate the Orang Asli is so strong that it has applied enormous pressure, sometimes even violating laws and the constitution, to get them to become Malays. Most Orang Asli strongly resent this pressure. They see no reason why they should not have the same rights as Malays and the Native Peoples of the Bornean states of Sarawak and Sabah without having to give up their religions and ethnic identities. As one Batek man said, "Why must we—and not the Chinese and Indians—be forced to become Malays?"

A crucial step in turning Batek into Malays is to get them to settle down in permanent villages. The JHEOA justifies its efforts to settle the Batek as necessary for efficiently providing social services, like health care, and economic improvements. However, the poor quality of the services provided to the Batek who have settled down casts doubt on this rationale. A more plausible reason is that confining the Batek to fixed locations would increase the ability of the JHEOA to control them and impose other changes on them. Department officials and ruling-class Malays in general abhor mobile people, whom they equate with animals, because they are too free. The Malay term *bebas*, which they often apply to people like the Batek, means "free," but with negative connotations, like "wild" and "out of control."

The JHEOA first tried to settle the Kelantan Batek at a site on the lower Lebir River in 1956. Field staff transported people to the site and provided rations while teaching them to do swidden farming. But when the rations ran out, the Batek immediately returned to foraging, which they preferred to the hard, hot work of farming. In the late 1960s, the JHEOA set up medical posts on the lower Lebir River (Post Lebir) and its tributary the Aring River (Post Aring). (The latter was closed in the 1980s.) At Post Lebir the JHEOA provided a lower primary school and a teacher, prefabricated cabins for the teacher and an advisor, and basic medical facilities and a medical assistant. In Pahang the JHEOA established a settlement—though without a school—at Kuala Atok on the Tembling River just outside the national park. The JHEOA repeatedly attempted to induce the Batek to settle at these and other locations during the 1970s, but met with little success. One problem was that a number of people died during those early attempts at farming because, Batek say, they could not tolerate the heat of working in the sun.

In the 1980s, when logging was fast reducing the ability of Batek to continue foraging, the JHEOA made Post Lebir the center of a regroupment scheme intended to become the home for all the Kelantan Batek. The JHEOA provided seedlings for rubber and fruit trees and houses for additional JHEOA personnel, and the Kelantan state Department of Religious Affairs built a Muslim chapel. The JHEOA expected the Batek to settle there and support themselves by tapping and selling rubber. But officials were reluctant to make major improvements at Post Lebir because they were unable to get secure rights to the land from the state government and make it an aboriginal reserve. Since the late 1980s, the government has been threatening to build a dam that would flood Post Lebir and the entire lower Lebir valley. A similar lack of secure land tenure for the JHEOA or individual Batek has inhibited the development of the Kuala Atok settlement in Pahang.

Most Batek De' strongly resisted settling permanently at Post Lebir and Kuala Atok as long as other alternatives existed. Until about 1990, the only permanent residents of Post Lebir were members of other Semang ethnic groups, the Batek Teh (or Mendriq) and Batek Te', whose land was logged off early on, but who did not have traditional rights to move into Taman Negara. Those Batek De' who did try living at Post Lebir soon discovered that they could not make an adequate living tapping rubber. They also disliked being pressured to become Muslims and being exposed to uninvited visits by curious outsiders. Many Batek considered the settlement unhealthy because increased contact with outsiders led to serious diseases, including tuberculosis and leprosy. Although some Batek De' built houses at Post Lebir and Kuala Atok, they generally used the settlements as base camps, spending most of their time in the forest hunting, gathering, and collecting forest products for trade, rather than using them as permanent bases for a market-crop economy, as the JHEOA intended.

Another part of the government's campaign to assimilate Orang Asli is education. Since the 1950s, the JHEOA has built lower primary schools (grades one through three) or central primary schools (grades one through five) in Orang Asli villages. Until 1995, when the Ministry of Education took over Orang Asli schooling, teachers were mostly JHEOA field staff—Malays and a few Orang Asli—who were not trained as teachers. The quality of instruction is generally very low, and only a tiny proportion of students move on to higher grades. All instruction is in the Malay language, and the curriculum is not adjusted to Orang Asli cultures or needs. Education thus conveys large doses of Malay culture and values, including the anti–Orang Asli prejudice of many teachers, along with the lessons.

The only school especially for the Batek is the one at Post Lebir, which was established in the late 1960s. In Pahang, the JHEOA expects Batek children to go to ordinary government schools like the one at Kuala Tahan, where most pupils are Malays. The popularity of the Post Lebir school has fluctuated widely over the years, depending on the competence and attitudes of particular teachers. Teachers in the early 1970s were quite good. Thanks to them, a group of Batek now in their thirties have basic reading, writing, and mathematical skills (though some later forgot what they learned). Later teachers have been generally less liked, and Batek parents have pulled their children out of school altogether for considerable stretches of time. Batek in Pahang generally refuse to send their children to local Malay schools, in part because of the discrimination they suffer from teachers and classmates. Most Batek parents say that they want their children to learn to read, write, and do mathematics, but they do not want their children to be taught to despise their parents and the Batek way of life. In addition, they will not allow teachers to hit their children, an integral part of traditional Malay education.

The most intrusive component of the government's assimilation effort is its attempt to convert Orang Asli to Islam. Although the Malaysian Constitution guarantees freedom of religion, officials claim that Orang Asli do not have religions (*ugama*), only beliefs or superstitions (*kepercayaan*). Therefore, politicians, government officials, and Muslim missionaries, who are mostly Malays, feel justified in using all their powers to pressure Orang Asli to become Muslims and to prevent them from adopting other world religions like Christianity. The Iranian revolution in 1979 led to an upsurge of Muslim consciousness and proselytizing in Malaysia. The JHEOA started a secret program in cooperation with state and federal religious bodies aimed at converting all Orang Asli to Islam. Although physical force or the threat of force has never been used, many other forms of pressure have been applied, including systematic "positive discrimination" favoring converts in all types of aid and development assistance. The most visible sign of this campaign is the Muslim chapels the government has built in at least 265 Orang Asli villages, often before providing crucial facilities like running water, and has staffed with "welfare officers" trained as missionaries. Despite these pressures, most Orang Asli have resisted conversion. Only about 16 percent had become Muslims in 1997.

In the mid-1970s, some JHEOA staff and former employees began telling the Kelantan Batek that they had to become Muslims. The Batek were worried and angry. They said that they could not live if they had to give up foods they depended upon, such as monkeys, which are forbidden by Islam. They also objected to having to pray five times a day, observe the fasting month, and (for men) be circumcised. In 1981, several young Batek men who had joined the Malaysian army discovered that they were expected to become Muslims at the end of basic training, so they left the army. In the late 1980s, the Kelantan Department of Religious Affairs built a Muslim chapel at Post Lebir and hired a religious teacher from the Malay village of Kampung Lalok to instruct the Batek in religion. The teacher diligently rode his motorbike to the settlement each day but usually found no pupils and returned home soon afterward. Some missionaries made day visits by four-wheel-drive vehicles to Batek camps in the upper Lebir valley. As logging and development exposed them more and more to outsiders, Batek became prime targets of official and unofficial proselytizers.

The results of this pressure is that some Batek De' and other Semang (the number is unclear) who live fairly permanently at Post Lebir have become at least nominal Muslims. Some men have gone for religious training courses in the state capital, Kota Baru, and a few have been circumcised. The extent of their understanding of and commitment to Islamic beliefs and practices varies widely. Some pray regularly and try to follow Muslim food prohibitions, while others are Muslims in name only. However, the majority of the Kelantan Batek De' have rejected the religion entirely and have withdrawn from the settlement into Taman Negara, where they can practice their own religion.

RESPONSE: STRUGGLES TO SURVIVE CULTURALLY

We Batek can't work in the heat like the Malays. We're not used to it. The superhuman beings intended for us to be cool [i.e., to live in the forest].
—A Kelantan man, Lebir River, 1976

I will never settle at Post Lebir. If you want to find me the next time you come, you will find me in the forest in the headwaters.
—A Kelantan man, Post Lebir, 1981

Batek responses to these changes and pressures range from intense resistance to cultural change, at one extreme, to wholehearted adoption of Malay culture, at the other, with intermediate positions in between. For the sake of description, these responses can be grouped in three categories: the cultural-preservation path, the assimilationist path, and the middle path. These paths should not be viewed as discrete categories, however, but as rough divisions of a continuum of strategies Batek follow for surviving in their changing world. In addition, particular individuals may change their patterns of behavior occasionally or frequently, thus appearing to shift from one path to another. For example, it would not be unusual to meet a man at one time living in a temporary camp deep in the forest, dressed in a loincloth, and hunting with a blowpipe, and to see him at another time dressed in a shirt and trousers and working as a tourist guide. Batek culture continues to emphasize flexibility and keeping many options open.

The Cultural-Preservation Path

The most culturally conservative Batek, both from Kelantan and Pahang, have moved into the interior of Taman Negara where they can avoid unwanted contact with outsiders. Some defiantly claim that they would rather die than become Malays. Like their ancestors, they live in temporary camps and subsist mainly by hunting and gathering. They deliberately maintain their traditional knowledge and skills, like making pandanus-leaf mats and baskets. They try to avoid depending on the outside world for food or material goods, although, like most Batek, they carry on some trade, especially for rice, sugar, tobacco, and metal tools.

Conservative Batek believe that it is their duty to continue the way of life laid out for them by the superhuman beings. They say that if they should stop living in the forest, following their prohibitions, and performing their rituals, the superhuman beings would destroy the world in a cataclysmic storm and flood. They believe that by continuing their traditions, they are performing a service for all humanity.

However, even the most conservative Batek have changed the way they view themselves and their way of life. Most notably, pressures to become Muslims have led them (and many other Batek) to begin thinking of their world view, which they previously treated as a commonsense understanding of reality, as a religion. They now consciously contrast their beliefs and practices with Islam. Some say that Allah is merely the god of Malays, equivalent to their Tohan. They compare their singing sessions to Muslim prayers and their food-mixing prohibitions to Muslim food taboos. They have also begun to conceal their religious beliefs and rituals from outsiders, probably to avoid having to defend them to Muslims. Batek living in Taman Negara generally deny to outsiders, especially when Malays are present, that they have any religion at all.

The Assimilationist Path

At the other extreme, the Batek who have settled at Post Lebir seem to have accepted the inevitability of change, and they are trying to minimize their losses while taking advantage of new opportunities. Among the Batek De', the decision on whether or not to settle down has been an individual one. Sometimes different members of families have chosen different paths. However, the Batek Teh and Batek Te' living at Post Lebir probably had little choice but to settle down, as their traditional areas have been completely developed and taken over by other people.

The core of the settled group seems to be the people who attended the Post Lebir school. They see the advantages of the market economy and sedentary living, and they have the confidence and skills needed to live in a world dominated by outsiders. Often on the weekly market day in the nearby Malay village of Kampung Lalok, a group of Batek men, women, and children, dressed in Malay-style clothes, make their way to the village, where they spend a festive morning shopping, eating, and strolling among the stalls. They have also learned to dislike the hardships of mobile life in the rain forest. In 1990, a young Post Lebir man visiting his parents, who were living in a forest camp, gestured contemptuously toward their thatched lean-to. "I would never want to live like that again," he said. When Post Lebir people occasionally visit their relatives who live on the border of Taman Negara, they travel by motorcycle or hitch a ride with a trader, and they usually stay only a few days before returning to the comforts of the settlement. Some Post Lebir youngsters are no longer learning the skills necessary for living in the forest.

Because the Batek living at Post Lebir are exposed daily to outsiders, especially Malays, they are trying to appear as much like rural Malays as they can. They build their houses in Malay styles and use store-bought materials, like corrugated metal roofing, if they can afford them. Like local Malays, they dress in sarongs, shirts, trousers, and shoes or "flip-flops." They avoid openly eating foods like pork and monkeys that are forbidden by Muslims. Even their gender roles have become more like those of the Malays, with women deferring to their husbands and eating after them, in the kitchen, when guests are present. However, they still use the Batek De' language among themselves, and they keep blowpipes and other artifacts of their former identity.

The Middle Path

The majority of the Batek are following a path between the two extremes of cultural preservation and assimilation. They are trying to preserve their

Batek identity, traditions, and core values while also taking advantage of new opportunities and possibilities. Typically they shift back and forth between traditional activities and activities oriented toward the outside world. Thus during the fruit season they may move into forest camps near groves of wild fruit trees, but at other times they may look for wage-earning jobs at the park headquarters or go outside the park to collect forest products to sell. They try to maintain their old skills and to pass them on to their children, as well as to learn new skills that are useful in the modern economy. They spend their earnings on foods and goods from the outside world that enhance their quality of life, as they perceive it, but do not impede the flexibility and mobility that they value. For example, they purchase flashlights, which enable them to fish, catch frogs, and hunt mouse deer at night. For entertainment, they buy portable battery-powered boomboxes. In general, they buy things that are easy to carry and avoid heavy or bulky items that would seriously impede their ability to move.

Some followers of the middle path have established settlements where they build small, Malay-style houses—raised structures with frames of wooden poles, split bamboo walls, and thatched roofs—and plant a few crops. Kelantan Batek have built settlements on the northern border of the national park. Some Pahang people have created a small settlement inside the park (against park regulations) at Kuala Yong, about an hour's walk from the park headquarters. Residents charge tourists a small fee to visit the village and take their pictures. But, contrary to appearances, the Batek treat Kuala Yong not as a permanent place of residence, but as a convenient place to stop from time to time to visit friends and relatives, to catch up on the news, and to look for temporary wage-paying jobs. When the people who built the houses are not in residence, other families are free to occupy them. Thus what appears to be a small permanent population is really an extensive group of people cycling through the settlement.

Like the cultural preservationists, Batek taking the middle path maintain their traditional religion and strongly oppose conversion to Islam. They pass on their beliefs and oral traditions to their children, observe the prohibitions, and perform the rituals necessary for maintaining harmony with the superhuman beings. They may join their more conservative relatives for singing sessions during fruit season and may turn to shamans for treatment of diseases. Despite their openness to some cultural changes, the middle-path Batek strongly believe in the traditional religion, which states that the proper place for the Batek is in the rain forest.

Tension between Cultural Preservationists and Assimilationists

The Batek who have chosen to preserve their traditional way of life see the assimilating Batek as a worrying portent and a threat to the continued existence of the world. They fear that there will someday be too few true "forest Batek" to carry on their way of life. They ridicule Batek who have adopted Malay customs, calling them by the term used for Malays, *gob*. Some Pahang Batek refuse to consider marrying the Malayized Batek from Post Lebir. Some even accuse Kelantan people of practicing sorcery against them. The Pahang Batek blame the "corruption" of the Post Lebir people on their having gone to school, giving that as a reason for not sending their own children to school. For their part, the Post Lebir Batek De' consider their Pahang brethren to be foolishly ignoring the realities of the changing world around them. Those who have adopted Islam seem to have lost any fear that the superhuman beings will destroy the world because of their behavior. Whether future developments will widen or heal this cultural and social split in the Batek population remains to be seen.

Methods Used to Preserve Batek Culture

Culturally conservative Batek are attempting to preserve their culture by withdrawing as much as possible from other peoples, a practice that has worked well in the past, but that may not be possible in the future as more and more tourists and government officials pour into the park. Batek taking the middle path, like their conservative relatives, concentrate on transmitting their values, practices, and lore to their children, but they also expose them to the outside world and help them learn to cope with modern pressures. Because of their relative isolation and lack of education, Batek have not yet begun working with the recently formed pro–Orang Asli organizations that promote Orang Asli rights and interests at the national level: the Center for Orang Asli Concerns (COAC) and the Persatuan Orang Asli Semenanjung Malaysia (Orang Asli Association of Peninsular Malaysia; POASM) (see the Resource Guide for details).

FOOD FOR THOUGHT

The Batek case shows some of the typical problems facing hunting and gathering (and swidden-farming) peoples in rapidly developing nations. A foraging economy requires large amounts of land to support a small population. With national population growth and development of primary industries, other groups covet the land and resources used by the foragers. Small groups without political representation have few means to resist the powers of the state (including the power to define people's rights) and those of wealthy, politically connected business people. The foragers nearly always lose their land and end up living in poverty on small reservations or even as marginalized day laborers or beggars on the fringes of modern society.

In addition, for political reasons, governments often try to force such peoples to make fundamental changes in their cultures and particularly to adopt the ways of the dominant group in society. But discrimination and lack of education, skills, resources, and political power may condemn these peoples to the lowest positions in society. This can lead to demoralization and social problems like alcoholism.

Questions

1. How would you define "indigenous" peoples? Should indigenous peoples have different rights than other categories of citizens in a country?

2. Should governments force indigenous peoples to assimilate to the dominant culture of the country? Compare the Malaysian government's treatment of the Batek with the U.S. government's treatment of Native Americans.

3. What sort of education would be useful to peoples like the Batek? Should they study the mainstream curriculum in the national language? Or should the curriculum and medium of instruction be adapted to their cultures and needs? Compare these issues with the controversy over non-English-language schooling in the United States.

4. What is the proper role of human occupants of national parks? Should they be removed? Should they be treated as part of the natural ecosystem? Should they be given jobs in the park?

5. What, if anything, can foreigners do to help indigenous peoples in other countries, like Malaysia? Do foreigners have any right to oppose the policies of other national governments?

RESOURCE GUIDE

Published Literature

Dentan, R. K., K. Endicott, A. G. Gomes, and M. B. Hooker. *Malaysia and the "Original People": A Case Study of the Impact of Development on Indigenous Peoples.* Boston: Allyn and Bacon, 1997.

Endicott, Karen L. "Fathering in an Egalitarian Society." In *Father-Child Relations: Cultural and Biosocial Contexts*, ed. Barry S. Hewlett, 281–295. New York: Aldine de Gruyter, 1992.

Endicott, Kirk. *Batek Negrito Religion: The World-View and Rituals of a Hunting and Gathering People of Peninsular Malaysia.* Oxford: Clarendon Press, 1979.

———. "The Economy of the Batek of Malaysia: Annual and Historical Perspectives." *Research in Economic Anthropology* 6 (1984): 29–52.

Lye, Tuck Po. "Knowledge, Forest, and Hunter-Gatherer Movement: The Batek of Pahang, Malaysia." Ph.D. dissertation, University of Hawaii. Ann Arbor: University Microfilms International, 1997.

Film

No professionally produced films or videos of the Batek exist. The JHEOA refuses to permit foreign filmmakers to film them, and local filmmakers apparently are not interested.

An early, rather staged depiction of a mixed Semang group in Perak state is the film *Nomads of the Jungle* (Victor Jurgens, director and photographer, Earth and Its Peoples series, Louis de Rochemont Associates, 1948). It is readily available in film libraries. Despite some distortions, it is a useful introduction to the Semang foraging and trading economy.

Internet and WWW Sites

The Orang Asli Assistance Fund (see Organizations) has a Web site at www.dartmouth.edu/~asli. Related information on the OAAF can be found at www.cs.org under "Special Projects."

Children of the Rainforest, a CD-ROM project by Peter C. Reynolds and Associates, has a Web site containing Batek material at www.cybermainst.org/one/mainstreetpages/rainforest.html.

Barbara Nowak and Peter Laird, anthropologists specializing on Orang Asli cultures, have established an e-mail list to enable interested parties around the world to communicate and share current news about Orang Asli. To sign up for the list, write "subscribe orang-asli" followed by your e-mail address, and send it to majordomo@massey.ac.nz.

Organizations

Center for Orang Asli Concerns (COAC)

P.O. Box 3052

47590 Subang Jaya

Malaysia

E-mail: coac@tm.net.my

COAC is a small, multiethnic, nongovernmental organization dedicated to helping Orang Asli achieve self-determination through development of community and regional Orang Asli organizations. It is especially active in organizing legal assistance for Orang Asli and in communicating with government officials and the public on Orang Asli issues.

Orang Asli Assistance Fund (OAAF)

Contact person: Dr. Adela Baer

Department of Zoology

3029 Cordley Hall

Oregon State University

Corvallis, OR 97331-2914

E-mail: baera@ava.bcc.orst.edu

Inquiries and contributions (designated for OAAF):

Cultural Survival

96 Mt. Auburn Street

Cambridge, MA 02138

Phone: (617) 441-5400

E-mail: csinc@cs.org

OAAF is a special project of Cultural Survival, an organization based in Cambridge, Massachusetts, that works for the rights of indigenous peoples around the world. OAAF was founded by some anthropologists and other scholars who have studied Orang Asli cultures. It collects funds from book royalties and contributions and uses them for a variety of small projects intended to help Orang Asli to achieve their own goals, including legal rights, economic well-being, education, and health.

Persatuan Orang Asli Semenanjung Malaysia (POASM)

Km. 24

Gombak Utara

53100 Kuala Lumpur

Malaysia

POASM is a broad-based association open to Orang Asli of all groups and has over 2,000 members. It is dedicated to securing Orang Asli rights and improving their general welfare. Founded by educated Orang Asli employees of the Department of Aboriginal Affairs, it tends to work "within the system," maintaining contacts with the JHEOA, the Orang Asli senator (the sole Orang Asli member of Parliament), and various government agencies and political organizations.

Map 8-1. Courtesy of George N. Appell.

Chapter 8

The Bulusu' of East Kalimantan, Indonesia

George N. Appell

CULTURAL OVERVIEW

The People

The Bulusu' are an ethnic group of East Kalimantan, a province of Indonesian Borneo. (The apostrophe is the symbol for a glottal stop in which the vocal cords are drawn quickly together to stop the flow of air.) Traditionally the Bulusu' have been longhouse dwellers and swidden (slash-and-burn) agriculturalists. Swidden agriculture involves cutting an area of the forest each year for fields—the swidden. The slash is burned to clear the fields for planting and to provide fertilizer for the crops. The Bulusu' villages stretch along several small rivers and streams in the interior of Borneo. Downriver from the Bulusu' and along the mouths of these rivers are coastal Muslim peoples who had been much like the Bulusu' in language and culture before they converted to Islam.

In 1981, at the time the study of Bulusu' society was made, the Indonesian government was in the process of forcing the Bulusu' to leave their village territories and move into resettlement centers. Their traditional culture and how it was being destroyed by government policies and actions will be discussed here.

The Setting

The Bulusu' lived in a tropical rain-forest environment that had no marked seasons without rainfall. Rivers were frequently in flood. The re-

123

gion was heavily forested by primary jungle. The Bulusu' traveled to their fields and other villages primarily by longboat with an outboard motor. They were skilled in navigating the various rapids that are found on their rivers. Their agriculture was sustainable, and there were vast tracts of forest that had never been cultivated.

Traditional Subsistence Strategies

The Bulusu' grew dry rice, cassavas, taros, sweet potatoes, sago trees, and a variety of vegetables in their swiddens. They also planted extensive fruit-tree groves in old swiddens. When there was a fruiting season, the Bulusu' sold their fruit to vendors in a town about six hours away by outboard motorboat. A considerable amount of time was devoted to fishing and the gathering of forest products for trading to the coast. Critical to the ecology of the Bulusu' agriculture was the land-tenure system.

The Bulusu' System of Land Tenure

The village held residual rights to the land in its territory. All members of the village had the right to cut their swiddens within this territory. Population pressure on the land had not yet arisen, and land therefore was not scarce. Consequently, other individuals were allowed to cut a swidden in a village area in which they were not resident as long as they notified the village headman and got his permission. They were not required to relocate their residence to that village. Such nonresident cultivators also were allowed to plant their swiddens with fruit trees at the end of the agricultural year, establishing a claim of long duration. Seldom did a headman deny the request of a nonresident to cut a swidden unless he was known as a troublemaker. When an individual wanted to cut a swidden in another village, it was usually because he or his spouse had relatives in that village, and they wished to join the relative's swiddening group.

No permanent cultivation rights were established by clearing the forest. Once a swidden area had all of its crops removed and the jungle began to grow back again, the area reverted back to the jurisdiction of the village. Anyone else in the village could use that area again for a swidden. However, if the swidden area was planted with fruit trees at the end of the swidden cycle, this removed that area from future swiddening until the fruit-tree grove was no longer used.

Fruit-Tree Groves

Rights over these fruit trees were usually inherited equally by all the children of the planter, both male and female. Villages were interlinked by a network of kin, and as a result, an individual might have rights to fruit trees in a number of closely related villages.

Fruit was a major foodstuff of the Bulusu' and an important source of income. It was regularly sold in the distant town. When there was a major fruiting season, once every four or five years or more, everyone gorged himself or herself on fruit. Swiddening activities might in fact cease at that time while the fruit was enjoyed and wild pigs attracted to the fruit were hunted.

Once an area was planted in fruit trees as part of the swiddening process, it remained in the hands of the owner and his descendants. Others could not intrude upon this area of fruit trees without incurring a fine. Such groves might last for as long as eight to ten generations, and when the fruit trees were no longer bearing well, they were cut, a swidden was made, and the grove was replanted. Fruit-tree groves were not planted every year, usually only when there had been a good fruiting year.

Forest Products

In addition, the Bulusu' hunted for various wild animals and gathered a variety of forest products for trading to the coast. These included rattan of various varieties, resins, and other forest products. Forest gathering constituted a substantial part of their economy.

The Bulusu' invested their agricultural profits and their return from the sale of forest products in a variety of movable property. These included beads and beaded headbands—all of which were woman's jewelry—and brassware, gongs, cannon, and old swords.

Social and Political Organization

Domestic Family Cycle

Marriage was normally monogamous. After marriage, the couple resided in the longhouse apartment of the groom's father. Some couples stayed there until they had had several children. Consequently, this longhouse domestic unit could include more than one married sibling with children. On the other hand, some couples wanted to build their own longhouse apartment shortly after marriage and did so.

Even if the son and his new wife did join the apartment of his father, they still made their own swidden and swidden field house. The field house provided a place where the newly married couple could carry on their domestic life if they wished. When they were sleeping and eating in the apartment of the husband's father, the cooking and providing of meals in this extended-family apartment was in the charge of the husband's mother, the senior female. Each nuclear family provided from its own swidden the necessary foodstuffs to make a joint meal, but each nuclear family used its swidden profits to buy its own household necessities and invest in jars and other forms of nondepreciable property.

A son and his father who were living in the same apartment frequently would have adjoining swiddens. They then would share the same ritual structure where they would call the rice spirits and the fortune of their ancestors to come and ensure a good harvest. Such a structure consisted of a large post, and its further elaboration depended on the size of the swidden. (A large one involved a raised platform and a small shelf at the post for the rice seed to be blessed.) This structure would have straddled the boundary between their swiddens.

By the time the second generation's children had reached marriageable age, the son of the founder of the apartment would have built his own separate apartment onto the longhouse of his father. However, the youngest son was expected to remain in the parental apartment to take care of his aged parents.

Before marriage a young man would visit a girl in the evening at her parents' longhouse apartment. Their meeting was similar to what in the English-speaking world is called a date, except that there was no place to go but to the longhouse apartment of the girl's family. They talked, laughed, and giggled far into the night. If things progressed, the boy might join the girl in her sleeping sarong. Sexual foreplay might go on. If this led to intercourse, the girl was supposed to tell her father. If she did this, or if they were discovered in the act, the girl's father would sue the father of the boy and would receive a fine of several jars and a small pig from the boy's family. The ear of the pig was slit, and the members of the longhouse, with the exception of the girl, were wiped with the blood of the pig on their legs to eradicate the ritual jeopardy. Even if the two married, there would still be a fine of property and a pig, but the fine was smaller. Residence after marriage in the village of the groom was justified by the bride-price paid. When Bulusu' were asked what the purpose was for bride-price, they stated that the union would have been considered fornication if a bride-price were not paid.

A man putting together a bride-price for the wife of his son got help from his network of kin. Each kinsman who could afford it offered to provide a jar, a gong, or a piece of brassware. This was repaid by the father at a later point when those who helped him needed help for a similar occasion. The father of the bride redistributed these bride-price items among his network of kin according to the help that they had given him in the past and the help that they had provided in the form of provisions for the wedding feast.

As a result, Bulusu' society was composed of a vast, intricate network of debts and credits. These were recognized by descendants even if they had been incurred three generations earlier.

The Bulusu' Village

Village organization was simple. There were no hereditary social classes, such as have been found in some other Bornean groups. The village, rather than being an explicit, well-defined territorial entity, was both a nexus of kin relations and a center of the power of an individual leader who, with the coming of the government, became the official village headman.

Village boundaries were marked by natural phenomena along a river, such as rapids, mouths of tributaries, or a large tree, and at the height of land between two river systems. It was customary when traveling to stop at each longhouse village and ask permission of the village headman to proceed through that village's territory. However, village boundaries became more strictly defined and asserted when the market for forest products rose and the gathering of these forest products became a very profitable activity.

The Longhouse

The inhabitants of a village lived in one or more longhouses, which were raised on posts eight to ten feet above the ground. A longhouse would include seven to twelve separate individually-owned domestic family apartments that were joined together side by side. Each apartment was thirty to thirty-five feet wide. One-half of each apartment was open. Joined together, these apartments formed a long walkway and working area the length of the longhouse. The other half of the apartment was enclosed and was the area where the family cooked, ate, and slept. The enclosed area was approximately 25 feet in depth. Through the door was the walking and working area of the same depth. In addition, those Bulusu' cultivating swiddens far away from the village longhouse might construct a smaller version of the longhouse structure to live in during the agricultural season and while they were using that area for swiddens.

Religion and World View

The Bulusu' had a complex religion with a creator god and a variety of spirits, some of which inhabited the natural world and some of which inhabited an upper world that consisted of a number of levels. The Bulusu' self was constructed of the body, multiple souls, and a celestial counterpart that dwelt on the mountain of the dead souls. The term "soul" was also used to refer to indwelling spirits of inanimate objects, such as jars or trees. Animals and plants were also believed to have souls.

Explanations for illness included soul capture and torment by capricious spirits. Spirit mediums, either male or female, would go into a trance to negotiate with these spirits for the return of the captured souls to cure the illness (Figure 8-1). Traditionally, in addition to raising pigs and chickens for food, the Bulusu' raised these to sacrifice to the spirits and to cleanse a village after incest. Incest resulted in floods, sicknesses such as colds, the destruction of crops by forest animals and insects, lack of prosperity with domestic animals, immaturity in tree fruits, and difficulty in accumulating

Figure 8-1. Two Bulusu' spirit mediums in a Bulusu' longhouse performing a curing ceremony for the ill. Courtesy of George N. Appell.

property such as gongs and brassware. Fornication, and particularly adultery, would make the village "dirty," causing similar but not as disastrous consequences. For those who fornicated, marriage rectified the delict, and a pig was sacrificed at marriage. To nullify the ritual delict of adultery, the adulterers gave pigs to the offended spouse or spouses.

At death the body was placed in a carved wooden coffin, which was kept in the longhouse apartment until the entombment ceremony. This ceremony could be delayed for several years until enough funds and supplies were accumulated to feed the large numbers of invited guests. There might be three or four coffins by that time. Coffins were placed either in a burial cave or in a raised, covered, wooden mausoleum that was decorated with various carvings.

THREATS TO SURVIVAL

Indonesia is culturally, geographically, and historically a very complex region. The country encompasses over 3,000 islands and stretches 3,400 miles along the equator from its eastern to its western border. There are over 400 languages, each representing an ethnic group. The capital is Jakarta on the island of Java. Java supports over half of the Indonesian population and is one of the most densely populated regions of the world.

After independence from the Dutch in 1949, the central government was faced with the problem of constructing a nation from this vast cultural diversity. To do this, it had to bring all these ethnic groups and regions under its control. This process involved various development plans to raise the standard of living of Indonesians and create a national culture and national language.

The national ideology of Indonesia is defined by five principles in its founding statement: belief in One Supreme God; just and civilized humanity; nationalism; democracy; and social justice. However, it is the belief in One Supreme God that is pushed with great vigor throughout Indonesia. Those religions that do not include the concept of One Supreme God are not considered to be "religions," and individuals without religion are feared to be Communists. It has been stated by the Indonesian Department of Information that the government has the duty to give guidance and assistance in religious development in accordance with all religious teachings and to conduct the supervision in such a way that the fulfillment of these religious teachings by each citizen and the development of religion can run smoothly.

Thus it is believed that isolated ethnic groups have no religion at all, and converting them to one of the eight acceptable world religions is required. In this process, Islam is preferred, and conversion to Islam is encouraged by various forms of pressure.

As it was thought that the Bulusu' were animists without the belief in a supreme being, it was critical that these peoples be "given a religion." The Bulusu' were gathered together and were told to choose a religion from one of the accepted ones. One district officer who participated in this was extremely proud of his part in "civilizing" these people.

A critical part of these development plans was the "socialization of primitive peoples." The Bulusu', like other swidden agriculturalists, were viewed as being "unsocialized" by the government because they were mistakenly thought to be nomadic and "primitive." The "primitive" designation was based on the fact that they did not wear clothes purchased at a shop, such as blouses and trousers, and they did not live in communities large enough to support schools and health centers. Being "socialized" was to live in organized villages such as those found in Java. This view has led many foreign scholars to consider that the various Indonesian development plans are attempts to Javanize, that is, to bring Javan culture to these other, more outlying ethnic groups. Critical to this process was spreading the Indonesian language and the developing national culture throughout the archipelago by establishing schools. As a result, many cultures and languages have been and are being lost.

This whole process of making the country modern was and is characterized by two words: *bangun* and *maju*. Bangun refers to "waking a people up," "to developing them." *Maju* refers to making them "progressive, forward looking." To forward this goal of modernization and "socializing primitive peoples," the government created three downriver resettlement centers where all the upcountry Bulusu' villages could be brought together and where government services such as schooling and elementary medical services could be provided. The government personnel, who were Islamic and came both from Java and from coastal Muslim villages downstream from the Bulusu', did not like to travel upcountry to bring government services to the people, so they brought the people to the government services. But there were other reasons and advantages in doing this. It opened up the forest in the territories of Bulusu' villages for exploitation by timber companies that paid considerable bribes both locally and nationally to get timber-cutting concessions.

The Bulusu' society was originally in a state of equilibrium with its ecosystem. This equilibrium was rent asunder by the Indonesian government's resettlement program and the attempts to integrate the Bulusu' more closely into the national economy, a process that included the capture by the government of Bulusu' resources, both forest and labor. Thus being moved to a resettlement center involved a drastic redesign of their economic life.

Consequently, the Bulusu' were reluctant to move to the centers because of the loss of their culture and their resources. They did not want to give up their traditional village territories, their fruit-tree groves, their fields, their gravesites, and their cultural symbols. As a result, the government had to force the Bulusu' to come into the resettlement centers.

In the resettlement centers, the Bulusu' were prevented from carrying on their traditional agricultural activities, family life, and rituals. They had to live in much more crowded conditions than they were used to in their own villages. They found the centers to be threatening and confusing because a number of different ethnic groups were also resident there, particularly members of coastal Muslim communities that had economically preyed on them and cheated them in the past. Fights had broken out between the ethnic groups, and this had tended to drive the Bulusu' back to their village longhouses. The center's were hot because all the trees had been removed in preparing the site. The most difficult aspect of resettlement was that it put the Bulusu' at the mercy of government representatives and their surrogates. They were constantly being ordered about like indentured servants and were used as labor for the economic benefit of the government officials and members of the local Muslim communities. The commandant of police of the regency said that the Bulusu' were brought to the centers so that "they could be watched and told what to do, and they will do it." To enforce their wishes, government officials constantly used threats to obtain compliance. When government representatives were not in residence, several coastal Muslims took up the responsibility of running the centers, ordering the Bulusu' around, using them for their own economic interests, and threatening them with government retaliation if they did not obey.

The restrictions put on the Bulusu' economy and culture created many hardships. They were not permitted to build their longhouses. Instead, they were instructed to construct single-family dwellings, which they were not skilled in doing and which were too small for them to carry on their usual family and ceremonial activities. They were prevented from performing their traditional burial customs. Burial now had to be in conformity with Muslim law, which required that a body be interred in the ground by nightfall of the day of death. This caused considerable conflict because according to the Bulusu' religion, if the dead were not properly cared for, their souls would not reach the afterworld but would wander among the living and cause disease and disaster. In addition, the courting customs of the Bulusu' were forbidden.

The Bulusu' also were not permitted to raise pigs because the government personnel and other residents were Muslim. Furthermore, there was not enough land in the resettlement area for the Bulusu' to cultivate their crops. As the Bulusu' were far removed from their traditional areas for swidden farming and from the fruit-tree groves that they had established, the availability of food became marginal. When Bulusu' from villages that had not yet agreed to move to the resettlement centers came down for visits to their kin, it was apparent that they were better fed. In comparison to the markedly thin residents of the centers, they were heavier and healthier.

To force the Bulusu' villages to move to the resettlement centers, the government used extraordinary means. The Bulusu' were threatened with various punishments. District officers threatened to burn down the village longhouses. In some instances, the Bulusu' were told that they would be arrested. In several cases, the militia was sent into a village and forced all the men to stand in the river up to their necks for hours until they were shivering while the militia shot over their heads. In one village, members of the militia shot their guns up through the roof of the longhouse before they forced the men into the river. Bulusu' were beaten, slapped around, and sometimes physically forced under the water to coerce them.

The critical point is that the Bulusu' could not make a living in the centers. They had to go back to their village areas to cut swiddens, but they were constantly being called back when government officers would come for a visit to the centers. Under these circumstances, it was difficult to carry on their farming activities, particularly since much of their labor was required to build the individual houses in the centers and to work to maintain the centers' grounds and facilities. Cash payments designated to buy materials for housing construction were embezzled by the local government representative. As a result the Bulusu' had to resort to finding funds of their own to buy the materials to construct the required separate houses. One Bulusu' was overheard muttering, "When the government officer says eat, we eat; when he says drink, we drink; when he says we are to have a celebration, we celebrate; we cannot do those things for ourselves."

The Bulusu' were constantly being bullied, threatened, hectored, harassed, and ridiculed to their faces with regard to their demeanor, intelligence, and way of life. This kind of psychological and physical abuse of ethnic and minority peoples and the violation of their human rights stems from previously held negative stereotypes of the dominant group. Thus the abuse of the Bulusu' was justified and validated by the stereotypes the government personnel and the nearby coastal Muslims had. The Bulusu' were held in contempt by both. The coastal Muslims in the region had a long history of treating the indigenous populations such as the Bulusu' in terms that dehumanized and intimidated them. They referred to the Bulusu' as "dumb," which sometimes meant that they had not had any schooling and at other times meant that they lacked the normal capacities for thinking. They were "dirty." They "smelled like pigs." Their food was disgusting, and this included their alcoholic beverage made with rice and/or cassavas. They ridiculed the Bulusu' traditional clothing and their burial customs. It was believed that the Bulusu' had a lot of sickness and a high mortality. It was claimed that they did not have soap. The coastal Muslims laughed uproariously at the thought that the Bulusu' might have a religion. They disparaged the traditional longhouse structures and claimed that they were unhealthy. This ignored the fact that the housing structures in the labor lines for the timber companies were equivalent in design to longhouses and in fact appeared from the distance to be longhouses. Yet nothing was said about these being unhealthy even though they were more so. It was also a frequent statement by government personnel that the Bulusu' only ate cassavas, and this indicated just how backward they were because they did not even eat rice. For example, the commandant of police of the regency said, "All the Bulusu' do is work a few hours in their gardens, come back and eat cassavas, and make children." This attitude ignored the fact that not only did the Bulusu' eat rice, but before the resettlement they had sufficient quantities to sell rice and other agricultural products to the town.

Prior to resettlement and the loss of their traditional clothing, when the Bulusu' had gone to the town six hours away by longboat in their loincloths, they had been harassed by the police, who had grabbed their testicles. In the resettlement area, one Bulusu' was put to "dry out" in the sun—that is, stand in the merciless midday sun—for wearing a loincloth. At one point, all the men were lined up and their loincloths were removed by government personnel. The loincloths were thrown into a barrel and burned, and the Bulusu' were issued shorts or revealing nylon briefs in exchange, which were perceived as being an acceptable substitute for loincloths. Some government personnel told the Bulusu' that foreigners would be made "ashamed" or "embarrassed" if they saw them in loincloths. Also, Westerners and Japanese would think that there was not enough cloth in the country. The men were forced to wear "clothes," and the women had to wear blouses. Bare breasts encouraged fornication, it was said. In addition, Bulusu' men were told that they were not permitted to wear their hair long.

In the process of "socializing" the Bulusu', the government personnel and the coastal Muslims took the position that they had to be taught. Thus at various times the Bulusu' were brought together to be lectured. At one such meeting, the Bulusu' were told by a government official that they were no longer allowed to invest their agricultural surpluses in jars, brassware, gongs, and the like, their traditional form of investment. They were to purchase mosquito nets, beds, mattresses, dressers for clothing, modern kitchen supplies, plates, and bowls. (They already had plates, bowls, mosquito nets, and storage trunks for clothes.) They were no longer to make large swiddens but to make small gardens for food only and to look for wage labor, which, however, was not available. They were also to make plantations and sell the yield to the town. But this they had been doing all along.

One of the arguments for bringing the Bulusu' into the resettlement centers was to provide medical facilities. However, the knowledge of medicine by the resident dresser was so inadequate that his work was dangerous. The procedures he used could in fact spread deadly diseases. In one river system, about one-third of the Bulusu' children died as a result of a measles epidemic. But the government was uninterested in providing inoculations for childhood diseases that were particularly dangerous for the Bulusu'.

As for schooling, when classes were held, much of the Javanese schoolteacher's time was spent teaching the children about Islam. Frequently antisocial behavior or unusual behavior was explained on the basis that the individuals had not had enough schooling where they would have learned "to think."

RESPONSE: STRUGGLES TO SURVIVE CULTURALLY

The Bulusu' were completely at the mercy of the dominant culture and the military authority of the government. No response was available except that many individuals tried to avoid contact with the government whenever possible by returning upcountry. This was not a successful strategy because they were rounded up, and this did nothing to preserve their culture.

Our last contact with the Bulusu' was in 1981. We have not returned to observe the final outcome for the Bulusu'. This is because violations of the Bulusu' human rights were frequently perpetrated right in front of our eyes to demonstrate, to us and to the Bulusu' themselves, who really controlled the situation and the country. This pervasive violation of human rights, the attitude of the government personnel who treated both the people and their culture as inferior, dirty, and unworthy of respect, and the poorly thought-out attempts to introduce change that in essence really meant conversion to Islam and changing the Bulusu' culture to conform to Javanese culture were just too painful to us to continue our study. Furthermore, it may have been dangerous for us and certainly not beneficial to the Bulusu' for us to be present, observing and recording these attempts to destroy Bulusu' culture and control the population. The government personnel were antagonistic to our study as they believed the Bulusu' and their culture were not worthy of any attempt to understand them and thought that our study might stand in the way of achieving attempts at modernization. Consequently, any further attempts to record and understand the Bulusu' culture might only increase the pressure by government personnel to destroy their culture and reaffirm government control over the people.

FOOD FOR THOUGHT

The Bulusu' had been developing as independent agricultural entrepreneurs, selling their surplus fruits, vegetables, rice, pigs, chickens, and forest products to the town. However, after resettlement, the amount of agricultural products and forest products sold in the town dropped approximately 40 to 50 percent. The region was no longer producing much of a surplus. As a result, Bulusu' for the first time had to begin to buy rice.

Thus the resettlement cut off the development of an independent farming class, economically viable and equivalent in income and assets to the urban lower middle class. Instead, the government has taken control of the Bulusu' land, sold the rights to harvest trees to timber companies, many of them foreign, and pocketed the profit. The government has forced the proletarianization of the Bulusu' by converting their agricultural labor traditionally done for their own benefit into labor for the benefit of the commercial activities. But wage labor was only occasionally available, as in the timber camps or when there were oil companies exploring in the area, and workers were needed to cut lines, build boardwalks through swamps, and the like. Worse, it was stated that the wages obtained were only sufficient to sustain an individual. Nothing was left over, unlike the situation in farming where surpluses had been invested in old jars, gongs, brassware, and other implements. In some instances, Bulusu' undertook wage labor and were never paid. Also, one of the worst disadvantages of wage labor was that when one was sick and could not work, he received no income. When a farmer is sick, if it is not for an extended period, he can still make a living because the crops continue to grow and the fruit trees continue to bear, and he can always rely on help from his family.

Thus the Bulusu' have been stripped of their property; they have been made poorer; they and their culture have been devalued and demeaned; they have been bullied into acquiescence; and they have been prevented from carrying on their own culture. As a result, their health has been put in jeopardy. One might expect that in a few years the Bulusu' will be discouraged, disoriented, and apathetic rural slum dwellers with little chance of ever moving out of that category, being at the very end of the line for opportunity. It is well documented that when individuals are put under psychological and physical stress, health impairments follow. First, an increase in psychological disorders appears, followed by an increase in behavioral deviancies, finally culminating in increased rates of physical impairments and disease. This case clearly delineates that in Indonesia, and elsewhere, development and modernization have become a religious movement rather than a rational approach to solving problems.

Questions

1. Does the Bulusu' experience differ from that of the Plains Indians as they were forced into reservations during the last half of the nineteenth century?
2. Why are indigenous peoples treated in this fashion so often even today?
3. When human rights have been violated, how can these violations be reported and to whom, and what sanctions are available to prevent this from happening?
4. Because verbal abuse and negative stereotyping of a people seem to precede various forms of physical aggression and the capture of their resources and labor, how can this abuse and stereotyping be stopped?
5. Has colonial imperialism really died?
6. How do resettlement centers differ from concentration camps?

RESOURCE GUIDE

Published Literature

Appell, G. N. "The Bulusu' of East Kalimantan: The Consequences of Resettlement." In *Modernization and the Emergence of a Landless Peasantry: Essays on the Integration of Peripheries to Socioeconomic Centers*, ed. G. N. Appell. Studies in Third World Societies Publication no. 33. Williamsburg, VA: Studies in Third World Societies, 1985: 183–240.
———. "Dehumanization in Fact and Theory: Processes of Modernization and the Social Sciences." In *Social Science Models and Their Impact on Third World*, ed. John A. Lent. Studies in Third World Societies Publication no. 45. Williamsburg, VA: Studies in Third World Societies, 1991: 23–44.
———. "The Health Consequences of Development." *Sarawak Museum Journal* 36 (1986): 43–74.
———, ed. "Resettlement of Peoples in Indonesian Borneo: The Social Anthropology of Administered Peoples." *Borneo Research Bulletin* 17 (1985): 3–21.
Centers for the Study of Human Rights. *Twenty-Four Human Rights Documents*. New York: Center for the Study of Human Rights, Columbia University, 1992.

Map 9-1. Karen homelands.

Chapter 9

The Karen of Burma and Thailand

Yoko Hayami and Susan M. Darlington

Now I want to tell you about Karen nationals. Karen are indigenous people in Burma. The Karen people are fighting for the freedom to live in peace. But [the Burman] government tried to divide the Karen people and tortured Karen people and they have killed some people's families in the front line. So some Karen people run to the forest and build houses and they live in the forest. So they can't learn at school and they can't read and write their own language. But in the future I want to learn English . . . and get education and I will teach . . . my Karen people.

—From a letter to an American pen pal by a twenty-year-old
Karen woman in the civil war zone in Burma

CULTURAL OVERVIEW

The People

The term "Karen" generally refers to a group of people who inhabit the hills and plains on both sides of the Thailand-Burma border. In Burma (officially called Myanmar), most Karen face a struggle for human rights, democracy, and self-determination. Some Karen have engaged in an armed revolution against the Burman government since 1949. In Thailand, the Karen face cultural and political discrimination as well as the destruction of their natural environment.

The question of who the Karen are is not easily answered. Some Karen in both Thailand and Burma have assimilated to the majority culture and may claim Karen descent but identify with the majority population. The term "Karen" (an anglicized form of *Kayin*, the Burmese term for the major Karen groups) is one that is used by outsiders, not by the people themselves.

The people labeled with this term actually belong to several different but related cultural and language groups with distinct identities. For example, people who speak the Sgaw Karen language, one of the major subgroups of the Karennic languages, call themselves "Pga k'nyau." The major subgroups recognized as Karen by scholars are the Sgaw, Pgo, Bghe, and Pa-O (or Taungthu). In Burma, the situation is more complex because ethnic labels serve as political labels for insurgent groups that may or may not share a common language. Some of the Pa-O and the Bghe (Karenni, meaning Red Karen), for example, have their own insurgent organizations in Burma and refuse to be associated with the other major Karen groups. In this chapter, the term "Karen" will be used to refer mainly to the most numerous of the subgroups, the Sgaw Karen, unless otherwise noted.

The past of the Karen and their migratory paths to where they now live remain unknown. What is clear is that they have lived on the edges of the lowland states of the Burmans, Mon, and Thai for generations. There has so far been no conclusive evidence that indicates Karen presence in the area now called Thailand prior to the seventeenth century. According to chronicles and other evidence, it seems that many Karen moved to the Thai side of the border early in the eighteenth century after heavy fighting between the Thais and the Burmans. Some of them were forced to settle on the Thai side, while others came voluntarily. They moved into the valleys and lower hill slopes to cultivate swiddens as well as wet-rice fields. Their cotton cloths and forest produce were traded in the lowlands, so they were relatively well off. Well into the nineteenth century, however, the centralization of administration by the Chakri dynasty in Bangkok and changes in the political as well as economic structure of the country took place. As a result, Karen lost their ties with the local lowland authorities whose polities were absorbed into the centralized administrative structure, and trade for forest produce diminished. At the same time, various hill-dwelling groups began to arrive in the northern hills, mostly from southern China, Burma, and Laos.

In the late 1950s, the Thai government began seriously to consider policies toward the hill dwellers. It was at this time that the term *chau khau* (hill tribes) began to be used in reference to ethnic groups, including the Karen. Against the background of the war in Indochina, the government feared Communist guerrilla activities in the hills, as well as problems of deforestation and opium production. Hill-tribe policies by the Thai government aimed to consolidate the border areas, preserve the forest resources, introduce cash crops in place of opium, and assimilate the hill population into Thai culture and society. At the same time, hill-tribe settlements along the border were sometimes burned and forcibly removed by the Thai army. Hill people who have arrived more recently from neighboring countries lack Thai citizenship, and their living conditions are extremely precarious. These include a large number of Karen refugees along

Figure 9-1. Karen tribe house north of Mae Sot, near Mai Sarit, Thailand, 1997. Copyright © Her Majesty in Right of Canada. All rights reserved. CIDA photo: Graham Sim, 1997.

the border who have fled from the battlefields and persecution on the Burma side of the border.

The Setting

In Burma, the Karen habitat ranges from hill forests, valleys, and plains to the cities and towns. They live in a wide area ranging from the eastern hills along the Thai border (known as the Karen homeland or *Kawthoolei* in Karen) to the central area of the Pegu Yoma Mountain Range north of Rangoon, and in the Irrawaddy Delta region. The Karen in the eastern region have retained more of their culture and traditional lifestyle, while those in the plains and cities have adapted to the dominant Burman culture. In the discussion of the Karen in Burma in this chapter, the people living in the eastern region are referred to primarily, as they face the strongest threats to their cultural and physical survival.

On the Thai side, Karen inhabit areas from the northernmost province of Chiang Rai, west to Mae Hong Son and Tak, southward along the Burma border to Kanchanaburi, and as far south as Phetchaburi (Figure 9-1). In Thailand, most Karen communities are situated on the lower-altitude hills as well as in valleys and lowlands, close to creeks and streams. Many of the hills on which the Karen reside are watershed areas for the major rivers of this region, especially the Chao Phraya, which runs through the central plains of Thailand. This river provides most of the irrigation water for wet-rice cultivation in central Thailand. Forest resources for timber, paper and pulp, teak, and pine resin, as well as minor forest produce, are abundant. The forest area in northern Thailand diminished from 69 percent in 1961 to 44 percent in 1993, and in central Thailand from 55 percent to 23 percent or less during the same period. Arguments regarding forest and environmental conservation inevitably involve the hill dwellers and their rights to land.

Traditional Subsistence Strategies

In terms of historical as well as ecological characteristics, the Karen are somewhere between the lowlanders and the highlanders. Karen in the hills cultivate swiddens as well as paddy rice in annual cycles. Maize, beans, taros, mustard greens, pumpkins, chili, and fruits of various kinds are also grown in the hill fields, around rice-paddy fields, and in home gardens. The Karen swidden method is characterized by the short-cultivation–long-fallow system, in which one year of cultivation is followed by several years of leaving the land fallow, allowing ample time for forest regrowth. Preparation of the hill fields begins in the dry season around February when they cut the already-drying vegetation in preparation for burning. In April, when the vegetation is amply dry, fire is set, with care being taken that it does not go beyond the designated area. Larger tree stumps are left untouched, and surface soil is hoed before planting the seeds using a pointed pole. After harvest, the field is ideally left for several years to allow some forest regrowth. The paddy fields in the valleys are fed by streams and canals, and small dams are constructed to control the water. Water buffaloes are used for plowing, and the rice is transplanted from seedlings around June. Various rituals are held at important phases of cultivation, such as before forest is cleaned for a new garden, at planting or transplanting time, before the rice begins to mature, and at harvest time.

Today, however, restrictions on swidden cultivation are severe in both Thailand and Burma, while rice-paddy fields and production levels have become diminished due to population pressure and low water supply, which in turn is conditioned by both climatic changes and forest deterioration. Cash-crop cultivation among the Karen is mostly on a small scale. In Thailand, many youths move out of the hills to the cities for labor and education. Thus there is both a population and a cultural move toward the society and culture of the Thai majority.

Social and Political Organization

The border between Burma and Thailand and the different political situations Karen face in each nation affect the political organization among the people on each side of the border. In the hills, the social organization and basic political structures are similar in both countries, but the ways in which small village communities see themselves as part of any larger political organization differ dramatically.

Among the hill Karen, the village community is the basic sociopolitical unit. Traditionally, each such community has its ritual leader who is primarily hereditary through the paternal line from the first settler of the community. He performs rituals of the community that ensure that the community is in good relationship with the spirit owners of the land. Ritual and social order in the community is guarded by this ritual leader as well as a gathering of male elders of the community. Administrative intervention in Thailand began in the 1950s under which some village headmen receive a stipend from the district and act as mediators between the Karen community and the Thai administration.

Except among the Bgwe Karen, where small chiefdoms are found, there were no Karen organizations that went across village boundaries until early in 1881 in Burma, when the Karen National Association was founded with encouragement from Christian missionaries. Although it was not founded as a political organization, it nevertheless became the basis for later nationalistic movements. There are also today Karen religious organizations on both sides of the border, such as the Karen Baptist Convention.

In Burma in 1949, the Karen formed what later became the Karen National Union (KNU) when they declared revolution against the central government. Today that group remains as the largest insurgency group still fighting the government. The KNU consists of both a civilian branch, which is responsible for humanitarian and social welfare within its region of eastern Burma, and an armed branch, which continues to fight for freedom from an oppressive government. The KNU provides a political structure and voice for people both in the small area it controls along the eastern border and within the areas under government rule. It officially represents only a fraction of the Karen within the country, however, because many people support its aims for political recognition, cultural autonomy, and democracy but fear reprisal from the government for any active involvement with the group.

Religion and World View

The religious world of the Karen is diverse in itself. The majority of Karen in Burma are Buddhist, while approximately 20 percent are Christian. A small percentage still follow their traditional spirit beliefs. In Thailand, also, Christianity and Buddhism are both widely received, the former amounting to approximately 10 percent of the population.

The traditional animist ritual system consists of two major complexes involving two realms of spirits: the spirit owners of the land and the family spirits. The former rituals are performed by male elders, led by the ritual leader. If the spirits of the land are made happy with the appropriate rituals, fertility of land and prosperity are promised. Moral and social misdoings as well as failure in performing the rituals will cause the spirits' anger, resulting in famine and epidemic. Thus the elders are responsible not only for the performance of rituals, but also for maintaining peace and social harmony within the community.

Animist Karen believe that there are thirty-three souls in a person's body, the soul at the head being the most vital to a person's life. When any of these thirty-three souls is affected by spirits or simply escapes the body, it is said to cause illness and weakness. At times of any bodily ailment or bad dreams, curing rituals are held to call back the spirit, sometimes also involving exorcising spirits that may have taken over the soul.

Karen believe that at birth a person comes from the other world, and at death she or he returns there. Birth and death are determined by the population balance of the two worlds. The other world is the reverse image of this world; for example, when it is daytime in this world, it is nighttime in the other. When a person dies, the deceased person's close family member prepares for the dead person's voyage to the other world by bringing all kinds of daily utensils to the cremation and burial ground and making sure that each item is broken or torn and unusable in this world so that it will be usable in the other.

Karen conversion to Christianity has become a legend in missionary history since the first conversion of a Karen man in Burma by an American Baptist missionary in 1828. Conversion occurred in great numbers in early-to mid-nineteenth-century Burma. Karen converts received schooling and learned to read and write, and many of them became elite members of Burman society. Karen Christians from Burma began to send missionaries to Thailand in the mid-nineteenth century, although growth on the Thai side was much slower.

Karen communities long in contact with lowlanders have also been influenced by Buddhism. Karen in Burma are predominantly Buddhist, but their Buddhist practices are mixed with some of the traditional Karen beliefs. The government and monastic orders in Thailand have sponsored projects for propagating Buddhism in the hills, and Karen have been major recipients of these efforts.

THREATS TO SURVIVAL

The threats to the cultural and physical survival of the Karen in Burma and Thailand differ significantly because of the very different political climates of each nation. Thailand is relatively stable politically and was so economically until the crisis of 1998. Rapid economic development has resulted in environmental destruction; population increase and limited arable land force lifestyle changes among swidden cultivators such as the Karen. People living within forested areas often find themselves facing eviction in the name of forest conservation. Burma, by contrast, has been ruled by a dictatorial military government since 1962. The human-rights abuses against all its citizens are among the worst in the world. The government has fought a civil war against many of its ethnic minorities, including the Karen, since 1949, only one year after Burma's independence from Britain. It has forbidden the use of minority languages and ethnic dress except for special occasions among most of the minority groups in an attempt to assimilate them into the majority culture and prevent ethnic nationalism. People who practice religions other than Buddhism have been persecuted. The struggles faced by the Karen within Burma and the refugees who fled Burma to camps in Thailand differ substantially from those faced by the Karen in Thailand, despite their linguistic and cultural similarities.

Present Demographic Trends

In both countries, life in the hills is becoming increasingly difficult due to environmental degradation, population increase, and restrictions on forest and land use. In Thailand, the Karen comprise only about 0.5 percent of the country's total population (their number was officially reported by the Tribal Research Institute as 320,000 in 1996). The daily life of hill villagers has been changing rapidly in the past few decades. Family structure has been altered as parents consider two or three children as the limit in order to provide sufficient support and education (Figure 9-2). In the past twenty years, various methods of contraception have been adopted, and the average number of children has decreased. Children from outlying villages whose parents have enough means are sent to study in towns in the hope that they will gain enough education to cope with life in Thai society. Young men, and increasingly women also, venture out to the cities for job opportunities. Many Karen villages in the hills are populated mainly by the elderly and the younger children. Administrative and economic involvement with the lowland Thai political and economic structures has increased, while education and religious propagation have brought social and cultural changes. Similar processes have occurred among Karen in Burma. In addition, it is difficult to estimate their numbers because the dominant ethnic Burman government tries to assimilate them into the majority population. Most estimates place their total population at about 4 million, or 10 percent of the nation's population. In the war-torn eastern region, some Karen (and other) villages have been forcibly relocated for economic and security reasons. People suspected of aiding the insurgents are summarily arrested or even shot. Over 100,000 Karen from Burma have fled across the border into Thailand as refugees from such abuses and civil war. Many other Karen live as internally displaced persons in the forests

Figure 9-2. Karen mother and infant, 1997. Copyright © Her Majesty in Right of Canada. All rights reserved. CIDA photo: Graham Sim, 1997.

of Burma, driven from their villages by persecution and war, yet fearing to cross the border into Thailand. Their numbers cannot be estimated.

Problems Facing the Karen in Thailand

The foremost problem of Karen in Thailand is that of land rights for swidden cultivators. The legal code concerning land rights presupposes long-term continuous use of land. However, since land use under shifting cultivation implies discontinuous use of a plot of land, legal rights cannot be held. According to Karen custom, villagers gain the right to cultivate swiddens through community membership. Such communally based rights are not recognized legally. Even if hill dwellers wanted to apply for use-hold titles to land, many of them lack Thai citizenship and identification cards, which are preconditions for such applications. Thus swidden farmers are considered illegal encroachers. In addition, the land on which they are encroaching is today increasingly recognized as a precious national and natural resource. Especially since the 1980s, problems of forest destruction have led the media and the public to begin to emphasize conservation and reforestation, and after a devastating flood in the south in 1988, a nation-wide debate culminated in the logging ban of 1989. The hills inhabited by swidden cultivators are the headwaters of many of the major rivers that feed the major lowland plains in the area. Even though much of the forest destruction is caused by illegal loggers, behind whom are officials and elites, swidden cultivators become easy targets for criticism. As pressure for forest conservation increases, restrictions on forest use, especially swidden culti-vation among the hill population, have become severe. Although methods and techniques of swidden cultivation vary among the different groups, the stereotypical image of swidden hill farmers as people who have recently crossed the border into Thai territory, who subsist on swidden cultivation with short fallow periods that destroy the forests, and who cultivate opium has been prevalent. Deterioration of forest resources is easily attributed to the hill population through this stereotype.

While the public image of swidden cultivators as forest destroyers is prev-alent and is often applied across all groups, researchers have recognized that among the hill dwellers there are different modes of land use concern-ing swiddens. The Karen system is known to be environmentally sustain-able if there is a sufficient amount of land to remain fallow. This means that the Karen system is more conducive to a sedentary lifestyle and the coexistent practice of wet-rice cultivation. Increasing pressure on forest land in the hills has led to conflict in localities where groups with different land-use systems and notions of territoriality live in close proximity. When more mobile people for whom land use is basically on a household basis move into Karen areas and land becomes scarce, there is bound to be conflict in which Karen, who recognize local communal rights and depend on wet-rice cultivation, lose out. Such competition for forest land is exacerbated by the delimitation of land by the Royal Forestry Department for refores-tation and conservation. Use of forest land has become increasingly limited, especially in the watershed forest classified as protected forest by the gov-ernment. In the face of these limitations, Karen themselves are forced to shorten their rotation, diminishing the sustainability of land and water re-sources. Forest policy whose purpose is primarily to maintain the forest and water resources thus actually pressures some swiddeners to abandon what might otherwise be sustainable practices.

As forest conservation has become a major issue in civil action, the rights of hill-dwelling minorities have become a topic of much debate since the mid-1980s. The voices of government officials, some conservationist groups, and the public blaming the "hill tribes" for forest destruction have become harsher. On the other hand, since the 1980s there has been interest among urban elites, monks, students, and intellectuals, represented by the activities of environmental nongovernmental organizations (NGOs), in decentralized forest management and communal access to forest land as a means of sustainable coexistence. The Karen have cooperated with environmental activists since the latter half of the 1980s. The earliest environmental movements involving students, through which various environmental NGOs were organized, arose from resistance to the construction of a dam in Kanchanaburi Province, a heavily Karen-populated area. In one incident, they successfully resisted relocation of Karen residents from the Thung Yai Naresuan Wildlife Sanctuary. More recently, cooperation between Karen and lowland environmentalists has been a strong force in the community forestry movement led by NGOs, intellectuals, and some forestry officials, as well as local residents. Despite such cooperation, some recent events illustrate the precariousness of Karen existence in the hills today.

Klity Mines and a Karen Village

In a Karen village within the Thung Yai Naresuan Wildlife Sanctuary in Kanchanaburi Province, water is contaminated by mines located upstream. The mines have existed for twenty years, but the overflow of lead-contaminated wastewater into the stream that feeds the village only became a concern several years ago. In 1989, it was found that the water near the mine factory contained 200 to 7,000 times more lead than the safety level. Fish floated belly up, livestock such as cattle died, and villagers suffered from headaches and diarrhea. After several ineffectual attempts to improve the situation through the factory manager, the villagers lodged a formal complaint with the Pollution Control Department. They had long kept silent, not daring to file complaints against the mine owner, an influential former member of Parliament. The factory had allowed the wastewater to flow out into the stream by building pipes that led out of the waste pond. The filing of this complaint has spurred discussion about allowing mines to be set up bordering wildlife sanctuaries in other areas. Yet in spite of such protests and problems, in August 1998, the mines were granted a ten-year renewal of their concession and rights to forest use by the Industry Ministry.

Protests of Lowland Farmers and Environmentalists

In April 1997, many protest rallies and long and laborious negotiations between the authorities and villagers under the Forum of the Poor resulted in three resolutions to settle land-rights conflicts in 107 forest communities in Thailand, including many "hill-tribe" villages. The resolutions allowed villagers who had been living in forests before they were declared national forests to remain there on the condition that they take part in forest conservation. Through efforts of various NGOs and the Forestry Department, the Community Forest Bill was drafted, recognizing the rights of conservation-minded communities to stay in forests.

Yet within a year these resolutions became severely challenged. The Forestry Department claimed that the resolutions had caused further forest encroachment, so the only solution would be eviction of forest dwellers. The claim is supported by some conservationist NGOs. Parties with political motives are also attempting to revoke these hard-won resolutions. An incident that brought this home to the wider public was the protest by lowland villagers in the Chom Thong district of Chiang Mai Province. This was the result of a conflict between highlanders on Doi Intanon Mountain Range and lowlanders on the southern foothills. Lowlanders blocked a road leading to Doi Intanon to urge the eviction of more than 20,000 hill-tribe people (in this case, Hmong and Karen) who were allegedly causing forest fires and drought. Seven hundred residents of Chom Thong stepped up pressure on the government to revoke the resolutions without delay or face a move to oust the prime minister. They accused the highlanders of the destruction of watershed areas, resulting in prolonged drought affecting the lowlands, when in fact there has been nationwide drought, not only due to forest destruction, but to climatic changes on a much larger scale.

The Sudden Arrest of Fifty-Six Villagers

Another incident one day in March 1998 also concerns hill dwellers' rights in the forest and the 1997 resolutions. Over one hundred fully armed and uniformed government officials (forestry officers) and police burst into a village in Chiang Dao, Chiang Mai Province, and began arresting people. Fifty-six villagers (including Karen, Lahu, and Lisu people) ranging in age from thirteen to sixty-six were taken away. They were charged with encroachment on a national forest reserve and forest arson. The incident began when the deputy agriculture minister looked down from a helicopter, noticed fires, and attributed them to the hill tribes. Upon investigation, it was discovered that 790 acres of national reserve land had been turned into mango plantations, and 600 illegally cut logs were found. That same day, the fifty-six villagers were taken to jail. Through this incident, the Royal Forestry Department attempted to show that it was concerned and that it would act for the environment, but at the expense of the most powerless. Reportedly, some of the fifty-six taken to jail were merely visitors coming from other regions, and many were children.

The Revocation of the Three Resolutions

Hill dwellers participated in press conferences with academics and gathered in June 1998 at Chiang Mai's city hall to hand a letter to the provincial governor to pass on to the prime minister protesting the revocation of the three resolutions. Environmental NGOs varied in their stances on the resolutions. While there were NGO groups and intellectuals critical of revoking the resolutions, there were also groups that fully supported revocation in the belief that the presence of "hill tribes" in the north posed a serious threat to watershed areas. These groups staged rallies supporting the relocation of "hill tribes." Such conservationist groups together with lowland farmers argued that "relocation of hill tribes should be done on the principle that development efforts would be made to ensure better livelihood for the affected hill-tribes people in their new homes in the lowlands. The hill tribes should prove their land claims. There is nothing to worry about if they have lived there for fifty or one hundred years as they claimed, because if that is the case, the government will give them the rights to stay where they are." It is, however, impossible for forest dwellers countrywide to produce any official documents to confirm that they settled on the land before they were declared protected or reserved areas.

In July 1998, a new cabinet decision authorized the Forestry Department to evict forest dwellers from vulnerable areas and endorsed the policy designed by the National Forest Policy Committee to return power over forest management to the Forestry Department. This would mean removing at least ten million forest dwellers living in sensitive zones nationwide. The cabinet resolutions from 1997 were scrapped, and new guidelines to prove land claims were adopted in 1998. Thus forest policy has basically returned to top-down policy making. These decisions and oppositions, involving parties with varied interests, are shaped by the political aspirations of parties in power. Whether a political ploy, a convenient scapegoating, or differences in conservationist ideas are behind these various turns of events, the hill dwellers' poverty and marginality keep their voices neglected, and the public image of the forest-dwelling "hill tribes" still persists.

Threats to the Survival of the Karen in Burma

The Karen in Burma face problems similar to those of Karen in Thailand due to the destruction of their forest environment. However, Burma suffers from worse economic conditions than Thailand, mostly because of the military regime's efforts to isolate the nation since 1962 until recently. Needing foreign investments to bolster its economy, Burma finally opened its doors to economic development in the early 1990s. The primary area of development is Burma's substantial natural resources, particularly natural gas and timber. Thailand, needing both, became a major consumer of Burma's natural resources. The development of these resources resulted in the destruction of forest land in southern Burma, an area inhabited by many Karen (as well as ethnic Burmans, Mon, and other peoples). For example, in 1993 the world's largest natural gas reserve was discovered in the Andaman Sea off the coast of southeastern Burma. Together with the American oil company Unocal and the French company TOTAL, the Burman and Thai governments built a pipeline to transport the gas from the ocean across southeastern Burma into Thailand. It cuts across a richly forested, mountainous region in Burma and through Thung Yai Naresuan Wildlife Sanctuary in Thailand, home to many Karen.

On the Burma side, Karen villages located along or near the forty-mile pipeline route were forcibly relocated, with no acknowledgment of their land rights or ownership or any compensation for lost land or crops. Some Karen were moved to small relocation camps where each family was given only small plots to cultivate. Those who refused to move were arrested, and some were reportedly even killed. Others fled to other forested areas or into Thailand, fearing persecution and suffering. The forest was cut for the pipeline, disrupting wildlife habitats and the natural forest environment. On the Thai side, construction of the pipeline destroyed the forest and wildlife habitats in the national park, while Karen villagers were forced to move their homes and fields. The struggle for forest dwellers to remain in their homes again came to the forefront of the fight over construction of the pipeline.

The construction of the pipeline is only one example of the problems faced by the Karen in Burma. Due to the civil war, villagers have suffered fear of violence, arrest, torture, or summary execution by the government military for alleged support of the insurgents. They have been forced either to pay fees equivalent to at least one year's income or serve one month as a porter for the army. Women are frequently raped or even gang-raped by soldiers. Crops are confiscated or destroyed and livestock are stolen by military units passing through villages. On a less violent scale, Karen in Burma are not allowed to study in their own language, wear their ethnic dress except for special occasions, or practice other aspects of their culture that distinguish them significantly from the Burman majority. In this way, they are denied their cultural and, in the case of many Christians, religious identity.

The Karen who moved into the regions of Burma controlled by the KNU to escape the direct oppression by the military government until recently lived in relative freedom compared with those still in government-controlled areas. Nevertheless, their lives are still dominated by the fact of living in a civil war zone. While they are free to learn and speak Karen, wear their ethnic clothes, and practice their religions, their existence is precarious. They must provide everything for themselves, from food to education and health care, because the government will not help them. In January and February 1997, the Burman military mounted a particularly violent offensive against the KNU, including any civilians living in KNU-controlled territory. Many villages were burned to the ground, and tens of thousands of people fled the violence. The Karen from Burma who fled as refugees into Thailand must live in camps established and controlled by the Thai government. Several times the Thais have threatened to return the refugees to Burma without any guarantee of safety once they return home. Some camps in Mae Hong Song and Tak provinces have also been attacked several times by a breakaway Karen army (with the implicit support of the Burman army) and burned to the ground, leaving the refugees without shelter or any belongings. All the refugees are dependent on relief aid from NGOs and, in the few cases the Thai government allows, the United Nations High Commission for Refugees. The Thai government does not allow the refugees to build permanent houses or cultivate any crops, despite the fact that some of the refugees have lived in the camps for years. Schooling for children is limited and insufficient.

RESPONSE: STRUGGLES TO SURVIVE CULTURALLY

Despite the suffering the Karen face in both Burma and Thailand, there are several examples of people working to solve their problems and change the oppressive situations in which they live. In Thailand, these efforts take the form of working to preserve the natural environment and maintain their rights to live in the forests in which they have lived for generations. In Burma, Karen have worked nonviolently (in addition to the armed struggle) for human rights, community development, and environmental conservation, both forming their own organizations through the KNU and cooperating with international NGOs, such as EarthRights International and the Burma Relief Centre. In both countries, the use and maintenance of Karen culture and language have actually played major roles in people's efforts to help themselves.

Response in Thailand

In western Thailand, a Karen village resisted the sale of a nearby forest to a wildlife park operator through mobilizing a network of communities and environmental groups. Karen Buddhist monks took an active part, holding an oath-taking rite in which village leaders and officials drank holy water and swore not to harm the forest. The same group then turned to the pollution-ridden Lower Klity village in the same province. The Karen network claims that the Thung Yai Naresuan Wildlife Sanctuary's status as a World Heritage Site exemplifies how Karen live in harmony with nature, protecting forest resources. It is outsiders with power to conduct mining and logging that bring damage. While forestry officials threaten to evict these Karen, they allow destructive mining to continue. The Karen claim to the outside world, "The forest is not only our home. It is the root of our culture and identity." Through the effort to secure rights to land on which they live and subsist, Karen come to voice their cultural identity in the face of environmental and social threats. A temple in the same district has become a locus of Karen activities where leaders and elders gather to express their problems. Karen songs and dances are performed. The monks often play an important part in negotiating with outsiders without using force.

In northwestern Thailand, there have also been small victories in the past. In northwestern Mae Chaem District, Chiang Mai Province, the state-run Forestry Industry Organization had planned a lumber project that would cut down the local pine forests. Villagers began protesting in 1992 with the help of the northern NGO network, students, academics, and concerned monks and succeeded in ending the project. The early 1990s saw a growth of such networks in support of community forestry, a recognition of local communities' roles in preserving and coexisting with the forest, which culminated in the land-rights resolutions mentioned earlier. In the case of resistance to destruction of the pine forest in Mae Chaem, local Karen, in coordination with their supporters, used various tactics. First, they identified with lowland interests: watershed conservation was foremost among their concerns, as it was for the farmers living downstream. Located at the headwaters of the major tributary of the area, the Karen in this area joined together with the lowland wet-rice cultivators. Even without consciously adopting the Thai environmentalist discourse, the Karen, who are themselves wet-rice cultivators, are well aware of the importance of conservation of the forest and water. However, there is also a conscious effort to merge their discourse with that of the Thais. The Buddhist and environmentalist practice of ordaining trees (inviting Buddhist monks to perform a ceremony in which yellow monk's robes are placed around the trunk, sanctifying the tree so that no one will harm it) was adopted enthusiastically in the pine-forest incident. Local Karen thus appeared in the media as Buddhist citizens, denying the often-cited image of the non-Buddhist "hill tribe." At the same time, however, there was emphasis on the fact that the Karen had inhabited the land for almost a century, and that the Karen helped preserve the forest. The land they live on today is the land they inherited from their forefathers and continue to cherish. Another important tactic is the emphasis on Karen culture. When the protesters appeared in the media, they always wore their traditional costume, although it is no longer worn daily. Together with the Buddhist imagery, Karen tradition and identity are emphasized in their struggle for land rights.

Karen villagers are experiencing ongoing rapid social and cultural changes. Many Karen are forsaking their customs in favor of Thai ways or Christian and Buddhist practices. Yet because Karen must make claims of their right of existence to a Thai state and society that still feed on past images of the "hill tribes," efforts are being made to review and selectively maintain Karen wisdom and customs. Among those involved in voicing communal claims to forests and participating in the network of community forestry rights are Karen people, elders from villages as well as educated younger persons, who consciously promote the maintenance of Karen tradition. Pau Luang Joni is one of the most prominent of these elders. He became a Catholic when he was eighteen, yet his mind is open to Karen traditional teachings, as well as to Buddhist ideas and rituals. He inherited wisdom from elders regarding the forest, plants, communal living, and Karen customs. With this ability to integrate knowledge and a keen eye for the practicalities of communal life, he has been one of the leaders of the community forestry movement in the north. Selectively integrating Karen wisdom with lowland ways, he mediates between villagers, NGOs, and lowland peoples. He emphasizes the importance of teaching Karen tradition, history, and language to the youths and has even designed education programs that integrate Karen teachings into the Thai curriculum.

Efforts made by Karen to promote their own traditions while adopting some lowland ways are recognized by some urban Thais as well. Thai NGOs and elites today use the Sgaw Karen term "Pga k'nyau" instead of "Karen" ("Kariang" in Thai) to refer to the Karen. Thailand experienced rapid economic growth in the 1980s and a sudden faltering of the economy in the late 1990s. Karen have recently been introduced as exemplars for dealing with some of the resulting problems as they live in peaceful coexistence with nature. The promotion of Karen traditional wisdom and culture is, at least among some Thai people, received enthusiastically as a path, an alternative way of living to the upcoming market-oriented new culture of the Thais.

Response in Burma

The Karen in Burma also work to maintain as well as use their cultural traditions and identity in their struggles for human rights, democracy, and the preservation of their natural environment. For example, the KNU runs several projects in its southernmost district of Mergui-Tavoy (the region through which the natural gas pipeline runs) to educate villagers in the Karen language, human rights, and environmental conservation. It publishes and distributes in villages a monthly newsletter in the Karen language (Sgaw) with information about the political situation in Burma, community development, and environmental conservation, as well as relevant world news. It also sponsors mobile medical teams. In addition to programs run by the Karen themselves, several international NGOs work to promote human and environmental rights in Burma as well as aid the internally displaced persons and the refugees who fled to Thailand. Some of this help takes the form of humanitarian aid, providing food, medicine, and other necessities to refugees. Other projects promote self-help, providing refugees and displaced persons with education, skills, and materials to help themselves. One such organization is the Burma Relief Centre (BRC), based in Chiang Mai, Thailand, which supports printing of educational texts in several ethnic Burmese languages, including Karen, on subjects such as language skills, mathematics, community development, agriculture, health, and HIV/AIDS. The BRC also runs community-development educational programs for people from Burma that enable them to implement community-development projects for themselves in many of the isolated war zones of Burma.

Because the Karen in Burma only recently learned about human rights as supported by the United Nations, they have limited knowledge of how to address the abuses or inform the world about them. Several people from other countries, including Canada and the United States, are helping the Karen work for their human rights. For example, working with a Canadian, the Karen formed the Karen Human Rights Group. This independent organization documents cases of human-rights violations throughout eastern Burma and produces regular reports on the situation. Another international nonprofit organization, EarthRights International, taught Karen to document the human-rights abuses that they face at the hands of the Burman government. Using this and other evidence, they sued Unocal Oil Company in international court for violating their human and environmental rights. Although the outcome is still undecided, this case is an example of how international organizations and indigenous peoples can work together to try to solve problems of human-rights abuses.

FOOD FOR THOUGHT

Although the name "Karen" stands for several related groups of peoples in both Thailand and Burma, there are similarities in their cultures and situations. The Karen people in both places, and the Karen refugees from Burma seeking asylum in Thailand, all face threats to their culture, language, traditions, and, in many cases, religious practice due to their treatment by the dominant cultures in the two countries. They are also threatened by the destruction of the natural environment in which they live due to economic development, national policies toward the forest and the forest-dwellers, and, in Burma, civil war. Despite the different political and social climates in Thailand and Burma, the Karen people in both countries are integrating elements of their traditional culture with aspects of Western and Thai or Burman cultures to adapt to their changing situations, preserve their cultural identity, and, most importantly, find ways to protect themselves from physical and cultural oppression. Through studying the various ways in which the Karen people attempt to ensure their cultural survival, we can learn lessons about the creativity of cultural adaptation and preservation and the obstacles that still threaten these peoples.

Questions

1. After reading how Karen hill dwellers struggle against the background of political gains and losses surrounding forest policy in Thailand, what do you think would be a fruitful approach to the problem, and where would you begin?

2. There is today an effort by some of the Karen people themselves to redefine and reconstruct their culture. Where can "authentic" Karen culture be located? What is tradition? Do you think that if the Karen are evicted from their forest environment, their cultural identity will be diminished or lost?

3. How do the problems faced by the Karen in Burma and in refugee camps compare with those of the Karen in Thailand? Are there ways the various Karen groups could help each other? What is the role of cultural identity in their struggles for survival?

4. This chapter opened with a quote from a young Karen woman whose family is involved in the civil war in Burma. Discuss her comments in light of what you have read about the Karen struggle for human rights in Burma. Why do you think she wants to learn English and to teach her people? How can education help in their struggle for human rights?

RESOURCE GUIDE

Published Literature

Hirsch, Philip, ed. *Seeing Forests for Trees: Environment and Environmentalism in Thailand*. Chiang Mai: Silkworm Books, 1997.

Marshall, Harry Ignatius. *The Karen People of Burma: A Study in Anthropology and Ethnology*. 1922. Bangkok: White Lotus Press, 1997.

Rigg, Jonathan, ed. *Counting the Costs: Economic Growth and Environmental Change in Thailand*. Singapore: Institute of Southeast Asian Studies, 1995.

Sanitsuda Ekachai. *Behind the Smiles*. Bangkok: The Development Support Committee, 1990.

Internet and WWW Sites

Report of the Special Rapporteur on the Situation in Myanmar to the United Nations Commission on Human Rights: http://www.unhchr.ch/html/menu4/chrrep/6497.htm.

Organizations

Burma Ethnic Research Group
PO Box 1865
Bangrak, Bangkok 10500
Thailand

Burma Relief Centre
PO Box 48
Chiang Mai University
Chiang Mai 50202
Thailand

EarthRights International
PO Box 12
Lard Phrao Junction
Lard Phrao, Bangkok 10901
Thailand
E-mail: earth@ksc8.th.com

The Karen Human Rights Group
Mae Sot
Thailand
E-mail: khrg@burma.neT
http://sunsite.unc.edu/freeburma/humanrights/khrg/archive/

Open Society Institute
Burma Project
400 West 59th Street, 4th Floor
New York, NY 10019
Fax: (212) 548–4655
http://www.soros.org/burma.html

The Thai Development Support Committee
409 3rd Floor, TVS Building
Soi Rohitsook, Pracharat-bampen Road
Huay Khwang, Bangkok 10310
Thailand

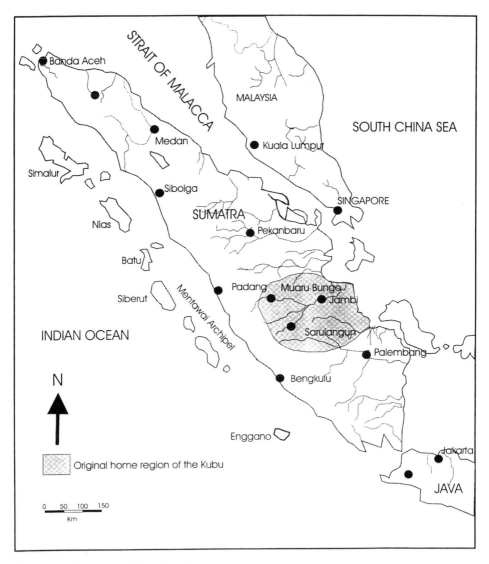

Map 10-1. Courtesy of Gerard A. Persoon.

Chapter 10

The Kubu of Central Sumatra, Indonesia

Gerard A. Persoon

Just let me go
My rice will consist of wild tubers
My buffalo in the forest: the tapir and the deer
My goat: the mouse deer and the boar
My chicken: the pheasant and the jungle fowl
I shall have a roof of leaves
I shall drink water from a wooden bowl
(and if I don't keep this vow)
The tree will bear no crown above
Have no roots below
And its middle will be gnawed away by beetles.

—Kuba vow

CULTURAL OVERVIEW

Ever since the Kubu were "discovered" in the dense rain forest of south and central Sumatra, travelers, colonial civil servants, and researchers have been worried about their survival. It was toward the end of the nineteenth century that outsiders started to actually meet and report on these "wild people" about whom so many stories were told. As hunters and gatherers, with very little material possessions, they made a pitiful impression on these strangers. According to them, the Kubu did not look healthy, and moreover, they suffered from slavery and oppression from the surrounding Malay population. That is why the Kubu preferred to stay away from village settlements and to look for food in the forest. The early writers predicted a future in which this interesting people would soon be swallowed by the encroaching civilization.

Though more than a century has passed and there have been incredible changes in technology and modes of forest exploitation, the forest-dwelling Kubu have not disappeared, but their chances for survival as a people or as an ethnic group are poor. Over the years they have lost land and resources and have never been able to generate internal strength to cope with outside pressures in an effective way.

Forest-Dwelling People

The origin of the Kubu, who themselves prefer the name "Anak Dalam" (People of the Interior) because of the negative connotation attached to the word "Kubu," is still much debated. Some scholars are of the opinion that the Kubu are really the original, indigenous people of Sumatra. Others, however, argue that in times past they belonged to farming communities. For various reasons, small groups of people are supposed to have alienated themselves from these communities. Economic reasons led some to become commercial hunters and gatherers. Another reason that is mentioned is the fear of slave raids organized by the sultanates in this part of the island. People fled to the forest to escape a life in slavery. Whatever the real origin, which is hard to reconstruct, there can be no doubt that centuries ago the Kubu developed into an ethnic group with big differences with their farming neighbors, the so-called Orang Melayu, the Malay people. These farmers live in permanent settlements. Their villages, equipped with small shops, are located on the banks of the rivers or along the roads. They all adhere to Islam and practice a variety of swidden (slash-and-burn) horticulture. But they also maintain permanent garden plots. The contacts with the Kubu used to take place through a Malay middleman called the *jenang*. The differences between the Malay people and the Kubu are in the areas of religion, housing and settlement, clothing, food, lifestyle, and social organization. The lifestyle of the Kubu was never much appreciated by the surrounding farming population. Their food, their housing patterns, the lack of a "proper" religion, the rejection of ordered village life, and the fact that they do not till the land make the Kubu in the eyes of the Malay farmers a lazy, primitive, and backward people. In all aspects of life, the Malay farmers consider themselves superior to the Kubu. The expression "You look like a Kubu" was and still is a powerful means to express disagreement with somebody's behavior.

As hunters and gatherers the Kubu are basically a nomadic people (Figure 10-1). They live in small bands that consist of only a few families.

The Kubu have a variety of dwellings. In case they only want to stay overnight and protect themselves against the rain, they build a simple lean-to. If they want to stay at a particular site for some time, they construct a small hut on little poles with a floor about twelve to sixteen inches above

Figure 10-1. Two Kubu boys in their forest homeland. Courtesy of Gerard A. Persoon.

the ground but without walls. These huts provide just enough place to sleep and store their belongings (cooking utensils, clothes, food). If they intend to stay still longer at a site, they build bigger huts or houses on higher poles with walls made from leaves or bark.

Traditional Subsistence Strategies

The staple food of the Kubu consists of wild tubers and starch obtained from various kinds of palms. Hunting is an important activity. In contrast with many other hunting and gathering tribes, the Kubu do not use bows and arrows or blowpipes. The only weapon that the Kubu have in addition to the bush knife is a long spear that is not thrown but pushed. Dogs are very important in hunting. The most important game animals are wild boars, deer, monkeys, tapirs, and numerous smaller animals. Traps and snares are also used for catching smaller animals such as monitor lizards, snakes, rats, and birds. In former times, the Kubu are known to have hunted elephants and rhinoceroses as well, but by now these animals have become extinct in this part of Sumatra.

The material wealth of a hunting and gathering people is limited because they have to remain highly mobile. Traditionally the Kubu do not have more than their bush knives, cooking utensils, and small quantities of clothes. In order to stay mobile, their material wealth cannot exceed the literal carrying capacity of the group.

At all times food is prepared at a cooking place just outside the hut. Every family cooks its own food, but in case a large animal has been caught, the meat is distributed among all band members. If there is excess meat, other bands might also profit from the successful hunt. In this way, meat, which may be smoked before it is given away, is widely distributed, sometimes even to relatives in other watershed areas.

The length of stay at a particular place depends mainly on the availability of food and other resources and varies between a few days and a few weeks. The population density in areas where foraging and some cultivation of roots crops takes place is between 0.2 and 1.0 square mile. For the Kubu who have taken up agriculture, the rhythm of moving is different. They build Malay-type houses on poles and take care of their crops. During all times, some members of the family will stay behind while others go out foraging or hunting. While foraging groups tend to be smaller in size, usually not more than five or six families, groups that practice swiddening might include more than sixty people. There is a tendency to clear fields in the forest relatively close to each other.

The Kubu have long maintained exchange relationships with the neighboring farmers. They exchange forest products such as rattan, resins, and honey for products like bush knives and spearheads, cloth, tobacco, tinned fish, salt, and batteries. In former times, this exchange took place through silent barter, a form of trade in which the parties do not actually meet. Products offered are put in a particular place, and if the goods offered in return are sufficient, they are taken away by the first party.

Of special importance for all Kubu is the time of the year when a particular forest fruit, the *durian*, is ripe. This fleshy and tasty fruit also attracts herds of bearded pigs, which are relatively easy prey when they cross the river. This is the time of abundance. It is also the time to have weddings and other meetings.

Social and Political Organization

Socially the Kubu live in small bands of a few families that may be part of a larger group. These larger groups are often called after a particular watershed area. Within each group, there is a structure for local leaders, but this leadership is relatively weak. In daily life, the bands are far more important. It is within these units that men hunt together, and that women of the group go out on forest trips to collect all kinds of products. Usually the members of such bands build their huts close to each other.

It is common practice for a daughter to stay with the group of her father and mother, so a husband coming from another unit moves into the residential group of his wife. Usually a man has one wife, but because of uneven birth ratios or special circumstances, a man may take another wife from his first wife's group. The second wife may be her younger sister or an orphan. Within the group, the father of daughters enjoys authority. Boys aged thirteen or fourteen live in a hut by themselves, even though they still eat with their parents. Aged or weak persons and widows are taken care of by the younger generation, although they continue to contribute to the food-production activities as much as possible. Because of internal conflicts or food scarcity, residential groups may split up. In particular, the in-moving husbands with children at marriage age may want to become head of a residential unit.

Though the Kubu do not have an elaborate material culture, they have a fascinating variety of little four-line poems called *pantun*. These are used to express all kinds of experiences and feelings, including feelings of emotions between boys and girls. They also express local wisdom. Not surprisingly, elements from their natural environment, plants, and animals and their characteristics play an important role in these poems, which are sung in a slow and drawn-out way.

Religion and World View

The religion of the Kubu was a great mystery for the early researchers. One researcher initially thought that he had finally discovered a society "without religion or religious beliefs." Later it became clear that this idea was largely based on a narrow definition of what a religion actually is. The Kubu, like many other comparable groups, do have a world view; they believe in a spiritual world and have ideas about the natural and social world that surrounds them. For the Kubu, the forest is not just a wilderness area full of dangers, including the tiger. To them, the jungle is above all a space to live in. They have developed means to make sense of this world and its visible and invisible aspects. They also have to make a living from the forest resources as well as cope with its hardships and dangers.

The Kubu differentiate between "this world," the material world in which they live, and the "spiritual world," which has its material manifestations but which is also invisible or "out there." They have shamans, or *dukun*, who are able to communicate with these spirits or deities. Particularly at times of illness or misfortune, communication with these spirits is extremely important. A major source of misfortune comes from the Malay world that surrounds the Kubu area. Through their activities, the people of this world may bring harm to the Kubu.

The Kubu use medicinal plants to cure a wide range of diseases, but they also believe that illness can be caused by the wandering away of the spirit of the ill person. In order to cure such a person, the shaman performs a ritual during which he tries to bring this spirit back to the sick person.

Magical spells play a very important role in these ceremonies, during which the shaman may fall into a trance. If a major ritual is being performed, the Kubu build a large platform in the forest on which the event takes place. Lean-tos are located in its neighborhood.

Of particular interest in their religion is the fear of death. The Kubu leave the bodies of the dead in the forest and never return to that same place again. This habit, called *melangun*, is based on a fear of the spirit of the dead person, which might bring harm to other group members. The survivors do not want to be remembered by the deceased members. This habit has frustrated many efforts to settle the Kubu in permanent villages. Death cannot be avoided, and that is why permanent settlement for Kubu who maintain the traditional lifestyle is highly problematic. On the other hand, *melangun* can also be used as an excuse for other motivations to leave a certain area. The period after someone has died is often also the moment that the composition of bands changes. People may move to other groups or relatives.

THREATS TO SURVIVAL

Demographic Trends

Exact population figures for the Kubu are hard to give. Throughout history, numbers have varied a great deal. The first estimate from the beginning of the nineteenth century was about "700 wild Kubu." During the census of 1930, the last that paid attention to ethnic affiliation, about 1,700 people classified themselves as Kubu, but numerous nomadic Kubu were not included. The Indonesian census data make no reference to ethnic groups, and it is hard to calculate the exact numbers of dispersed groups like the Kubu. Estimates of the Department of Social Affairs indicate that the total number of Kubu is between 12,000 and 15,000, but the numbers have varied widely over the years. These variations reflect more lack of accurate data and administrative purposes than demographic changes.

Health Conditions

The general health conditions of the Kubu are not very favorable. On the one hand, they face the loss of means needed for their physical survival. Over the years, they have lost much of their forest resources (fruits, vegetables, root crops, and wild game), which has led to a decline in food intake. This even led to serious attention in some Indonesian press media some years ago. Under the title "Death in the Forest," the weekly *Tempo* described the serious state of the Kubu in the degraded forest and also pointed out how ill designed some of the development programs were.

Figure 10-2. Logging moves deeper into the forest. A bulldozer pulls a little house for the drivers and chainsaw operators to a new site. In the back, some Kubu wait for their share of cigarettes or food. Courtesy of Gerard A. Persoon.

Moreover, it was reported that in the recent past the Kubu had lost more than 988,400 acres of forest land to logging (Figure 10-2), transmigration sites, and newly established plantations. On the other hand, access to polyclinics in villages and transmigration sites and medical care provided by the missionaries have increased. This may help to cure people in case of illness but does not do much to promote physical well-being for those who are not ill. Through their own activities, economic interaction with the village communities, the proximity of the gardens of the Malay peasants, and some emergency foodstuffs, the Kubu can meet their demand for food in general. In some cases, missionary organizations or the government provide food through relief programs. However, a noticeable decline in the quantity and quality of the food over a longer period of time is undeniable, and since the forest fires starting in 1994, the situation has become much worse. In the recent past, there have been a number of critical periods during which the Kubu suffered severe casualties because of rapidly spreading diseases (cholera, typhus, smallpox, or flu). Infant mortality is also high among the Kubu, but this has been the case throughout history.

Unlike some other tribal communities, for example, in the Philippines and Australia, the Kubu are not exposed to alcoholic drinks, which, in deplorable circumstances, might aggravate the declining health conditions and social misery. Due to the fact that most of the village people are Muslims, alcohol is not easily available. The Kubu do not prepare alcoholic drinks themselves.

Environmental Changes

Changes in the environment of the Kubu are caused by swiddening, logging, transmigration, and the expansion of large-scale plantations. Jointly they contribute to the impact of forest fires.

Expanding Agriculture

An important part of the landscape in this part of Sumatra has been modified by the activities of the local farmers over many decades. They practice a kind of expansive agriculture in which they cut down the forest, burn the trees, and plant rice and corn for a few years. Once weeding takes more and more time, they start to cultivate rubber on that piece of land. Gradually the rubber trees dominate the vegetation, and a new piece of forest is cleared for food crops. Later, villages might split up, and satellite settlements might be built on the fringe of the forest. Over the years the area under cultivation has greatly expanded, as has the variety of plant communities: gardens with rubber trees of various age classes, fields with rice, woody patches, fallow fields, and fruit gardens with bananas and numerous other fruits.

This mosaic type of landscape also attracts much wildlife. Deer, wild boars, monkeys, and birds are attracted to these gardens with a relative abundance of food and shelter. Malay farmers consider these animals and particularly the wild boars as pests. They are not really interested in hunting these animals because in Islam these animals are forbidden, *haram*. These circumstances have provided the Kubu with an opportunity to profit from the activities in the forest by the farmers. Often, at a small distance from the settlements of the farmers, the Kubu settle down in the gardens of the farmers. Here they can hunt more easily or collect some food products. Once in a while they are also hired as daily laborers by the farmers for clearing the forest, weeding or harvesting crops, or tapping rubber. Sometimes they receive money, but they can also be paid in kind (foodstuffs like rice and cassavas, tobacco, or other items). In this way, many Kubu have adjusted to the changing environmental conditions. On the one hand, the modification of the forest has led to a reduction of many so-called nontimber forest products like rattan, honey, and resins. On the other hand, new modes of obtaining food or income have become available.

Logging, Transmigration, and Plantations

Another factor that has contributed greatly to changes in the environment is commercial logging. Though logging and mining have been going on in this part of Sumatra for many decades, the scale and impact of these activities rapidly increased in the 1970s and 1980s. Large areas of forest were granted to logging and mining companies. The sparse local population was never a serious reason to withhold the issuing of concessions. According to the Indonesian forestry laws, primary forest belongs to the state. Hunters and gatherers do not have property or use rights over these lands. As a result of this policy, the extensive lowland forests were opened up for logging activities. Roads were built and logging camps were established. In some cases the Kubu could temporarily profit from these camps: camp managers were willing to provide cigarettes and food to the Kubu as compensation for loss of wildlife or in exchange for labor. Kubu were hired as guides or to look after bulldozers and other equipment during nighttime.

Often the logging activities were only the first phase in a longer process of forest conversion. Large tracts of logged-over forest were given a new use as sites for transmigration or for the establishment of plantations for industrial crops like rubber and palm oil. If the land was designated for transmigration, this process implied total clearing of the forest in order to make room for the migrants from the densely populated islands of Java, Madura, and Bali. These farmers were given a small piece of land meant for permanent agriculture. They also received a house in newly built settlements equipped with all sorts of facilities like schools, mosques, community buildings, and a marketplace. Sometimes the Kubu are also offered houses and pieces of land in these transmigration projects, but they always turn these offers down. They do not want to live in this kind of environment. They prefer the forest and reject the regularities of closely supervised village life. Moreover, they would only form a tiny and despised minority.

Other areas are designated for growing rubber and oil palms. These huge areas of monocultures provide little chance for survival for the Kubu after a phase of land clearing. Wildlife has almost completely disappeared in these plantations, and there are no fruit trees or other forest products to be collected.

The rain-forest area is considered a relatively useless form of land by certain sectors of Indonesian society. It is classified as "empty land" to be put to more productive uses. The very limited number of hunting and gathering people inside the forest is hardly a reason to refrain from converting forest land into agricultural sites. Moreover, it is very hard for the hunting and gathering people to obtain legal titles to the land because Indonesian law does not have any provisions for this type of land use. The law is based on the idea of permanent and intensive agriculture, so uncultivated land is by definition state property and available for logging, agriculture, and plantation purposes.

Road Construction

Mention should also be made of the extensive building of infrastructure in the area, with the Trans Sumatra Highway and all its feeder roads, bridges, bus terminals, and booming marketplaces as the core. Along this highway, a whole new web of roads has been built to connect old settlements with new transmigration sites, sawmills, and boomtowns. Former logging roads have been turned into all-weather roads. These road-building activities, often financed by the World Bank or other donor agencies, have led to an influx of farmers from elsewhere. The general attitude has always been that primary forest land is state land, and that this "empty land" could be granted to new settlers. Roads have served as an important facilitator to stimulate this process of colonizing the land. Gradually the land formerly occupied by the Kubu has been cut into ever-smaller pieces surrounded by roads through which migrant farmers obtain easy access to the forest.

Forest Fires

The environmental changes brought about by logging and encroaching farmers have turned the forest land into a mosaic of other forms of land use. Together these have led to heavily degraded forests. An important instrument in this process of forest conversion by various users is fire, the most powerful agent to change the landscape. Shifting agriculturalists use it for burning the trees and branches and clearing the land before planting. Big companies also use fire as a cheap tool to clear the forest and prepare the land for transmigration sites or planting industrial crops. In 1994–1995 and particularly 1997–98, fires from numerous sources burned out of control, and extensive areas of already-degraded forest were totally destroyed. South and central Sumatra were among the most affected areas. The thick layer of peat, which is very hard to extinguish, contributed to the prolonged burning of forest land. These forest fires have without doubt further aggravated the situation of the Kubu, who, in addition to acute health problems, have to face further degradation of the remaining forest resources.

Civilization and Development Activities

Apart from the environmental changes, two other kinds of change need to be mentioned in relation to the survival of the Kubu as a people. While the environmental changes influence the lifestyle of the Kubu indirectly, missionaries and civil servants try to persuade the Kubu in a straightforward manner to give up their nomadic lifestyle and become modern peasants.

Missionary Activities

As early as colonial times, missionary organizations were stimulated to work among the Kubu and convert them to Christianity. By doing so, the colonial government tried to prevent the Kubu from becoming Muslims, like the neighboring farmers. Conversion to Christianity was preferred by the Dutch colonial state. This process went hand in hand with efforts to settle the Kubu in permanent villages. These efforts have not been very successful, however. In most cases, the Kubu left the villages again after a few weeks or months. The impact of "gifts and beautiful words," as one missionary stated, did not last.

Since Indonesian independence in 1949, the religious policy of the government has changed somewhat. In Indonesia, everybody in the country should adhere to one of the five officially acknowledged religions, which are Islam, Protestantism, Catholicism, Hinduism, and Buddhism. Tribal religions, animism, or "natural religions" do not qualify. People who adhere to their belief systems are described as "not (yet) having a religion" and thus as "pagans." By this definition, all Kubu are "pagans" and subject to missionary activities. A large number of Indonesian Protestant organizations are active among the Kubu, often with financial support from abroad. Through these missionary activities and through the severe competition between the churches, small Christian enclaves have been created amid the dominant Muslim Malay population. In addition to bringing Christianity to them, the missionaries also try to stimulate the Kubu to settle down, to start agriculture, to send their children to school, and to give up the lifestyle of their ancestors.

Development Programs

Though the colonial government now and then expressed great concern for the survival of the Kubu and about the exploitation of the Kubu by the Malay farmers, few effective measures were taken to change things for the better. Some of the civil servants thought that there was no better alternative than gradual assimilation into the Malay community. The fate of the Kubu and other tribal minorities who were under various kinds of pressure was never defined as a major issue for the government of the colonial state.

A few years after Indonesian independence, responsibility for the tribal minorities in the country was entrusted to the Department of Social Affairs. The tribal groups are mainly looked upon as "isolated communities." The Indonesian government carefully avoids words like "indigenous people" because according to Indonesian law all Indonesians are indigenous, the Javanese and Balinese just as much as the Kubu or Papuans. Together with some 1.5 million people in the country, the Kubu are classified as isolated, backward, and in urgent need of "development." Particularly since the 1970s, a large-scale, uniform program has been designed to bring all of these communities into the "mainstream of Indonesian social and cultural life." Though the diversity of these tribal communities is enormous and ranges from hunter-gatherers and sea nomads to agriculturists with an elaborate material culture (such as the Dayak and the Mentawaians), this development program is aimed at only a single image of a modern Indonesian citizen. The core of this program consists of the resettlement of the tribal people and the implementation of a development and civilization agenda. This program is being implemented through settlement and development projects which last for five years. During each five year period people are acquainted with new housing, permanent agriculture, modern clothing, a new religion, the system of public administration, modern education, and health care. According to the Department of Social Affairs, about 75 percent of the Kubu population has been reached by the program up to now. The department hopes to have reached the remainder within a few years.

The lasting effects of this program on the life of the Kubu, however, are limited. Most of the Kubu left the resettlement projects once the flow of food, tobacco, and other products was reduced. They went back to the forest or to the fields of the Malay farmers. The restrictions of ordinary village life, the supervision of civil servants and administrators, the hard labor in the fields, and the lack of freedom are mentioned as reasons for leaving the project sites. Often they were also more or less pushed out of these projects by village people or migrants from elsewhere, who look down on the Kubu as primitive and backward people.

RESPONSE: STRUGGLES TO SURVIVE CULTURALLY

In one of the writings about the Kubu dating from the beginning of the twentieth century, it was stated that "a Kubu wearing fine shoes and clothes, drinking lemonade from a bottle and smoking good cigarettes is no exception anymore." This image was also taken as an indication that before long most Kubu would gradually come out of the forest and integrate into village society. They would experience the advantages of "modern life," and it would be a great relief to be exposed no longer to the hardships of the jungle. According to one colonial civil servant: "These poor desperate people will soon be with us and no special policies are necessary to achieve this. They will give up their freedom and laziness, and their hunger will drive them out of the forest. Assimilation needs to be stimulated because the state of nature of the Kubu is not so ideal after all."

Almost a century has passed, the "blessings of modern society" have been multiplied, and numerous development projects have been implemented. Still, the Kubu, if given an opportunity to speak out, recall the vow taken by their ancestors. They prefer a life in the forest to living in dense settlements and to being surrounded by people of other ethnic groups and other lifestyles. There can be no doubt that retreat has been the main response of the Kubu toward outside pressure. Sometimes the Kubu accept the benefits in the form of food, tobacco, and clothes from the outside world that come along with missionary activities or resettlement schemes implemented by the government. But in most cases, the flow of goods is reduced after some time, and then the Kubu also lose their interest in staying in the new settlements.

A closer look at how the Kubu react to outside pressure reveals that the response of the Kubu depends largely on their social and ecological circumstances. These circumstances vary widely. In some cases, when they still have some forested area at their disposal, they flee in that direction. Others maintain close relations with the Malay farmers in an intensified economic exchange relationship but stay spatially and culturally at a distance. They are hired as daily laborers or control animal pests in the forest fields. As a result of this, they rely more heavily on the farmers for food and other items. There are also Kubu who have made the transition to become farmers. They have taken up farming in a way comparable to the Malay farmers, using swidden agriculture to grow rice, cassavas, and corn and engaging in some extensive rubber cultivation. Finally, there is a group of Kubu who have lost most of their forest resources because of the establishment of transmigration and plantations. These people have no opportunities for developing a kind of symbiotic relationship with the Javanese farmers or plantation workers. Wildlife has become extinct in these areas. These people hang around at bus terminals along the Trans Sumatra Highway or at big marketplaces. By begging or by selling medicinal plants or some bush meat, they try to make a living. They may also "collect" food from the fields of Malay farmers. Once in a while, they have also forced cars and buses to stop on the highway. In exchange for some tobacco, food, or money, they allow the vehicles with their astonished passengers to continue their trip.

Throughout the history of outside interventions, the Kubu have never been able to forcefully resist these pressures. They could not generate the organization to fight encroaching farmers. They have also not developed the negotiating skills to discuss their fate at the right level in the Indonesian bureaucracy in order to generate more support and more protection. Kubu have sometimes filed complaints against logging companies for felling their highly valued honey trees. Together with their Malay middlemen and supported by some local officials, they have succeeded in securing better compensation. An interesting meeting took place in August 1985 between a group of Kubu and officials from the Indonesian Department for Nature Conservation in relation to the establishment of a protected area in the province of Jambi. In this case, the Kubu successfully argued that their presence in the protected area did not harm the overall status of the park, and the officials were receptive to this idea. The Kubu won the right to stay in the area in spite of its protected status.

These are exceptions in the long history of Kubu people in interaction with the outside world. Usually they have been on the losing end. They have been deprived of vast areas of forest land, including all its resources, and have received little in return. Thousands of migrant farmers from various parts of Indonesia have entered the area. They have colonized the land and pretend to be culturally superior to the "forest people." By now these farmers also outnumber the Kubu. What was offered to the Kubu in return for these losses did not have a long-lasting attraction. Given these social and ecological circumstances, it is remarkable how strongly the Kubu have maintained a lifestyle different from that of their neighbors. Assimilation did not come about automatically.

FOOD FOR THOUGHT

The combined effects of environmental changes and imposed development have left the Kubu with little choice but to adjust to these new circumstances. Their way of coping with new circumstances has always been characterized by retreat and adaptation. They have never openly resisted these forces, but still they have managed not to disappear or give up their preferred lifestyle altogether. In retrospect, it is surprising that the future of the Kubu predicted in the beginning of the twentieth century—total assimilation or extinction—has not come about even though the processes of change have been much more powerful than one could have imagined at that time. The Kubu have proven to possess a greater capacity for adaptation, to be more creative in coping with extremely difficult circumstances, and to be much more reluctant to adopt a lifestyle that they think is not attractive.

The first lesson to draw from this experience is that predicting the future is far more difficult than is often assumed. Moreover, the image of the future that is given is usually only that of the author or the researcher, not the one of the people concerned. People continuously make the best out of changing circumstances, while predictions of the future are often based on the cumulative effects of projections into the future. People, however, make decisions on a day-to-day basis, and even under very unfavorable circumstances they are more creative and innovative than one would expect.

Questions

1. Why would many Kubu like to retain a lifestyle of hunting and gathering in spite of the alleged blessings of modern Indonesian society?

2. Predicting the fate of the Kubu has been extremely difficult. In the past, most

researchers have been wrong. What do you think will become of the Kubu in the future?

3. If you were put in charge of the "isolated communities" in Indonesia, including people like the Kubu, would you continue the "development and civilization" program or take a different approach?

4. If you had to choose between granting a plot of forest land to one Kubu family in order for it to continue its traditional lifestyle or allocating that same piece of land to twenty-five landless farmers and their families from Java, what would you do? What would be your reasons for that decision?

5. Why is it that a tribal group like the Kubu in Indonesia escapes international attention while similar groups elsewhere (e.g., Punan in Borneo, Tasaday in the Philippines, and Kayapo in Brazil) can become the focus of heated debates and extensive media attention? What does this tell us about people in the West?

RESOURCE GUIDE

Most of the old literature on the Kubu is written in Dutch and German because most of the authors were employed by the civil service of the Dutch colonial administration. In addition, German, Swiss, and Austrian travelers and researchers have had a long-term fascination for "primitive tribes" like the Kubu, who were even classified as the most primitive tribe on earth, without a religion and many other traits of civilization. In recent times, scientific research among the Kubu has been rather limited.

Compared to some other tribal people in Indonesia, the Kubu have never received a great deal of attention from the world of the mass media or from organizations for indigenous peoples. No films have been made, and there has been no campaign to secure rights to forest land. An exception that needs to be mentioned here is the work done by Down to Earth, International Campaign for Ecological Justice in Indonesia, a London-based project that is part of the Asia-Pacific People's Environmental Network. The newsletter *Down to Earth* regularly pays attention to issues related to the indigenous peoples in Indonesia, including the Kubu. Within the national context of Indonesia, other issues like East Timor, the Papuans of Irian Jaya, the Dayak of Kalimantan, and the Mentawaians of the island of Siberut have attracted much more external attention. Also, within Indonesia, the Kubu do not have academics or people in the mass media who are prepared to speak out about particular issues on their behalf. Newspaper coverage is very limited. Kubu do not appeal to the interests of the audience. So far, no Kubu has been able to find his or her way into the Indonesian bureaucratic system and become an intermediary between the Kubu and policymakers. The Christian churches are too divided among themselves to draw attention to the plight of the Kubu as a people.

Published Literature

Persoon, G. A. "Indigenous Peoples or Isolated Groups? Indonesia and the International Discourse." *Bijdragen tot de Taal-, Land-, en Volkenkunde* 154, no. 2 (1998): 281–304.

———. "The Kubu and the Outside World (South Sumatra, Indonesia): The Modification of Hunting and Gathering." *Anthropos* 84 (1989): 507–519.

Sandbukt, O. "Kubu Conceptions of Reality." *Asian Folklore Studies*, 42 (1984): 85–98.

———. "Resource Constraints and Relations of Appropriation among Tropical Foragers: The Case of the Sumatran Kubu." *Research in Economic Anthropology* 10 (1998): 117–156.

Schefold, R., and N. de Jonge, eds. *Indonesia in Focus: New Times. Old Traditions.* Meppel, The Netherlands: EduActief, 1988.

Organization

Down to Earth

5 Athenlay Road

London SE15 3EN

United Kingdom

E-mail: dte@gn.apc.org

Phone/Fax: 44 171 732 7984

Chapter 11

The Okinawans of the Ryûkyû Islands
James E. Roberson

From the Chinese era to the Japanese era
From the Japanese era to the American era
This Okinawa sure does change a lot.
> —Kadekaru Rinshô, "Jidai no Nagare" (The flow of time)[1]

What I would like to say before anything else is that among the people of Okinawa, the longing for peace is strong.
> —Governor Ota Masahide, testifying before the Japanese Supreme Court on July 10, 1996, about his decision to refuse to sign documents necessary for the forced lease of land for U.S. military bases[2]

CULTURAL OVERVIEW

On October 21, 1995, an estimated 85,000 people of all ages, of varying occupations and political persuasions, affiliated with numerous citizens', labor, management, women's, and other groups, individuals and families, gathered in a park in the small town of Ginowan, Okinawa. They were there because they were angry. They were there to protest against the rape the previous September of a twelve-year-old Okinawan girl by three American soldiers and to demand, among other things, that the Japan-U.S. agreements regarding the presence of American military forces in Okinawa be reviewed and revised. To understand this event, we need to go back in time, not just to the preceding September, nor even to the post–World War II establishment of American military bases in Okinawa. To more fully understand these and similar current events, actions, and emotions in con-

173

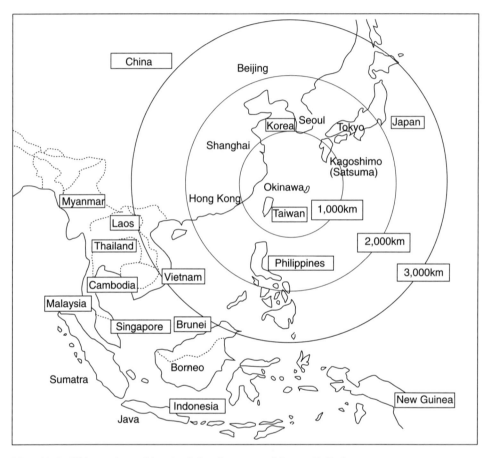

Map 11-1. Okinawa's position in Asia. Courtesy of James E. Roberson.

temporary Okinawa, we must go much further back into the history of Okinawa and the Ryûkyûs.

Locating Okinawa

When Americans talk about "Okinawa," they are usually referring to the main island of "Okinawa Prefecture" of modern Japan. The island of Okinawa is the largest of the 300 or so islands, one-third of them inhabited, in the Ryûkyû archipelago. The Ryûkyû Islands stretch some 800 miles from just south of Kyushu, Japan, to just north of Taiwan and include four major groups of islands: Amami, Okinawa, Miyako, and Yaeyama.

The people of the Ryûkyû Islands share various linguistic and cultural characteristics. While the Ryûkyûan dialects have common roots with Japanese, it is estimated that they separated from Japanese sometime between the third and sixth centuries. Ryûkyûan dialects share basic grammatical structures and root words with Japanese, but have three vowels (*a, i,* and *u,* pronounced as in Spanish) to Japanese's five vowels (*a, i, u, e,* and *o*). There are also distinct Ryûkyûan words not found in Japanese. The relationship between Ryûkyûan and Japanese has been compared to that between Portuguese and Spanish. Common Ryûkyûan cultural characteristics include native religious beliefs such as the existence of a "paradise" (*nirai kanai*) across the seas from which the gods and other spirits visit and to which the dead travel. The traditional roles of women as the primary native religious and ritual specialists is another well-known characteristic of Ryûkyûan culture. Music (instruments and scales) also helps tie the islands together culturally. Throughout this chapter, translations of lyrics from contemporary songs are provided that describe the sociopolitical position in which Okinawa has found itself and the problems that Okinawan people have been facing.

Currently, some 1,300,000 people live in Okinawa Prefecture. Thus Okinawans are not "endangered" in the same way as other peoples and cultures described in this volume. Okinawa, the largest and politically and culturally most important island in the Ryûkyûs, is very centrally located in relationship to other countries and cultures in East and Southeast Asia. This has made Okinawa's location "strategic," and this has in turn been of great positive and negative importance to the culture and history of the Ryûkyûs. In tracing the processes that have led to the present endangerment, five major historical periods, stretching from 1429 to 1998, will be focused on.

Ryûkyûan Kingdom (1429–1609)

In the period leading up to 1429, Okinawan society was politically characterized by the emergence of numerous local leaders who fought with each

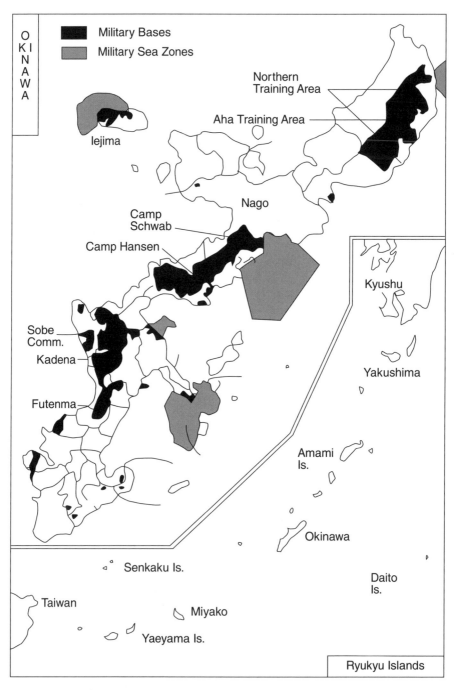

Map 11-2. Ryûkyû Islands and U.S. military bases on Okinawa. Courtesy of James E. Roberson.

Figure 11-1. Palace-castle at Shuri, Okinawa. Courtesy of James E. Roberson.

other to gain control of land. During the fourteenth century, the main island of Okinawa eventually became divided into three separate "kingdoms": Hokuzan, Chûzan, and Nanzan. In 1372, Chûzan was able to establish tributary relationships with China that were politically, economically, and culturally important and that were maintained for some 500 years, until 1872. In 1429, Shô Hashi of Chûzan succeeded in unifying the main island of Okinawa. This marks the beginning of the Ryûkyûan Kingdom, with its center at the palace-castle of Shuri (Figure 11-1). The Ryûkyûan Kingdom eventually came to include the islands from Amami Oshima in the north to Yonaguni in the south.

The "golden age" of Chûzan and then the Ryûkyûan Kingdom lasted from the fourteenth to the sixteenth centuries. This was a period of political independence, economic prosperity, and cultural development during which Ryûkyûan people were able to peacefully benefit from the centrally strategic location of their island country. From the end of the fifteenth century to the beginning of the sixteenth century, local leaders were required to live in the Shuri area, and the possession of weapons was prohibited. The Ryûkyûs became an essentially weaponless state, absorbed in the pursuits of cultural refinement and trade and in the maintenance of proper relations with China. Beginning in the fourteenth century, Ryûkyûan merchants, acting as middlemen, expanded their trade routes throughout East and Southeast Asia, trading at ports in China, Korea, Japan, Vietnam, Thailand, Malaysia, Indonesia, and the Philippines. Some of the items Ryûkyûans traded included porcelain, textiles, and metal wares from China; swords, fans, and folding screens from Japan; ceramics and books from Korea; pepper and other spices from Southeast Asia; and horses, sulfur, and other items from Okinawa.

Dual Subordination (1609–1879)

However, the vulnerability of the peaceful Ryûkyûan Kingdom to outside military power became apparent when the Satsuma feudal domain of southern Japan invaded in 1609. The last time that there had been a general call to arms and widespread fighting in the Ryûkyûs had been some two centuries earlier. The pretext given for the invasion was that the Ryûkyûs had failed to acknowledge their submission to the new Tokugawa government in Edo (now Tokyo). However, Satsuma's real intentions were, in part, to gain control over Okinawa's profitable tributary relationship with China. While still maintaining basic sovereignty, the Ryûkyûan Kingdom entered a 270-year period of "dual subordination." Various economic hardships were imposed upon the Ryûkyûan people, but cultural production flourished from the mid-seventeenth to the mid-eighteenth centuries as Okinawans combined native, Chinese, and Japanese influences. Ceramics, textiles, and mother-of-pearl–inlaid lacquer ware became highly developed, as did bridge-stone masonry. *Ryûka* (Ryûkyûan poems) also became popular and refined and were generally written as songs to be danced to, accompanied by the *sanshin*, a three-stringed banjolike instrument that had first been introduced from China during the fifteenth century. The development of classical Ryûkyûan dance forms and the *kumi-odori* dance-drama also mark this period.

Okinawa Prefecture I (1879–1945)

The arrival of Commodore Matthew Perry in 1853, on his way to "open" Japan to Western trade, marked the beginning of the end of dual subordination. It is significant that Okinawa's first major encounter with the United States was with the American military and that Okinawa was thereby placed between the United States and Japan. It is also significant that Perry essentially forced the Ryûkyûan Kingdom to accept the presence of a small naval operations station during 1853–54 and that during Perry's second visit in 1854 an Okinawan woman was raped by an American sailor.

Perry's visits to Okinawa and Japan helped set in motion a series of changes that led to the end of the Tokugawa shogunate and the establishment of the modern Meiji government in 1868. The Meiji government was sensitive to the threat posed by the Western powers and to the strategic location of the Ryûkyû Islands at Japan's southern border. In 1872, the Meiji government unilaterally declared the Ryûkyûs to be a "domain" within Japan. In 1875, tributary missions to China were forbidden, and despite the Ryûkyûan king's protests that this might attract hostile actions from foreign powers with which Okinawa itself had no conflicts, a Japanese military garrison was established in Okinawa. In 1879, the Ryûkyûan king, Shô Tai, was deposed, and Okinawa was declared to be a "prefecture" of Japan. The Okinawan people thus came under direct Japanese control. They suffered economically as the result of a combination of land privatization—until then, land had been held communally—increasing taxation, and agricultural development in which profits were returned to investors in mainland Japan.

The annexation of the Ryûkyûs represented only the first of imperial Japan's forced appropriations of foreign territories. Japan gained control over Taiwan in 1895 and over Korea in 1905, formally annexing the latter in 1910. In the 1930s, Japan started its bloody attempt to conquer China, and in the early 1940s, the Japanese military expanded throughout much of Asia. When Japanese planes bombed American military installations in Hawaii (itself an independent kingdom until 1893) in 1941, the United States finally entered the war against Japan. By late 1944, American forces were approaching Okinawa, and on Easter morning, April 1, 1945, they landed on the main island of Okinawa. The Battle of Okinawa will be further discussed subsequently.

American Occupation (1945–1972)

At the end of the war, the United States took control of Okinawa. From 1945 to 1950, the Ryûkyûs were placed under an American military government, and in 1950 the United States Civil Administration of the Ryûkyûs (USCAR) was established. In 1952, an Okinawan civilian-run Government of the Ryûkyû Islands (GRI) was established under USCAR supervision.

While the U.S. occupation of mainland Japan ended in 1952 as a result of the San Francisco Peace Treaty, American control of Okinawa continued for another twenty years. Many Okinawans felt that they had been "sold out" by both America and Japan—the price paid by Okinawans for the sake of America's world military interests and Japan's "peace constitution," Article 9 of which forbids Japan from having armed forces other than those necessary for self-defense. Still, most Okinawans came to support reversion to Japanese control, in part because of various kinds of discrimination experienced under the Americans.

Okinawa Prefecture II (1972 to the Present)

On May 15, 1972, Okinawa became a prefecture of Japan once again. However, reversion to Japan did not mean the removal of American military bases. Many people, including then Governor Yara Chôbyô, felt that Okinawa had once again been sold out to American and Japanese interests.

Since 1972, life in Okinawa has changed and improved in many ways. The Japanese government has sponsored a series of economic development programs, and roads, schools, public utilities, and many other dimensions of everyday life have benefited. Okinawa today receives over 3,000,000 tourists every year and because of this is now less economically dependent than ever before on agriculture or on employment related to the American military bases. However, Okinawa still remains the poorest prefecture and the prefecture with the most U.S. military bases in Japan.

THREATS TO SURVIVAL

> The view from Agarizaki
> reminds me of the Okinawa of old
> Now, everything has changed
> these living islands, Okinawa
> Oh sea, oh mountains
> Don't let the hearts of the people change
> Forever, forever, like this Agarizaki Point.
> —Kina Shoukichi, "Agarizaki"[3]

Looking back at past crimes by American soldiers in Okinawa, the number of violent crimes is shocking. Even now, fifty years after the war, crimes by American soldiers are still occurring. Is this really acceptable? I just don't understand why all of the incidents up to this time have been ignored by people on the mainland [of Japan].
> —Third-year Futenma High School female student speaking
> as high-school student representative at public rally,
> October 21, 1995

During the "golden era" of the Ryûkyûan Kingdom, Okinawa's strategic location was a great benefit to the peaceful development of its people and culture. However, Okinawa's geographic advantage has also attracted the outside powers of Japan and America. While this has in turn brought benefits, there have also been several severe and continuing threats to Okinawa's sociocultural survival and integrity.

Militarization

Perhaps the most critical experience in Okinawa's long history was the Battle of Okinawa during World War II. The battle is referred to as "the

Table 11-1
Deaths during the Battle of Okinawa

American Armed Forces	12,520
Japanese Defense Forces	65,908
Okinawan Conscripts and Draftees	28,228
Okinawan Civilian Combat Participants	55,246
Other Okinawan Civilians	38,754
Okinawan Subtotal	122,228
Okinawan Total (including deaths from starvation and disease [malaria])	150,000+

Source: Okinawa Prefecture, *An Oral History of the Battle of Okinawa* (Naha: Okinawa Prefectural Government, 1985).

typhoon of steel" in Okinawa because fierce fighting continued for over ninety days, from late March until early July 1945. The battle involved some 180,000 American ground troops, backed up by nearly 360,000 naval and support personnel, and approximately 100,000 Japanese troops, of which about one-third were Okinawans, though only 4,500 of these Okinawans were trained and armed combat personnel. Both American and Japanese forces suffered very heavy casualties, as shown in Table 11-1.

As Table 11-1 also shows, however, Okinawans suffered the greatest losses of life and of property as well. The 150,000+ Okinawan deaths represented approximately one-fourth of the total prefectural population at the time. The Japanese government in Tokyo did little to prepare Okinawans for invasion, and the Japanese military in Okinawa made little effort to protect or separate noncombatants. Okinawan civilians were killed when they became caught in cross-fire and while attempting to find safety in buildings and even in caves. Hundreds died as the result of *shûdan jiketsu*—group "suicides" essentially resulting from ideological indoctrination—while others were murdered by Japanese soldiers desperate for their own lives. Among the Okinawan Civilian Combat Participants were students such as the members of the Himeyuri high-school girls' nursing corps. There remains a strong feeling among many Okinawans that Okinawan lives were discriminatorily sacrificed by the Japanese imperial government for the sake of averting or at least delaying invasion of the Japanese mainland.

Although the Battle of Okinawa ended in July 1945, and although the war in the Pacific ended that August, in many ways the war has never really ended for the Okinawan people. There are many reasons for this. Okinawa remained under American control for another twenty-seven years, until 1972. During the Battle of Okinawa, some 200,000 tons of explosives (bombs, bullets, and other weapons) were used. An estimated 10,000 tons were left unexploded. In 1974, one such bomb exploded during work on an underground water pipeline, killing four people and injuring twenty others. As of the early 1990s, some 3,000 tons worth of explosives had still not been recovered, and it is estimated that it will take another fifty to sixty years to fully clear the islands of this danger.

Furthermore, even now, more than fifty years after the war and twenty-five years after reversion to Japanese rule, Okinawa remains occupied by extensive American military bases that present many important problems for Okinawans. The current population of Okinawa Prefecture is around 1,300,000 people, or 1 percent of the total population of Japan. The land area of Okinawa is approximately 922 square miles, no more than 0.6 percent of the total for Japan. However, some 75 percent of all the U.S. military bases in Japan are located in this small island prefecture. Some 20 percent of the main island of Okinawa remains occupied by U.S. military installations. This is another reason that many Okinawans think that they and their land continue to be discriminatorily sacrificed for the sake of uncaring mainland Japanese, the U.S.-Japan Mutual Security Treaty, and the "peace constitution" of Japan.

Although American bases in mainland Japan were reduced to one-quarter of their previous size between 1952 and 1960, this was in part accomplished by moving facilities to Okinawa, where during the same period bases doubled. The expansion of U.S. military bases during the 1950s occurred under American rule and often with the use of force—many in Okinawa recall the use of "bayonets and bulldozers" in the forced appropriation of valuable farm land. Under the terms of various mutual security and cooperation agreements between America and Japan, the United States is guaranteed the use of land for its military bases in Japan. Individual Okinawan landowners have been legally forced to lease land to the U.S. bases. While the bases continue to be an important source of lease revenues for some Okinawan landowners and were formerly more important for the Okinawan economy as a whole, base-related revenues amounted to only 5 percent of total prefectural revenues in 1996. Still, the military bases remain a reminder of the war and, as will become clearer subsequently, are a hindrance to economic change and development and to the achievement of local and individual rights of self-determination.

There are also several other important social and human consequences of the continuing presence of American military bases and personnel in Okinawa. Okinawan people have been injured or killed by accidents that occur during military training and other routine exercises. There have been 121 such accidents since 1972, including artillery and mortar shells that missed their marks and military aircraft crashes. For example, in 1959, a military jet crashed into a school, injuring 121 and killing 17 students.

In 1995, there were some 27,121 American soldiers in Okinawa—including 16,200 marines; 7,252 air force personnel; 2,794 navy personnel; and 875 army soldiers—representing over 61 percent of all U.S. forces in

Japan. One of the unfortunate consequences of the presence of American soldiers in Okinawa, as in many other places with American military bases, has been the occurrence of various crimes committed by these soldiers. Between 1972 and 1995, there were nearly 4,790 reported crimes committed by American soldiers in Okinawa. While the majority have been petty thefts, there have also been 255 robberies, 111 reported cases of violence (including rape) against women, and 12 murders. The rape of the young schoolgirl in 1995 mentioned at the beginning of this chapter, like the famous 1955 rape and murder of a six-year-old girl called Yumiko-chan and the rape committed in 1854 by one of Commodore Perry's sailors, must be seen as an example of the threats to life and to freedom from fear that have been constantly posed by the presence of military forces in Okinawa. Furthermore, these cases of rape show that many of the victims of such acts are women.

Some Okinawan women, as mothers, also suffer difficulties related to the children that they bear from relationships with American men. Reports indicate that a high percentage of these Amerasian children grow up in economically disadvantaged single-mother households, their American (military) fathers failing to take even monetary responsibility for their children. Often called "half" (the English word is used, meaning half-Japanese/half-foreign), Amerasian children and adults in Okinawa, especially those whose fathers are African American, commonly face discrimination at school (where they may be bullied), in employment (both in getting a job and in getting promoted), and in marriage. Recently, the problem of educating "dual-citizenship" children has been reported in Japanese newspapers and was discussed by Governor Ota in a 1998 trip to Washington, D.C. Many children would like to attend Department of Defense schools operated on American military bases in Okinawa in hopes of improving their English-language skills and using these as a social asset in overcoming discrimination. However, high tuition costs for nonmilitary personnel make attending difficult. The problems that these children and their mothers face, while suggesting that Okinawan society itself contains discriminatory attitudes towards those who are viewed as different, also remind us of the very human consequences of the continuing American military presence in Okinawa.

Political Threats

When the Meiji government of Japan annexed the Ryūkyūan Kingdom in 1879, it did so in part because of Okinawa's location, providing Japan with a strategic defense zone. During World War II, Okinawans suffered heavily when Japan and the United States fought there as Japan protected its homeland from the American forces. The continuing presence of U.S. military bases in Okinawa is similarly seen by many as a sacrifice that

Okinawan people are forced to make for the geopolitical interests of Japan and America.

Okinawa is thus caught between these two larger powers. Agreements and treaties such as the U.S.-Japan Mutual Security Treaty and the Agreement on the Status of the United States Armed Forces in Japan are legal documents drawn up and signed by the United States and Japan and do not involve the participation of Okinawa Prefecture. This has left the Okinawan people out of decision-making processes that directly influence their fate. Most recently, the U.S.-Japan Special Action Committee on Okinawa (SACO), formed to consider the reduction, reorganization, or removal of American bases in Okinawa, likewise places Okinawa Prefecture outside the formal decision-making process.

Furthermore, even when Okinawans do have some say in decisions, this is often limited and subject to the final authority of the Japanese government. This is the case, for example, in the legal process regarding the forced lease of land for use by American bases. There are two points in this five-step procedure at which local Okinawans are able to exercise some local authority: when land-survey documents are to be signed, and when final documents approving the forced lease of the land are to be signed. At both of these points, if the landowners refuse to sign, then local city or town mayors may do so instead; and if the mayors refuse, then the prefectural governor can do so. However, if even the governor refuses to sign, the Japanese government can use various legal means to require him to sign or even to sign in his stead. Thus even if people in Okinawa want the military bases removed because of the disadvantages and dangers associated with them, the Japanese government retains final authority over the issue.

Economic and Environmental Threats

Since World War II, three important economic changes have occurred that have affected the lives of people in Okinawa and the natural environment in which they live. The first of these, of course, is the presence of U.S. military bases, which have forced people from their land and continue to present an important obstacle for prefectural economic development. During the long American occupation of Okinawa, the economy became very dependent on income received directly from working at the bases or from land rents and indirectly from services provided outside the bases, such as bars and cabarets. Secondly, after its reversion to Japan, Okinawa experienced a construction boom in the early 1970s, when the Japanese government initiated the first of a series of ten-year development programs that, as mentioned earlier, did much to improve the economic infrastructure of the islands. The third, and perhaps the most important, major change in the postwar Okinawan economy has been the rise of tourism (Table

Table 11-2
Tourism in Okinawa, 1972–1992

Year	Visitors	Revenues (¥100 Millions)
1972	443,692	324
1977	1,201,156	991
1982	1,898,216	2,010
1987	2,250,700	2,534
1992	3,151,900	3,442

Source: Terunobu Tamamori and John C. James, *A Minute Guide to Okinawa: Society and Economy* (Naha: Bank of the Ryūkyūs International Foundation, 1995).

11-2). Tourism now represents some 20 percent of prefectural income (nearly 60 percent of Okinawan prefectural income comes from the national government), compared with only 5 percent being military related. Approximately 94.5 percent of all tourists to Okinawa are people from mainland Japan, for whom Okinawa is now a tropical island resort "paradise" similar to Hawaii.

Each of these "developments," however, has produced a situation in which the Okinawan economy remains heavily dependent on only one or two kinds of industries and on investments from the outside. This is typical of many other "third-world" countries and other "peripheral" places located outside the "center" of economic and political power.

It is true that people in Okinawa are now better off economically than they have ever been since at least 1879, when the Meiji government deposed the Ryūkyūan king and established Okinawa Prefecture. However, as it was then, Okinawa remains the poorest prefecture in Japan. Per capita income is 73 percent of the mainland average; the ratio of household debts to savings is 60 percent, some 10 to 20 percent higher than in the rest of Japan; Okinawa ranks forty-second out of forty-seven prefectures in home ownership and forty-fifth in the size of homes (already small by American standards); the rate of unemployment has consistently been twice the national average; and average monthly wages are 20 percent lower than on the Japanese mainland. Such statistics reflect the marginalized status of Okinawa within the Japanese economy—a status and a relationship that is very similar to those of third-world societies.

Furthermore, there have been many negative environmental consequences of economic change and "development" in Okinawa, as is often the case elsewhere. Japanese government-financed construction and the building of tourist resort and leisure facilities, for example, have increased the erosion of soil. This, in turn, has led to cases of severe water pollution and to the unrecoverable destruction of the coral reefs surrounding and protecting the islands. Some 90 percent of the coral surrounding the main island of Okinawa has been killed by pollution caused by various public works, housing, and resort-development construction projects. American armed forces have also caused several environmental problems, including soil erosion resulting from artillery and aircraft bombing practice. Between 1972 and 1994, there were at least sixty-six reported incidents of ground and water pollution resulting from chemicals stored on the bases. Included were two cases of pollution by toxic polychlorinated biphenyls (PCBs) on the Kadena Air Base. Severe noise associated with takeoffs and landings of military aircraft in close vicinity to the residential districts of Okinawan cities has resulted in low birth weights among newborn babies and impaired hearing among local residents. All of these problems represent immediate or future threats to Okinawan ecological systems and/or to the pursuit of peaceful and healthy lives.

Cultural Threats

The final threats to survival are to cultural integrity and pride. Soon after the Meiji government took over control of the Ryûkyûs in 1879, it initiated a series of assimilation policies that were designed to make the Okinawan people "Japanese." These policies included prohibitions on speaking the Okinawan language in schools and on other cultural practices such as the traditional hand tattooing done by Okinawan women. Prewar educational policies attempted to indoctrinate the Okinawan people as "imperial subjects," and since the war this has been blamed for many unnecessary deaths during the Battle of Okinawa.

Since Okinawa's reversion to Japan in 1972, the Japanese government has once again been attempting to make Okinawans "Japanese" citizens. Since the 1980s, for example, the Japanese Ministry of Education has required the use of the (unofficial) Japanese national anthem ("Kimigayo") and flag (the Hinomaru) at all public school entrance and graduation ceremonies. Although until the 1980s such use was lowest in Okinawa among all Japanese prefectures, since that time Okinawa has come more in line with national trends. Similarly, the singing of "Kimigayo" and the display of the Hinomaru flag have been increasingly required and common at events involving national sponsorship. The cultural dominance of Japan is also revealed in clothing, music, other fashions and tastes, and language use. Accounts from the Meiji era to the postwar period describe the use of "dialect tags" (hôgen fuda), placed as a penalty on children who were caught speaking their local dialect while at school. People now speak some combination of local Okinawan dialect and Standard Japanese. Such cultural domination, however, does not mean that people in Okinawa do not maintain their own cultural uniqueness and pride, nor that they have simply and passively accepted their domination by either the United States or by Japan—and this is true whether one is speaking of culture or politics.

RESPONSE: STRUGGLES TO SURVIVE CULTURALLY

We will shout—Okinawa!
This is ours—Okinawa!
Return Okinawa!
Return it to Okinawa!
      —Daiku Tetsuhiro, "Okinawa e Kaese" (Return it to Okinawa)

Looking back on those days, I am convinced anew that we might need to fight again. Without opposition, we cannot improve our situation as being a territory for U.S. bases. I firmly believe that unless tens of thousands of people stand up to protest, exploding with anger against authority, we cannot change this reality in Okinawa and truly win peace.
      —Chibana Shôichi, *Burning the Rising Sun*

Because of the advantageous location of their islands in relation to much of the rest of Asia, Okinawans and other Ryûkyûans have found themselves caught between the political and military interests of larger and more powerful nations, particularly Japan and the United States. Because of this, people in Okinawa remain exposed to several threats to life, land, and liberty. Okinawans have reacted to and resisted such domination and such threats with two general kinds of resistance: political and cultural.

Political Demonstrations and Protests

When the American military government used "bayonets and bulldozers" in the 1950s to force Okinawans to give up their land for the expansion of U.S. military bases, it sparked the anger of many people throughout the islands and, for a time, in mainland Japan. The *shima-gurumi* movement begun in 1956, which protested against the forced taking of Okinawan land, was one of the first widespread antibase protest movements. Since that time, a series of groups and movements have continued to protest against the presence of the military bases, the forced taking and use of Okinawan land, and the crimes committed by American soldiers. There have also been protests against Japan because of the Okinawan people's experiences under Japanese imperial rule up to World War II and because of continuing Japanese support of the American bases since the war.

Prominent among the people protesting against the American military bases have been pacifist "antiwar landowners" groups. While the numbers of landowners participating has fluctuated, the antiwar landowners have resisted the forced appropriation of their lands and the economic terms under which this has been done by, for example, refusing to sign the necessary legal documents allowing the Japanese government to arrange for the lease of their land to the U.S. military. One interesting development along these lines was the beginning, in 1982, of the "one-*tsubo* landowners movement" in which people in Okinawa, and then throughout Japan, were encouraged to purchase small parcels of land from other antiwar landowners in order to complicate and so resist the legal procedures necessary for the forced lease of land for the bases.[4] Though the Japanese government has occasionally attempted to arrange for longer lease periods of up to twenty years, leases have generally been for terms of five or ten years. This means that when these leases end and are to be renewed, landowners may choose to refuse to sign. A few of the antiwar landowners have in fact refused to sign the forced lease documents at various times since Okinawa's reversion to Japan in 1972. In 1992, for example, some one hundred landowners refused to sign.

Until the 1990s, either the local mayors or the governor of Okinawa then signed, allowing the lease despite the landowners' disapproval. However, in 1995, first the mayors of the towns of Okinawa City (Koza), Yomitan, and Naha refused to sign the lease documents, and then so did the governor of Okinawa, Ota Masahide. Ota had first been elected governor in 1990 under an antibase slogan, and although he had earlier signed such documents, by 1995 he had become frustrated with the Japanese government's lack of progress toward removal of the bases and concerned about the necessity of removing the bases in order for Okinawa to achieve a more balanced and independent economic development.

More recently, Ota has expressed his disapproval of plans agreed upon by Japan and the United States to construct an offshore helicopter-port facility near Camp Schwab in Nago that is supposed to "replace" the heliport at the U.S. Marine Corps Air Station at Futenma. Ota and many others in Okinawa, including a majority of Nago residents participating in a local referendum, object to this project because it is only a "transfer" of bases within Okinawa and is not "removal" to places outside the Ryûkyûs. The planned heliport (4,921 feet long by 1,968 feet wide and capable of stationing over 2,500 marines) also poses an ecological threat to the fragile coastal environment of the area. Because most of the coral surrounding the main island of Okinawa has already been destroyed, any further destruction is all the more disastrous. Furthermore, sea turtles lay their eggs along the coast near the proposed heliport site, and the area is also home to a number of endangered species, including the dugong, a sea mammal protected by international and national law.

The actions of Governor Ota and the mayors of Okinawa City, Yomitan, and Naha are important recent examples of official political protests against the continuing U.S. military presence in Okinawa. In April 1996, the Central Okinawa Mayors Association, composed of the mayors of thirteen towns and cities, also issued a declaration against the transfer of military bases inside of Okinawa Prefecture. Between 1972 and 1995, the Prefectural Assembly issued no less than 125 official statements of protest against accidents, crimes, and other incidents associated with the American bases and military personnel in Okinawa.

At the beginning of this chapter the rally organized in October 1995 to protest the rape of a twelve-year-old girl and to demand the removal of the American bases was described. The protests against this rape case included early and widespread participation by various women's groups. While the October rally of some 85,000 people was certainly one of the largest gatherings in Okinawan history, it was not the only such large-scale protest. In June 1987, approximately 25,000 people made a human fence nearly eleven miles long surrounding Kadena Air Base. In a similar event in May 1998, some 16,000 people joined hands in surrounding the Futenma Marine Corps Air Station. During the late 1960s and early 1970s, there were frequent protests against American use of bases in Okinawa for the war in Vietnam, including their use for direct bombing missions by B-52s newly stationed in Okinawa. In December 1970, at the height of the Vietnam War and of the movement for Okinawa's reversion to Japan, anti-U.S. riots broke out in the city of Koza (now Okinawa City).

In addition to these and other protests against the American military presence in Okinawa, there have also been protests against Japanese governmental policies and the government's military history and background. Perhaps the most famous of such incidents is one that, like the protest at Kadena, took place in 1987. On October 26, 1987, at the opening ceremony of the Youth Softball Competition during the Okinawan National Athletic Meet, Chibana Shôichi, the owner of a small grocery market in Yomitan village, pulled down and burned the Hinomaru flag of Japan. This athletic meet was part of the fifteenth-anniversary celebrations of Okinawa's return to Japanese control, and various Japanese officials had pressured the Okinawans to display the Hinomaru and sing the "Kimigayo" anthem. Prior to this event, Chibana had become active in educating people about the group suicides and other horrors of the Battle of Okinawa that had resulted from Japanese militarism and nationalism. His action in burning the flag was a protest against that history and against increasing Japanese nationalist control since Okinawa's 1972 reversion.

Finally, it should be noted that not all political responses to the American bases and Japanese nationalism have taken the form of protests and demonstrations. The prefectural government of Okinawa has recently begun to formulate plans for the future development of Okinawa after the military bases are removed. The prefectural "Action Program" for the removal of the bases involves three steps, with all bases to be gone from Okinawa by the year 2015. The prefecture also envisions the development of Okinawa as an "International City," once again making peaceful use of Okinawa's historically strategic position for purposes of trade and international exchange. Though problems with these plans have been pointed out, they still represent positive, future-oriented forms of political response to the political and economic difficulties Okinawa continues to face. It is interesting that in drawing on Ryûkyûan cultural and historical distinctiveness, these plans appeal for more local Okinawan autonomy.

Cultural Pride and Resistance

The cultural and historical uniqueness of Okinawa has also been emphasized by two recent construction projects. One of these involved the restoration of the Shuri palace-castle (Fig. 11-1). From the fourteenth to the late nineteenth centuries, Shuri was the residence of the Ryûkyûan kings and the center of politics and culture. During the Battle of Okinawa, the Japanese army built an underground headquarters beneath the castle, which was completely destroyed by heavy American bombardment. After the war, the University of the Ryûkyûs long occupied the site. The restored palace-castle was opened to the public in November 1992. The restoration of Shuri may be seen as one way in which Okinawans, as Ryûkyûans, have been able to restore their cultural heritage and pride. Especially given the fact that its Chinese-based design makes it very different from Japanese-style castles, Shuri is a sign of the distinctiveness of Ryûkyûan culture, pointing to Okinawa's differences from the rest of Japan.

The other project of cultural and political significance in pointing to the distinctiveness of Okinawan experience and identity is the construction of a war memorial at the Okinawa Peace Memorial Park in Mabuni. The war memorial is similar to the Vietnam War Memorial in Washington, D.C., in that it consists of blocks of polished black granite on which are written the names of those who died during the Battle of Okinawa. The Okinawan memorial, however, includes the names of all 234,183 people who died—Okinawans, Japanese, Americans, and others (many Koreans, however, have refused to have their family members' names inscribed because of a continuing sense of disgrace over the fact that most Korean victims were either male laborers or female sex slaves—the so-called comfort women—forced to work for the Japanese army). The Okinawan names, furthermore, include those of people who died from war-related causes during the fifteen years of war beginning with Japan's earliest invasions of Chinese territories in the 1930s. While the memorial has been criticized for including the names of Japanese officers and soldiers responsible for many Okinawan deaths, the memorial should also be seen as a reminder of the costs paid by Ryûkyûans during Japan's war and as a symbol of the Okinawan people's hopes for peace.

In addition to these forms of physical and symbolic protests and revitalization of cultural pride, more everyday forms of cultural protest and resistance may be heard or seen in contemporary Okinawan music and on Okinawan television and radio. For example, television and radio shows feature the use of Okinawan dialects or a unique blending of Okinawan dialect and standard Japanese. Such language use may be understood to represent ways in which a distinctively "Japanese-but-Okinawan" identity is both created and maintained. In Okinawan music, vigorous regional and subregional folk-music traditions survive. Numerous popular groups combine the use of traditional Okinawan instruments with rock-and-roll instruments, perform in distinctively "Okinawan" clothing, and sing many of their songs in Okinawan dialects that require Japanese translations in the CD liner notes. Some of these groups have made revised rock or reggae versions of traditional Okinawan folk songs; several groups have created songs that either directly or indirectly comment on various social and political issues facing Okinawans today. Excerpts from some of these songs appear in this chapter. As among many other peoples throughout the world who have experienced political, social, and cultural domination, such creative uses of native language and music are important in the re-creation, the renaissance, of local cultural pride and identity.

FOOD FOR THOUGHT

We had the American era
We had the Japanese era
We had the Okinawan era
We had the Chinese era
Even if the world changes
Even if everything changes
Don't forget your gentle kindness.
—Rinken Band, "Yu-Yu-Yu You-You-You"
("Yu" means "era/world/time")

Don't forget; Never forget
The spirit of the Island Child
Don't throw away your heart
Don't throw away your love
We are the Children of these Islands
Don't throw away the spirit of the Island Child
Don't forget the spirit of the Island Child.
—Kina Shoukichi, "Shimagwa Song" (Child of these Islands song)

Okinawa's geographically advantageous location has placed it in an economically, politically, and militarily strategic position. Especially since the late nineteenth century, this position, together with the Ryûkyûans' non-militarized political and sociocultural systems, has been exploited by Japanese and American imperialisms for their own advantage. Ryûkyûan people have been subjected to various forms of externally imposed political and military domination, economic subordination, and sociocultural discrimination. However, for a number of reasons and in various ways, Okinawan people have also accepted, made use of, or benefited from the presence of Japanese and Americans. Especially since the end of World War II, Ryûkyûan people have continually protested against and resisted forms of exploitation, domination, and discrimination. Finally, despite all of the changes and troubles that Ryûkyûan people have been through, they have retained and indeed are even reviving and re-creating their culture and their cultural pride. The example of Okinawa and the experiences of the Ryûkyûan people should lead to thought and reflection on a number of related examples and issues.

Questions

1. What political-historical connections and similarities can be found in other places, among other peoples and cultures, not just in Asia but throughout the world, and especially that involve the United States? A very instructive comparison may, for example, be made with Hawaii, which has experienced similar problems with militarization and outside control because of its "strategic" location.

2. What are the implications of the continuing American military presence abroad? Whose interests and rights and whose liberties and lifestyles are being (or should be) protected or sacrificed?

3. What are the implications of the continuing American military presence in bases abroad (and at home) for gender and ethnic discrimination and exploitation?

4. How should issues of local autonomy and national interest be addressed? Whose interests should come first? At what cost? To whom?

5. What really constitutes "economic development"? What kinds of economic development are desirable? For whom? At what costs to local cultures and local environments?

6. How are cultural pride and cultural creations or performances in other locations also politically significant, sometimes directly or indirectly acting as protests or acts of resistance to exploitation, domination, and discrimination?

NOTES

1. Unless otherwise noted, all translations from the Japanese are by the author.

2. *The Ryûkyûanist*, no. 35 (Winter 1996–97): 2. In November 1998, with Okinawa's economy in recession, Ota failed in his attempt to be re-elected for a third term as Governor of Okinawa. He lost to Inamine Keiichi, a more conservative businessman and politician who ran on a platform emphasizing jobs and economic revival over political issues such as the American military bases.

3. This song is a lament for the environmental degradation accompanying economic development in Okinawa during the 1970s.

4. A *tsubo* is the equivalent of approximately 3.95 square yards.

RESOURCE GUIDE

Published Literature

Barrell, Tony, and Rick Tanaka. *Okinawa Dreams OK*. Berlin: Die Gestalten Verlag, 1997.

Field, Norma. *In the Realm of a Dying Emperor*. New York: Pantheon, 1991.

Higa, Tomiko. *The Girl with the White Flag*. New York: Dell, 1992.

Lebra, William P. *Okinawan Religion*. Honolulu: University of Hawaii Press, 1966.

Nakasone, Ronald Y., ed. *Reflections on the Okinawan Experience: Essays Commemorating 100 Years of Okinawan Immigration*. Fremont, CA: Dharma Cloud, 1996.

Okinawa Prefecture. *An Oral History of the Battle of Okinawa*. Naha: Okinawa Prefectural Government, 1985.

Ota, Yoshinobu. "Appropriating Media, Resisting Power: Representations of Hybrid Identities in Okinawan Popular Culture." In *Between Resistance and Revolution: Cultural Politics and Social Protest*, ed. Richard G. Fox and Orin Starn. New Brunswick, NJ: Rutgers University Press, 1997: 145–177.

Tamamori, Terunobu, and John C. James. *A Minute Guide to Okinawa: Society and Economy*. Naha: Bank of the Ryûkyûs International Foundation, 1995.

Internet and WWW Addresses

Contemporary Okinawa: Politics, Economy & Society: http://2.gol.com/users/johnrach.

Map 12-1. Courtesy of George N. Appell.

Chapter 12

The Rungus Dusun of Sabah, Malaysia

George N. Appell

CULTURAL OVERVIEW

The People

The Rungus live in northern Sabah, Malaysia. They refer to themselves, their culture, and their language as "Rungus." As their language forms part of the widespread family of Dusun languages in Sabah, the Rungus are frequently referred to as Rungus Dusun. Traditionally they were longhouse dwellers and engaged in a form of agriculture called swidden agriculture. This involved cutting the tropical forest for fields, burning the slash, which provided fertilizer for the crops, and then planting hill rice and other crops.

Until 1963, the Rungus lived under the jurisdiction of the British colony of North Borneo. Then Sabah was joined by the British to the State of Malaya, creating the new Muslim country of Malaysia.

In describing traditional Rungus society, the period prior to 1960 will be the initial focus. Then the changes that have occurred as the result of an authoritarian government system and other processes of modernization that did not take into consideration the values of Rungus culture or the needs of the Rungus will be detailed. The Rungus culture was unnecessarily destroyed, and many valuable aspects of it were lost.

The Setting

The Rungus live in a hilly region varying from 700 to 2,600 feet in elevation. The region was originally covered with secondary forest, which was cleared temporarily for agricultural purposes. After the removal of crops, usually after one agricultural season, the areas were left to return to forest. They would not be reused again for seven or eight years after sufficient forest had grown up so that when cut and burned, it would provide adequate fertilizer for the new crops. This secondary forest was broken by patches of primary forest. The forest was tropical rainforest, but that now only exists in small patches as a result of the recent development of plantations of coconut, oil palm, and rubber. There is a marked dry season between monsoons.

Traditional Subsistence Strategies

The traditional farming system of the Rungus was a complex and sustainable agroecological system composed of various food crops, fruit trees, plants for raw materials, domestic animals, and wild animals. The farming unit was the domestic family. After cutting the forest and firing the slash, the domestic family planted maize, various varieties of rice, and cassavas. In addition, if the female founder of the family was skilled in weaving, a couple of varieties of cotton and dye plants were planted.

When the crops were harvested from the swidden, the area reverted again to forest. In the forest and old swidden areas, a variety of wild animals, including monkeys, reptiles, and ungulates could be hunted. Dogs were kept to help in the chase. The domestic family also raised pigs and chickens and in some cases water buffaloes. Men would hunt in the forest for wild pigs and deer. The domestic animals and the animals hunted provided an important source of protein. The domestic animals also formed an integral part of the domestic family ecosystem through the cycling of nutrients. Waste products, remnants of the food processing, pieces of fruit, and excess vegetable products from the fields either fell through the longhouse floorboards to be eaten by the pigs and chickens or were fed directly to them. And the animals in turn provided an important source of food for the domestic family.

A large variety of fruit trees were planted by village members in any part of the village reserve not already in use. These included papaya, banana, tarap, lansat, and durian. In the late 1930s, a small number of Rungus began developing wet-rice fields.

The land-tenure system was critical to the ecology of the domestic family. The Rungus village held residual rights over a territory. Only village members could cultivate fields and plant fruit trees in the village territory. No permanent-use rights over a swidden area were established by cultivation. After the crops were removed, the area reverted to the village to be used in subsequent years by any village member when the forest had again recovered.

Social and Political Organization

The major Rungus social units were the family, the longhouse, and the village. Rungus society was egalitarian with no hereditary social classes.

The Family

The nuclear family was the primary production and consumption unit of Rungus society and is therefore referred to as a domestic family. Marriage was normally monogamous. Occasionally a wealthy man might have two or three wives, but this was thought not to be appropriate. Residence after marriage was initially in the wife's village.

When a son desired to marry, a substantial bride-price of gongs, brassware, and ceramic ware was provided for him from assets of his domestic family. The institutions that led up to marriage and the eventual foundation of a new domestic family were justified by the major value premise in Rungus society: all sexual relations, unless they are properly entered into through a marriage, are potentially dangerous to the participants, their families, the village as a whole, the swiddens, and the domestic animals in the village. Extramarital relations caused illness in the village and infertility of crops, domestic animals, and people.

After residing a year with the bride's domestic family, the couple built a separate longhouse apartment, ideally onto the longhouse where the bride's family resided, and founded their own domestic family. Thus the Rungus domestic family most frequently consisted of the two founders or the two founders and their children.

The division of labor in the activities of men and women is shown in Table 12-1. Among the Rungus, male and female work were viewed as complementary. The contributions of each were considered equivalent in value. On this interdependence of roles rested the prosperity of the domestic family. Children at an early age participated in the domestic family's economy both in household tasks and in agricultural work. Young girls started imitating the work of their mothers at about the age of three years, and by the time they were around twelve, they were accomplished in all housekeeping tasks. As soon as they could handle the responsibilities of the household, they freed their mother for work in the swiddens. Young boys did small chores around the household, and by the time they were ten or twelve years old, they started helping in the swiddens.

Profits from the household ecology were invested in gongs, brassware, jars, and other ceramic wares. This property was owned corporately by the domestic family and served as an investment that could be liquidated for food and clothing in times of poor harvests. Some of the agricultural surpluses were also sold to Chinese shops to repay debts, for various necessities, or for cash. The Rungus depended on these shops for items such as sugar, kerosene, cloth, cookware, and tinned fish.

Table 12-1
Male and Female Activities among the Rungus

Male Activities	Female Activities
Agricultural Activities	
Clearing and burning for swiddens	Help in clearing up small debris prior to planting
Planting swiddens	Planting swiddens
Weeding swiddens	Weeding swiddens
Harvesting swiddens	Harvesting swiddens
Care and Raising of Domestic Animals	
Dogs	Pigs
Water buffaloes	Chickens
Hunting and Gathering Activities	
Hunting with spears for large game	Gathering snails and shellfish
Fishing with baited traps and nets	Fishing with scoops for small fish and prawns
Gathering honey and orchard fruit	Gathering wild roots, berries, and vegetables
Domestic	
Collecting firewood	Husking the family's rice supplies
Tending children	Carrying water
Making knives, rope, fish traps, and carrying baskets	Tending children
	Weaving, dying, sewing, and making rice-winnowing baskets
Property Accumulation	
Marketing of agricultural surpluses	
Bargaining for purchase of property	
Birthing and Child Rearing	
Midwifery	Ritual aspects of birth
Child rearing and nurture	Child rearing and nurture
Ritual	
Ceremonies for swiddens	Communication with the spirit world through spirit familiars
Ceremonies for property	Ceremonies for health and illness of the domestic family
Minor ceremonies for longhouse	Major ceremonies for the longhouse
Political Activities	
Participation in village moot	
Headmanship	

The Longhouse

The longhouse was in essence a condominium, composed of various apartments joined together but built and owned by the individual domestic families. The entrance area of each apartment and its working space were

Figure 12-1. Interior of traditional Rungus longhouse during the day when most of the members were working in the fields. Behind the door to the right are the sleeping, cooking, and eating areas. The area to the left is where people sat to talk, weave, prepare food, or make baskets. The walkway is where the women husked rice by pounding it in wooden rice mortars like the one the woman is sitting on. Courtesy of George N. Appell.

joined on to the next, forming a contiguous open area where the members worked, gossiped, tended children, and visited (Figure 12-1).

The Village

The number of inhabitants of a village varied from 40 to approximately 400 people. There was no formal political organization above the village level except for temporary alliances between villages that arose from time to time as the result of an outstanding political leader. A village was composed of one or more longhouses. These were either located together or scattered in various hamlets in the village territory.

The territory of the village, or the village reserve, usually encompassed a drainage area of one of the small streams that run out of the height of land forming the backbone of the Rungus region. This village reserve contained a number of sacred groves with indwelling spirits.

Religion and World View

The Rungus believed in a creator god and a number of other divinities. These included the rice gods and the *rogon*. The *rogon* represented aspects of the physical and social environments. Thus they were found in sacred groves around springs and in the hearth of the household itself. The *rogon* were easily offended and when angry could cause illness and misfortune. A *rogon* living in a sacred grove became angered if his grove was intruded upon and cut to plant swiddens. He would vent his anger by making the culprit or another member of his family ill.

Illness was believed to be the result of the capture and torture of an individual's soul by the *rogon*. Alternatively, it could be the result of the soul wandering away. To retrieve the soul and cure illness, a priestess would be employed to diagnose the source of the illness. Then a ceremony was held to sacrifice pigs and chickens to the appropriate *rogon*. The priestess would officiate at this ceremony, chanting and singing the long and beautiful ritual texts that told of the works of the supernaturals. During the ceremony, the priestess would go into a trance and with the aid of her spirit and helper would retrieve the soul.

Priestesses officiated at other ceremonies to sanctify marriages and to promote the fertility of swiddens, family, and village. These established a state of goodwill between the spirit world and the domestic family and village.

THREATS TO SURVIVAL

The first thing that strikes a visitor to the Rungus now is the amount of roads that have been built through their lands. Then comes the shock of the lack of tropical forest and the disappearance of the sacred groves. Instead, there are miles and miles of coconut palms, rubber plants, and oil-palm plantations. Then one notices how dry the country has become. Where rivers ran before, there are now dried-up stream beds that grow small trees. There are no longhouses. Every hamlet is composed of scattered individual family houses and has either a church or a small mosque. Conversion to Christianity has predominated. Also here and there one sees a rural medical dispensary. Many bird species are now not found in the area, and there are no longer any wild animals to hunt. How did this happen in so few years?

It is difficult for small, indigenous populations such as the Rungus to withstand the expansion of the global economic and political systems. Everywhere indigenous peoples are faced with attempts by those in economic and political centers to gain control of their land, their labor and their natural resources to maximize their profits. There are certain universal processes whereby this is accomplished. Characteristically, these indigenous populations are viewed as flawed and inferior, with cultures that have nothing of value. This attitude provides the justification for those in the economic and political centers to take control of the labor, land, and resources of these indigenous peoples. The means used would be considered a violation of human rights if they were done to the people in the economic and political centers. This process of taking the resources of indigenous peoples at the same time makes such populations dependent, for which they are again disparaged.

This process begins with labeling by those in power in terms that dehumanize and debase these indigenous peoples. They are considered dirty, dumb, lazy, backward, and poor. They are frequently referred to as being sexually loose, tending to drunkenness, riddled with incest, and rife with criminal behavior. The destruction of a population's sense of its worth and self-esteem removes its motivation to control its own destiny. Even worse, it has been found that individuals with lower self-esteem, without a healthy sense of self-worth, are more frequently ill. Attacks on an individual or population do have health consequences. They erode that individual's or population's capacity to adapt to life's challenges.

The psychological attacks on the Rungus as a people went hand in hand with attempts to destroy their culture and erode their land base. This process began with the colonial government but was accelerated with the arrival of Christian missionaries. The missionaries argued that if the Rungus converted to Christianity, they could cut their sacred groves, homes of the *rogon*, with impunity. They could then plant these fertile areas with crops and make a large profit. However, the missionaries had no idea of the ecological function of these groves and made no attempt to find out. These groves were situated around springs and seeps in the forest. Their destruction contributed to the drying up of the environment. The springs stopped flowing. With less forest, the amount of particulates exuded from the leaves into the air diminished and lowered the air density of nuclei in the air around which raindrops could form. The destruction of vegetation facilitated the rapid runoff of rain. A forest grove can slow down the fall of rain to the earth by eighteen or more hours as the water drips from leaf to leaf.

It was also claimed that conversion to Christianity would allow the Rungus to sell their chickens and pigs to the Chinese shops and thereby make a profit rather than saving them for sacrifice to their gods and spirits. The missionaries ignored the useful protein that this provided.

One of the more persuasive arguments was that conversion assured a life after death. The missionary group started an agricultural school. It was run by a missionary who admitted that he knew nothing about tropical crops. He maintained that he would teach the Rungus how to plant fruit trees. He could not see the myriad groves of cultivated fruit trees that stood out in the cultivated areas and the forest. This represents another aspect of creating dependent people. Those people on the peripheries do not get the most up-to-date information and technology.

Then the missionaries handed out discarded clothes from Western countries, supplanting the native dress, which included beautiful hand-woven skirts and blouses and embroidered sarongs. To those viewing the Rungus in these cast-off clothes, the Rungus looked like the most desperate of the poor.

The next step in the destruction of Rungus culture involved efforts at modernization taken by the British colonial government. Government schools were established at various centers. Children were told that they had to buy school clothing and knapsacks to carry their schoolwork in. They were told that if they wore their native dress or carried their native baskets, exquisitely well made and now a scarce item for the tourist shops, they would be laughed at. This illustrates just one of the steps that resulted in developing an unnecessary dependence on a cash economy and integration to the national economic system.

At the school, teaching was done in Malay, and it was expected that the Rungus would learn Malay, the national language. The Rungus language was forbidden, with the result that members of the younger generation began to lose touch with their own language. The Rungus language now spoken is no longer as elaborate and beautiful as it once was. Oratory has become a lost art, and along with it much of the traditional vocabulary has vanished. The extensive, incredibly beautiful and aesthetically complex oral literature used in ceremonies, the folktales and legends, and the oral history of the Rungus are all now being lost, a major calamity for world literature. The schooled generation now makes fun of its elders who carry on the old traditions when they can. They have become a source of ridicule rather than a source of knowledge, wisdom, and cultural history.

Along with schooling, the British government mistakenly decided that the Rungus were not using all their land and opened it up for commercial agriculture. Prior to that point, the introduction of commercial agriculture around the towns had forced many Rungus to move deeper into their territory and join already-existing villages. This increased the pressure on the sustainability of their agriculture. With little knowledge of the land and population necessary to maintain the Rungus livelihood, the government planned to bring in Chinese to open up commercial plantations and "shock" the Rungus into modernization. The Chinese wanted plantations close to Rungus villages so as to have a ready supply of agricultural laborers. An anthropologist was able to largely forestall this plan by explaining the land-tenure system of the Rungus to the district officer.

One scheme the government initiated was to take land from three villages to use as an oil-palm plantation. The villagers were promised that all those who settled on the scheme would receive ten acres of oil palms after the trees had begun to fruit, but those who agreed never did receive their allotment after laboring to open up the plantation. Furthermore, the settlement was unsanitary, and the planting of fruit trees was prohibited. As a result, most Rungus became discouraged and moved out to seek a livelihood.

The British also required individuals to take up permanent title to a small allotment of land. This process was continued by the subsequent Malaysian government. The shift from temporary use of land by domestic families to permanent land ownership by individuals removed land from the control of the headman and village. The owner could then sell the land to anyone, village member or urban investor, without any approval of the village. Thus the village has suffered the loss of control over its land and an erosion of its social solidarity. It is no longer a village of kinsmen but now includes absentee landlords.

With the formation of Malaysia, in which the government was dominated by the Muslim Malay peoples, many Rungus were either enticed or forced to convert to Islam. This was done by providing opportunities for schooling and government jobs primarily to those who were Muslim.

As development progressed, the government took the remaining land of the Rungus communities that individuals had not taken up. Ignoring the village ownership of land, the government took village land for plantations of oil palms, rubber plants, coconuts, and trees for wood products. The Rungus began to see that they were being changed from independent farmers to what they termed "coolies," landless peasants forced to labor on their own land for others. As part of the national development process, the government also converted the dominating mountain of the country, a sacred place to all Dusun speakers where their souls went after death, into a resort. Now, where people once feared to tread, tourists from all nations gaily climb up and down through this sacred place, unaware of its sacredness.

RESPONSE: STRUGGLES TO SURVIVE CULTURALLY

The response of the Rungus people to their psychological debasement and devaluation was not to fall into apathy or develop personality disorders. Instead, the development process of integrating the Rungus into the modern world system was in the view of the Rungus not all bad. They did not draw back from the challenges that development brought after the 1960s, including the possibility that they could lose control over their economic futures. Instead, many took realistic action. Rungus families sought out as much education as possible for their children. They perceived that they would be able to fight their political and economic domination through education and the new job opportunities. They wished to get Rungus representatives elected to government, into the higher echelons of government service, or into well-paying jobs in the private sector.

Thus while land had been of great importance to the Rungus and still is, they realized that power came from political position and access to cash income. Under the old method of subsistence agriculture, cash had been in short supply, and cash came to have a higher value than its actual monetary value. To achieve their goals, Rungus families gladly gave up the labor of their children in the fields so that they could attend elementary schools. They searched for the funds to support their children in secondary education through residential schools in the major towns, even though this cut the family income by an amount estimated at over 60 percent.

Others, not liking the opportunities of schooling, moved to the city to take up menial jobs as day laborers. Many, however, disliked being laborers, particularly the older Rungus who were accustomed to their independent entrepreneurial livelihood based on agricultural activities and the trading of gongs, brassware, and ceramic ware. Thus many Rungus still find their livelihood in agriculture: swiddening, wet-rice farming, selling copra from their coconut plantations, part-time market gardening, and raising and selling pigs, chickens, and water buffaloes, supplemented with occasional income from sporadic, short-term government employment in village improvement projects. Cash income is also supplemented not only by government agricultural subsidies but also by old-age assistance and by support to widows with children and to the needy. Some parents are supported partially by income from their children working elsewhere. There are also many Rungus entrepreneurs in the new economic sectors. A few have borrowed money to buy lorries or pickups to go into the transportation business either full-time or part-time. Several individuals in one village have learned how to make gongs out of culvert and water-tank metal, and these have become a fast-selling item throughout the country. Others have gone extensively into part-time trading with other ethnic groups. Some now expect the government to provide their major source of financial support. They have become largely dependent on the government programs to subsidize their agricultural activities, to modernize their houses, and to provide various necessities.

However, the growing economic prosperity of the Rungus and the increase in availability of cash has not resulted in improvidence such as a splurge of consumer spending and material display. Battery-powered television sets are common in the village, but they are relatively cheap. There are a few motorbikes, but these are used to take people to work in other villages or in town. Education is the major investment. Furthermore, some Rungus put any extra cash that they have in a bank savings account. This is an extension of their traditional economy into the modern one, as previously Rungus would invest their agricultural surpluses in gongs, jars, brassware, and similar items.

The population of one Rungus village grew from 356 to 681 individuals in a twenty-three-year period (1963–86), and the number of domestic families resident there grew from 71 to 111. The population increase has put additional pressure on the land base, and many Rungus perceive that there will not be enough land for their children. This increase in population, as well as the betterment of the physical health of the Rungus, was the result of bringing modern medicine to them with the availability of a dispensary in their area and a hospital at the district capital.

However, this medical delivery system focuses primarily on physical illness. Psychological illness or the part it plays in physical illness is ignored. The important work of the priestesses is thus disregarded. One way of valuing the work of priestesses, even for those who completely subscribe to a material cause of illness, is to note that placebos cure symptoms in 20 to 70 percent of cases. A view of medicine that ignores indigenous practices runs counter to what has been occurring in other areas, such as among the North American Indians. There the indigenous methods of curing are incorporated into the health delivery system. For example, among the Navaho there are facilities in the hospitals for native curers to do their work.

There is a deep-rooted attitude among the Rungus that they must maintain their land base. However, the home village to the Rungus is more than just land. It is a close network of kin and a source of support when outside sources of a livelihood fail. But as land has become scarcer and as other economic opportunities have arisen, swiddening has become less important. There has been a breakdown of kinship-based communities, with many strangers marrying or moving in. The range of economic activities has vastly increased. Those individuals who depend solely on monoculture or wage labor are more vulnerable to economic vicissitudes that are beyond their control and are driven by events outside the village and even the country. Such individuals may be less able to cope with economic change. This goes against the Rungus culture, in which individuals kept all their options open so that if they had a bad experience in one aspect of their economic activity, they had others to fall back on. This is why the land-development schemes that depend on monoculture and do not consider the human ecology of the Rungus domestic family are not popular.

It is true that over 70 percent of the Rungus traditional culture has been lost, much of it unnecessarily. For instance, the missionaries discouraged the traditional wedding ceremony in which the man and woman fed each other balls of rice. Instead, marriages are devoid of such symbols, and the couple get married in city clothes, with the bride wearing a white gown.

Furthermore, the attacks on the traditional Rungus culture that have led to its destruction and loss of its rules have resulted in an increase of various antisocial acts. Drinking, which was prohibited except during a short period after the harvest when weddings and festivals took place, now has become a problem. Many Rungus have become alcoholics. Drunken brawling and fighting, originally almost nonexistent, have become commonplace. Suicide rates have risen markedly especially among young people. Homicides are now occurring where they did not before. The breakdown in the rules of behavior between men and women, especially the erosion of the belief that sexual relations should only occur in marriage or the community will suffer the supernatural sanctions of infertility and crop destruction, has had a major impact. Promiscuity is now commonplace; illegitimacy, which did not occur previously, now is not uncommon, and prostitution now occurs. The Rungus used to say that prostitution only occurred in Christianized villages. Wife abuse and divorce rates have risen. There has been an increase in death and disability from accidents of all types.

All these behaviors represent a growing psychological dysfunction in the face of a strange and unpredictable future. What is surprising is that there is not greater psychological, physiological, and behavioral impairment, such as is found in many similar situations of change. Frequently associated with such impairments are social movements to recapture the lost culture that provided guidance and certainty. But this has not occurred. There has not yet been social bereavement over what has been lost, as is often found in other situations. Will this occur? And when it does, will it be too late? There has not yet been a crisis of Rungus ethnic identity, perhaps because there is still hope for a better future and, with growing educational and economic opportunities, the chance to move out of their devalued psychosocial position. But if this hope fails, if a better future does not become available, or if there is an economic crisis so that many Rungus are unemployed or unable to sell their commercial crops for a reasonable price, then the Rungus will have to deal with this loss. At that point, with these new frustrations and the loss of hope, social problems and health impairments—behavioral, psychological, and physiological—may rise precipitously as a consequence.

FOOD FOR THOUGHT

The Rungus have been subjected to religious and economic missionaries, both of whom have been proselytizers for modernization. The latter group is composed of politicians, government employees, and various elites who believe that a profit can be made from Rungus labor and land or whose status is improved by instituting change. Most of the Rungus have accepted the view of the world espoused by these agents of change, for they believe that by becoming modern for they will raise their status in the country and gain economic advantage. None of these people—politicians, government agents, missionaries, and the Rungus themselves—understand the consequences their decisions and actions will have on the environment, their health, or Rungus society and its members, and no one has suggested bringing in experts for planning more appropriate methods of social change. Are these ill-considered changes a violation of human rights?

Questions

1. How can indigenous societies on the peripheries of political and economic centers enjoy the advantages of modern society, such as modern medicine and ed-

ucation, without losing their culture or control over their labor and scarce resources?

2. Why are agents of change such as missionaries and development planners insensitive to the local culture, with the result that valuable aspects of it are lost? How do we prevent the loss of what is beautiful and useful in cultures during the process of modernization? What mechanisms are available to preserve the culture of a people undergoing change? How can change occur without the social dislocations that are usually associated with the loss of a people's culture, such as increases in drunkenness, acts of aggression, including homicides and rapes, psychological disorders, accidents, and so on?

3. Why is there not greater concern that the human rights of indigenous peoples are being violated? Why is there not greater concern over the pejorative labeling of others? Not only does this dehumanize them, but it is a clear signal that their rights are being put in jeopardy. How can we prevent such forms of verbal abuse?

4. Do economic measures of the productivity of a society provide a realistic profile of the health of that society, including the well-being of the members of that society?

RESOURCE GUIDE

Published Literature

Appell, G. N. "Individuation of the Drives of Sex and Aggression in the Linguistic and Behavioral Repertoire of the Rungus." In *Female and Male in Borneo: Contributions and Challenges to Gender Studies*, ed. Vinson H. Sutlive, Jr. Borneo Research Council Monograph Series, vol. 1. Williamsburg, VA: Borneo Research Council, 1991: 57–120.

———. "Land Tenure and Development among the Rungus of Sabah, Malaysia." In *Modernization and the Emergence of a Landless Peasantry: Essays on the Integration of Peripheries to Socioeconomic Centers*, ed. G. N. Appell. Studies in Third World Societies Publication no. 33. Williamsburg, VA: Studies in Third World Societies, 1985: 111–155.

———. "The Rungus Dusun." In *Essays on Borneo Societies*, ed. Victor T. King. Hull Monographs on South-East Asia 7. Oxford: Oxford University Press, 1978: 144–171.

Appell, G. N., and Laura W. R. Appell. "To Converse with the Gods: The Rungus *Bobolizan*—Spirit Medium and Priestess." In *The Seen and the Unseen: Shamanism, Mediumship, and Possession in Borneo*, ed. Robert Winzeler. Borneo Research Council Monograph Series, vol. 2. Williamsburg, VA: Borneo Research Council, 1993: 3–53.

Appell, Laura W. R. "Sex Role Symmetry among the Rungus of Sabah." In *Female and Male in Borneo: Contributions and Challenges to Gender Studies*, ed. Vinson H. Sutlive, Jr. Borneo Research Council Monograph Series, vol. 1. Williamsburg, VA: Borneo Research Council, 1991: 1–56.

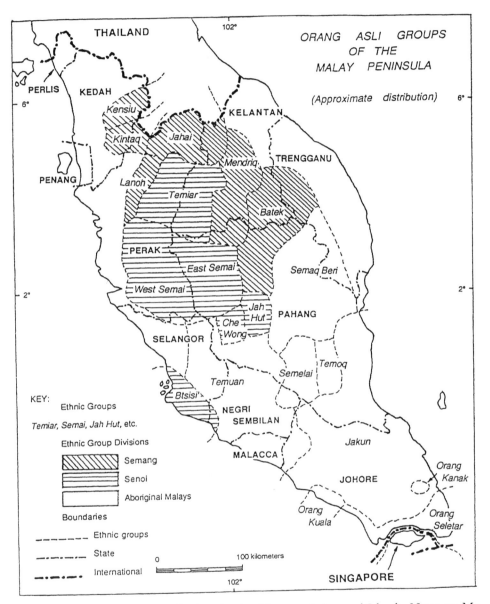

Map 13-1. Adapted from Geoffrey Benjamin, "Between Isthus and Islands: Notes on Malayan Paleo-Sociology," paper presented at the 12th Congress of the Indo-Pacific Prehistory Association, Penablanca, the Philippines, January 26–February 2, 1985. Courtesy of Robert K. Dentan.

Chapter 13

The Semai of Malaysia

Robert K. Dentan

We stay poor, and everybody else gets rich. The Chinese get rich. The Indians get rich. The Malays get rich. And they all get rich off the land that belongs to us hill people. That's fair?

—Bah Tungkoinc, Mncaak River, 1963

CULTURAL OVERVIEW

The People

The Semai are the largest group of Orang Asli, the earliest indigenous people of Peninsular Malaysia. This part of Malaysia, the western half, stabs downward from the southeasternmost corner of Asia like the tip of a wobbly spear into the scattered islands of Indonesia. The dominant people of western Malaysia, the Malays, are of Indonesian origin. They arrived in Malaysia around Shakespeare's time, a century or so before Europeans started to colonize the Americas. The Orang Asli were in Malaysia a millennium or two before that. The name "Orang Asli" means "Original People."

Counting people in towns, there are almost 100,000 Orang Asli, divided into over a dozen language groups, each with its distinctive way of life. It is hard to tell the exact numbers because the census counts them as Malays and the Department of Orang Asli Affairs only deals with rural people. Orang Asli make up about 0.5 percent of Malaysia's population, about the same as Native Americans in the United States. Their languages are or were related to the languages of Cambodia's Khmer and Thailand's Mon and are unrelated to the Malayo-Polynesian languages of later-arriving immigrants like Malays, Chinese, and Tamils from India.

Figure 13-1. Elderly Semai woman, Te-lom, 1962. Courtesy of Robert K. Den-tan.

There were about 30,000 Semai in 1998. They call themselves Senoi, "Humans" (Figures 13-1 and 13-2). Sometimes they call themselves "Hill People" because of where they live, or "Poor People" because they are the poorest people in Malaysia, at least in terms of money values.

The Setting

This is what we call our "heritage land." Maybe we don't build a settlement here, but we bury our children here. I buried my father in this land. I buried my grandchild. I buried my older brother. When I die, my wife will bury me in this land. . . . All of us have always been buried here from the beginning of time. When I die, my children will replace me. When they die, my grandchildren will replace them. I don't want to live anywhere else. Next time, if there's a war, tell them to leave us alone. So we die here, so what? I don't want always to be "regrouped" back and forth. I just want to stay here.

—Lgoos, Telom River, 1962

There is some evidence that the Semai used to have more complicated political and social arrangements than they do now but that, overwhelmed by immigrants from Indonesia, they developed a simpler way of life in order to live in the mountains that run lengthwise down the peninsula. A few Semai still live in enclaves on the southern flood plains of the state of Perak.

Figure 13-2. Semai family, Telom, 1962.
Courtesy of Robert K. Dentan.

Most live in the nearby foothills and mountains of southern Perak and the northwest part of the state of Pahang, which adjoins Perak to the east.

The mountains and valleys used to be covered with two types of rain forest, loosely called "lowland" and "upland" forest. Malaysian jungles may be the oldest in the world, spared by the glaciers that destroyed forests elsewhere during the ice ages. Perhaps for that reason they are the most diverse, with an enormous number of species (e.g., more than 5,000 species of flowering trees, 800 species of orchids, well over 100 species of snakes, and almost 100 species of bats). But there are only a few members of each species: there are not large herds of animals or great stands of two or three species of trees, as in temperate climates. The rains in Malaysia are about ten times heavier and occur about ten times more often than in most of the United States or Europe. Being out in a heavy rain there is like standing under a waterfall.

The trees average about three times the size of temperate-forest trees. A large white pine in the northeast United States nowadays is over 100 feet tall; a Malaysian forest gaint is over 300 feet. Because the Malaysian trees are larger, they need more nutrients. The soil under the trees is relatively poor, and to get enough food, the trees run their roots parallel with the surface of the earth instead of having deep tap roots. That makes them unstable, so the screaming monsoon thundersqualls can blow them down, although the trees grow huge buttresses, like those of Gothic cathedrals, to hold up their trunks. A whole traditional Semai band, a dozen or so adults and as many children, can stand between two of the buttresses. To chop a tree down in the old days, men had to build platforms up above the buttresses, where the trunk narrowed a little. Even then, it would take two men at least a day to chop down a rain-forest giant.

Traditional Subsistence Strategies

We want the jungle to be left as it is. We prefer to live near the jungle, as we have no skills to work outside the settlement. We don't like to be estate laborers because we have been cheated of our wages in the past.

Moreover, we don't like to work for others. We like to be free and live off the jungle. We don't fight among ourselves over the trees because we can identify which tree belongs to whom.

—Headman Yen, Bersih River, 1987

Traditional Semai did cut trees down. They cleared their fields, which anthropologists call "swiddens," in the heart of the rain forest, but they usually targeted areas where trees were still small enough to cut down easily. Thus they usually cleared swiddens in secondary forest, where they had cleared fields a dozen or so years earlier. They spared trees that produced valuable products, like fruits or blowpipe-dart poison. They also planted or tended such trees in their fields or in the forest. Anthropologists call such a way of making a living "agroforestry." The result was a forest rich in valuable species of trees, with a greater variety of plants and animals than untouched forest could sustain. This adaptation lasted for thousands of years.

When the possibility of joining the Malaysian mainstream economy emerged, Semai responded by adapting their traditional agroforestry. They began to grow trees as cash crops. But as time went on, Malaysian governments "regrouped" most Semai into densely populated regroupment schemes (RPSs) and turned their orchards and forests over to loggers and developers. The land base of regrouped people averages between 1 and 2 percent of their land before regroupment. Moreover, developers have usually removed whatever natural resources (ore, trees) are easily exploited. It does not take the dense population long to exhaust whatever natural resources remain, like fish or game.

Social and Political Organization

Shaman. Let me give one answer to your question [about why Semai traditionally commit so little violence]. When someone does something wrong, like stealing, we don't beat them up badly or kill them. We bring them to judgment under our laws. We are one family, one people. Maybe we fine them, but only a little. And we bawl them out, urge them to change their ways, not to set a bad example for the children. We don't want to kill people. We would be ashamed. And, number two, we would be like the beasts that kill people.

Old man. Right. What we think is, if we hit them, we lose out, we lose a friend. So, in our withdrawal and silent suffering [*kra'dii'*] we feel bad. But we need help in clearing swiddens, in feeding ourselves. We realize, if we kill our friend, we lose.

—Waar River, 1992

We *br-mage'* [share, especially small portions of food]. We're not like Malays. Look, when my daughter cooks, she sends food to her mom's house; when her mom cooks, she sends food to my daughter; and to the assistant headman or *rhii's* parents.

—Headman, Waar River, 1992

We never hit our children. Malays are always hitting hitting hitting their children. That's why our children are sturdy and healthy and Malay children are like baby rats [always whining and scrawny].

—Mrlooh, Telom River, 1962

Early European and Malay observers described Semai as timid. Although there were trade ties between Malays and Semai, patrons often exploited their Semai clients. Their timidity was a reasonable response to their political environment, which, especially when the colonial government sought to develop the country in the 1870s, involved increasing displacement and enslavement by Indonesian immigrants who had no ties with Semai and who exterminated other groups of Orang Asli. Slavers particularly targeted Semai children because they were easy to steal and domesticate as slaves for physical and sexual abuse. As a result, Semai become deeply distrustful of outsiders and still teach their children to fear and flee from strangers for fear they will be taken away.

Because the outside world had become so fearsome, Semai turned inward, developing an ideology in which loving one's friends and neighbors became a matter of survival, and quarreling a threat to one's life. A number of ways emerged to minimize violence within the society. People shared what they had with each other. There was a taboo on calculating how much one shared with a particular person, so that in theory one could not build up resentment. Traditional Semai usually talk about violence as ludicrous and stupid. Although the people are capable of violence in situations where it is safe and necessary or appropriate, they prefer peace. They deserve their reputation as one of the least violent people known to anthropology, but they do not much like that reputation. They know that most other Malaysians see Semai peacefulness as cowardice, not as the extraordinary cultural achievement it is.

Before coming into close contact with Malays and Europeans, Semai were egalitarian. They said that forcing people to do what they did not want to do would hurt them spiritually, and that the spiritual hurt could lead to their injury or death. No one has a right to coerce anyone else. When a child refuses to follow a parent's order, the parent has to accept the child's refusal. Trying to coerce children would spiritually damage and perhaps kill them. For traditional Semai, all coercion was violent, and all violence was dangerous to the only society in which Semai could live in peace and security.

The Semai knew, however, that as people grew older they accumulated experience and became wiser. Their age-grade system distinguishes between children, adolescent boys and girls (*litaw* and *mnaleeh*), mature people, and old people. Even now, any adult who is especially knowledgeable about a particular activity—hunting or fish poisoning, say—and who can convince other people of his skill can be a leader as long as the activity continues. When the activity stops, however, the person stops being a leader. Outsiders, especially bureaucrats, find this total democracy frustrating. No Semai speaks for anyone else, and no one even listens to anyone he or she does not want to hear. The outsiders' solution was to recognize someone—a man brave or greedy enough not to flee from outsiders—as "headman." They then rewarded this man by giving him some power in their scheme of things, although usually his power within the community went away as soon as they did. Failure to respect these differences in political organization has led to many misunderstandings.

Religion and World View

We're very careful about hurting people. We avoid it. We did the same smart thing [Semai in Pahang state] did during the Emergency [when Chinese Communists staged an uprising against the then British government in the 1950s]. The British usually stayed in town. When they came through here, we gave them help. The Communist terrorists killed a teenaged girl, but we gave them tapioca and other food when they passed through. We really hate getting mixed up in other people's squabbles. We want to live *slamad*, in peace and security.

That's why we don't steal things. Malays are always stealing things, but we don't. The funny thing is that it's the richer peoples who steal things, not us. We don't want trouble. Besides, we don't want to be rich. As long as we have enough to eat, that's enough. If you're rich, you get endless hassles, no *slamad*. That's why we don't want to be rich. We want *slamad*.

—Klip, Rias River, 1992

Traditional Semai religion resembles early Hinduism. Both religions may grow out of an ancient religion that once spread from southern China through Malaysia and into India. In Semai thinking, animals are people, though not human people. The souls of animals are *nyanii'*, "demons," from a word meaning "pain" or "sickness." They fall into the domain of the thunder god Nkuu', a vicious, ludicrous, and stupid tyrant whom Semai both mock and fear. He brought sickness into the world.

Long ago, Semai say, they tricked Nkuu' into sharing his power with "Humans," their word for themselves. Since then, a human may gain a demon "wife." An adept's "wives" appear in dreams, attracted by his (rarely, her) beautiful body, and give him melodies. The adept can then lure his demon wives in seances to help diagnose and cure patients. In some areas, after a successful hunt, Semai hunters go through a ceremony to thank and placate their "hunting wives." Midwives, the usually female equivalent of the usually male adepts, either have spirit guides of their own or appeal to the seven "Original Midwives." When an adept or midwife seems to have lost spiritual power, for example, if a child he or she has been caring for falls sick, he or she may be ritually bathed.

When a settlement needs spiritual refreshment or several people are pregnant or sick, Semai hold seances. The people still sometimes perform sanitized versions of these ceremonies in the daytime for tourists and government officials, but the seances themselves have become secret and rare as people seek to avoid offending their Muslim neighbors and the government agents who seek to convert the people to Islam.

THREATS TO SURVIVAL

> We live, always, under the authority of other people. The government, always, uses its authority not to make things easy for us but to make them hard, one minute this way, the next minute that, until making a living in the forest also becomes hard. Nowadays even food is hard to come by because now the forest isn't ours any more, it's the government's. What we knew, in the days of our ancestors, was that the forest was ours. But now it seems that people in the cities own the forest. And they have power over us.
>
> —Semai from the regroupment scheme at Betou,
> quoted by Hasan Mat Noor in his article
> about them in *Akademika*, 1989

Recent History

In the 1970s, the Indigenous People's Department (JOA) came completely under Malay control; as Orang Asli personnel died or retired, Malays replaced them, and the organization was renamed the Department of Indigenous People's Affairs (JHEOA). Worries about a ragtag Communist movement in southern Thailand plus a realization of economic opportunities in the hills prompted the government to draw up a comprehensive plan for "regrouping" Semai and other Orang Asli in remote areas that had been mined out and logged over, that is, wastelands. The idea was ostensibly to facilitate surveillance and the delivery of government services. The land the regroupment schemes (RPSs) occupied was usually less than 3 percent and often less than 2 percent of the area Semai had originally lived on. By the 1990s, about 2,000 Orang Asli families were crowded into 10 RPSs, officially 24,647 people. The people did not own the land they were moved to; the government retained ownership. Less than 1 percent of Orang Asli own their land; in 1998, only about 0.2 percent of them had land titles.

The deputy head of the JHEOA, Yahya Awang, said in August 1997 that his department will let some Orang Asli stay "in their traditional villages which we plan to upgrade through a programme to rearrange scattered Orang Asli settlements of which the current regroupment scheme will be a part. We want to introduce basic amenities in areas which have not received supplies yet. At the same time we want to promote and preserve their positive cultural values." It is unclear how the "rearrangements" will differ from the current pattern of displacement and dispossession. The "amenities" promised would not be hard to deliver. In 1992, a visiting anthropologist lived in a Semai settlement perhaps one hundred yards from a Malay settlement. The Malay settlement had bus service, electricity, safe water, and postal service. The Semai settlement had none of these amenities. Even the road narrowed abruptly as it left the Malay settlement and entered the Semai one. Thus it is not surprising to learn that in 1997 only 22 percent of Orang Asli villages had electricity and only 16.9 percent had running water.

Studies by Malaysian scientists reveal that a third to more than half of the Semai children in regroupment areas suffer from malnutrition and that the general health of the people is declining. Tuberculosis cases among Orang Asli went from 88 in 1987 to 243 in 1991, a rise of 176 percent. Semai say that besides making it easy to spread diseases, the crowding creates tensions and quarrels. Non-Semai men routinely harass Semai women with impunity.

More than three-quarters of Orang Asli are poor, half of them *termiskin*, the official term for "the poorest of the poor." In March 1997, the JHEOA conceded that 80.89 percent of Orang Asli lived below the Malaysian poverty line and that 49.9 percent of these poor people were *termiskin*. Later that year it said that the figure was an "overestimate." Only 7 percent of the poorest families were Orang Asli, it said, not stressing the implication that this figure means that the rate of poverty among Orang Asli is fourteen times that of the population as a whole. This sort of creative use of numbers, common to bureaucrats everywhere, seems particularly prevalent in statistics the JHEOA supplies.

Since feudal times, Malay governments have regarded Orang Asli as their dependents, whether as slaves or, nowadays, as landless country day laborers. The British colonialists found this arrangement reasonable. Apologists for the old slavocracy point out that although kidnapping the children of Orang Asli in order to use them sexually or as forced labor was "admittedly cruel," the children's children, if any, were allowed to assimilate into the lowest class of Malay society, unlike African Americans. In this view, ethnocide, the destruction of a people's ethnic identity, is a sort of kindness.

This "kindness" continues. The government talks about "spiritual" as opposed to "economic" development. They have done all the economic development the people need, say some politicians, Spiritual development means converting Orang Asli to Islam. That makes assimilating them into the Malay population much easier. Assimilation, which will be discussed, has been a goal of the Department of Indigenous People's Affairs since the 1980s. Because this policy does not fit very well with the religious-freedom clauses of the Malaysian Constitution, it was covert until the early 1990s. Even now it presents the department with some public relations problems.

Environmental Crisis

Why give us seeds and fertilizers, if you give us no right to the land we work? We have planted the land before with [orchards] and rubber without any help from anybody. But the land we have worked has been taken arbitrarily by outsiders. We don't want to plant again for others.

—Johan, 1990

Land Tenure

The Malaysian government has chosen to continue the British colonial legal fiction that Semai land belongs to nobody. The state therefore has complete control over all traditional Semai land. By this fiction, Semai are squatters wherever they live, no matter how many generations of Semai have occupied the land. The government can dispossess them for any reason or no reason at all, without paying them anything for the land or its forests. The government also sets the price for any "improvements," like orchards, that Semai have made to the land. The only trees Semai get paid for are those that Malays also plant and those that Semai have planted Malay-style, in plantations, not scattered among forest trees. The absence of secure tenure plus the government policy of turning over Semai land to private developers means that Semai are punished for attempting to become self-sustaining.

There is a way for Semai to get official recognition that lands are traditionally theirs, even though the recognition gives them no security. The process is called "gazetting" and requires appealing to the local state land office. But gazetting ground to a halt in the 1970s, and between 1990 and 1996, about 5,000 acres of Orang Asli land were degazetted (Table 13-1).

The government's solution is to let people buy the land as individuals.

Table 13-1
Gazetted Orang Asli Lands, 1997

Status	Acres	Percentage	Acres per Person
Gazetted	51,046	17	0.61
Approved for gazetting	89,108	29	1.07
Applied for	165,537	54	1.98
Total	305,692	100	3.66

Note: The calculation uses the estimated population of Orang Asli in 1990 (83,453) so the figures per person are high. Estimates of aboriginal Semai population density range from 5 to 25 people per square mile, much higher than the density for foraging peoples like the Batek, discussed elsewhere in this volume. If the government had gazetted all the ancestral lands Orang Asli asked for, the density would be about 174 people per square mile, that is, many times higher because the land area the government would recognize as belonging to the Semai is so much smaller than the land area on which Semai have traditionally lived.

Source: "Gazette Orang Asli Reserve Land Quickly," *New Straits Times*, May 11, 1999.

Since Semai are *termiskin*, few have enough money to do that. The JHEOA puts the number of Orang Asli with title to their land at 0.2 percent. Since the lands available to Semai are already overcrowded, this solution seems destined to increase the number of impoverished landless rural day laborers, of whom there are already many among Semai. Wherever in the world this sort of unskilled work force exists with no secure employment, crime, suicide, and alcoholism rates rise. There are strong indications that this same sort of transformation is occurring among Semai, as the JHEOA admits.

"Slash-and-Burn"

One of the terms anthropologists used to use for the sort of agriculture Semai traditionally did is "slash-and-burn agriculture." Nowadays it is called "swiddening" because the Malaysian government has managed to use the more dramatic term to cover massive corporate clearing of the forest for commercial development. Putting the two completely different activities into the same category allows developers to equate the sustainable "slash-and-burn" of Semai with the environmentally disastrous "slash-and-burn" of the huge Malaysian corporations that actually managed to set fire to the subsoil of Indonesian rain forests while clearing land for plantations. Although rain forests are normally dark and wet, clearing them for timber, golf courses, and plantations dries them out and leads to disasters like the 1997 fires that burned a million or so acres of Indonesia and blanketed Southeast Asia in a choking haze.

Calling both activities "slash-and-burn" lets developers and their government sponsors blame people like Semai for deforestation. When reading statistics about Semai, it is wise to remember that they change to suit the interests of the people using them. Since Semai have no power to correct any of the statistics powerful people use about them, officials apparently sometimes just make the numbers up out of whole cloth. Official figures on forest destruction by swiddening are an example. Thus in July 1989, the Perak Forestry Department accused Semai and Temiar swiddening of having "to date" caused Malaysian Ringgit (MR) $22.2 million worth of damage, destroying 61,750 acres of rain forest (then, almost U.S.$10 million); two years later, the damage "to date" had ballooned to MR $93.4 million, but the amount of forest destroyed had shrunk to 54,340 acres. Legal logging in Perak involved 29,640 acres annually, and illegal logging was completely out of control, so that the Semai and Temiar contribution was negligible anyway.

Although many studies have shown that swidden agriculture is not only sustainable but actually beneficial for forests as long as population density is low, governments have always hated it. The reason seems to be that it allows people to move around. If people are mobile, and a government wants to enslave them, tax them, or draft them into the army, they simply move away from government control. Therefore, one of the first things governments in Southeast Asia do in the name of "development" is to settle people into permanent villages.

The villages are "permanent" in the sense that the people are not supposed to move any place else. They are not "permanent" in the sense that the people are secure there. The government can still take the land any time it wants. There is a "permanent" Semai settlement through which outsiders have built superhighways and hydroelectric lines and on which they have developed an openface tin mine and dump for mining by-products. About as much land on the "reserve" belongs to non-Semai as to Semai. Another part of the reserve is to be opened to a rural redevelopment scheme for Malays. When local officials were asked whether Semai would be allowed to take part in the redevelopment scheme, they said that no one was interested. But the Semai said that no one asked them.

Even if Semai wanted to continue traditional agriculture, they no longer have enough land to do so. At the same time, as fewer and fewer Semai plant swiddens, there is less and less demand for the services of shamans who know how to placate local earth spirits so that they will allow such planting. By the 1990s, people in many Semai settlements said that they could not plant swiddens because there was no one left with enough religious knowledge to soothe the local spirits.

Highland Highway

The most serious new threat to the Semai is the proposed 137 mile Highland Highway. The highway is to link three hill resort areas that feature golf courses and luxury hotels catering to foreigners, especially Japanese. The northern part of the highway would run through Semai country. The roadbed is planned to follow the highest ridges of the Titiwangsa range, at about 4,125 feet above sea level, across very steep slopes that range from 30 to 70 degrees. The builders plan to clear at least 2,700 acres of hill forest. That does not count the rubble dumped down the slopes to clog the streams on both sides, nor the permanent runoff of litter and pollution. Naturalists and environmentalists are protesting the road despite the fact that "ecotourism" is one of the main reasons for building it in the first place. In February 1996, the Malaysian prime minister suggested that the road builders use tunnels rather than cutting into the sides of the steep hills in order to prevent destructive erosion. It is unclear what would happen to rock blasted from the tunnels, which are not part of current plans, or why tourists in search of beautiful unspoiled landscapes would enjoy driving through a network of tunnels. Even Semai downstream from the road would be threatened by runoff and erosion.

In 1997, a currency crisis in Southeast Asia led to a sharp drop in Asian stock prices. The prime minister of Malaysia blames the setback on a conspiracy of foreign Jewish currency speculators. The loss of capital means that plans for the Highland Highway are on hold.

Sociocultural Crisis

> I hope the public doesn't think that the JOA is so generous as to come forward to support my family and me. The only assistance we get from the department is medical care and education for our children. Even then the teachers who are sent to our settlements have low qualifications
> —Bah Chim Pok, 1987

Education

Traditionally, Semai adults did not hit children, even disobedient ones, and they did not expect children to hit each other. The children thus had no model for violent behavior. Adult skills came gradually as the children tagged along after their parents, playing at adult skills. There was no difference between playing, learning, and work.

Government schools are a big change. The government plan was "to instill confidence in Orang Asli with regard to education for their children and skill development for themselves." Islamic education of the sort the Malaysian authorities press on Semai children relies heavily on rote learning; understanding the material is secondary. In the early 1990s, Semai children wanted a few visiting anthropologists to give them English lessons. They would draw up lists of English words to be tested on. But the idea of actually using English, except in response to specific arbitrary demands, was alien to them. For Semai children, the "hidden curriculum" is to get used to having a Malay authority coerce them into performing apparently senseless tasks, to be obsequious in the presence of their "betters," and to want to become like Malays. When a child was teaching the anthropologists something in turn, he would waggle his forefinger and cry, "Stupid! Stupid!" the way his teacher did to him.

The school shows the children how to become inferior Malays. The language of instruction is Malay. Almost all the history books begin with the Malacca Sultanate, when Malay rule began in Malaysia, with no mention of Orang Asli, let alone Semai. Like Malay children—but unlike children from other ethnic groups, whom the Malaysian Constitution forbids the government to proselytize without parental permission—Semai children have to learn Arabic script so that they can read the Koran. Although they are not Muslims, the Malaysian government has decided that their destiny is Islamic. For that reason, too, the little Semai girls have to wear Muslim dress, curb their normal boisterousness, and defer to males.

This experience is common among colonialized peoples. But Islamic education in general and, in the old days, Malaysian education in particular stress also "corporal punishment," a polite way of saying that adults beat children with rattan canes, usually on the buttocks (sometimes naked) or on the palms of the hands where there are many nerves. When a Malay father turns his child over to a religious teacher, he ceremonially hands the teacher a cane with which to beat the child, the way traditional Malay parents do. Lat, a Malay humorist from Perak, recalls:

My enrollment in the class was made in the traditional way. I can still remember clearly what happened. Dad handed over to Tuan Syed a bowl of glutinous rice, a fee of $1 and a small cane and then said: "Tuan, I am handing over my son to you in the hope that you'd teach him the Koran. Make him as if he is your own child . . . if he is stubborn or naughty don't hesitate to punish him with this cane—as long as it doesn't reach the extent of breaking any of his bones or blinding his eyes." Tuan Syed took the cane and nodded. Thus end[ed] the formality. But I noticed the teacher already had his own cane. (Lat 1977, *the kampung boy*)

Caning was novel and abhorrent to Semai children and adults. Although the Department of Education has officially abandoned the policy of corporal punishment, Semai still talk of Malay-style education as involving teachers who beat students. It is traditional, of course, in the sense that Malay slavemasters beat kidnapped Semai children into submission and assimilation in feudal times. That practice and the insults and browbeating that are the new practice do teach Semai children that powerful people (teachers, Malays, adults) think that it is okay to humiliate less powerful people (pupils, Semai, children) and to hurt them physically, and that the Semai children themselves can survive violence. Occasional beatings by their Malay classmates, who always outnumber them, reinforce this lesson in civility. The Semai children, of course, try to respond in kind, as the Malay teachers expect them to do and punish them for doing. Thus from a situation in which adults do not expect physical violence from children and do not punish children with physical violence, the children move into one in which physically violent adults expect them to be physically violent too. Psychologists say that the first sort of situation is one that is the most likely to produce nonviolent people; Americans know how well the second one works. Young Semai men are getting into brawls more and more often.

Many of the Malays in charge of Semai education are aware of how Semai feel about beating children and coercive schooling. It is, they say, "a problem," but they see it as a Semai problem, not their own. Semai, they say, do not appreciate the value of education. The parents need to be taught that by Malays. The parents allow their children to help them out during fruit season, the Malays say. They do not force the children to attend school when the children do not want to go, perhaps out of fear of being beaten. Many Malays add, in total error, that Semai kids are not very smart anyway.

Although many Semai children run away from boarding schools or play hooky from day schools, often with parental support, the school does represent their link to all the rewards of modern Malaysian society. Because children cannot go into the forests or orchards with their parents if they are going to school, the system of education does, whatever its other failures, make the children so ignorant of traditional skills that they cannot revert to the old Semai ways. In other words, their education makes them unskilled in two societies.

Religion and Identity

Malays have special privileges in Malaysia. These privileges stem from the legal fiction that they are the "original inhabitants" of the country, "princes of the earth," *bumiputera*. In Malaysia, even the descendants of Indonesians who immigrated under British protection in the nineteenth century are *bumiputera*. That is, they are officially the aboriginal inhabitants.

In ancient Hindu law, aborigines merited special status. The mere existence of Orang Asli, people who were in Malaysia long before Malays arrived, is a tacit challenge to Malay rule, an embarrassment. The first prime minister of Malaysia acknowledged that Orang Asli were the first inhabitants but said that since they had no culture worth the name, the later-arriving Malays deserved to be thought of as "original inhabitants." That position had uncomfortable echoes of European colonial policies in the Americas that Malaysia's government officially condemns.

The simplest solution is to assimilate Orang Asli into the Malay population. As a Semai leader remarked, "When all the Original People become Malay, the Malays will finally really be the original people." Recently, government forms have eliminated the category "Orang Asli," counting the people as Malays. In late 1997, the outgoing head of the JHEOA denied that Orang Asli had arrived before Malays. Everyone in the legally and ethnically vague category of *bumiputera*, he argued, was equally indigenous: Orang Asli, Malays, and the Malayo-Polynesian speakers of the Bornean states of Malaysia. In late 1993, the deputy prime minister said that the sort of oppression of indigenous people that occurred, tragically, in the Americas, could not happen in Malaysia because Malays and Orang Asli and the indigenous people of Borneo like the Punan were all equally indigenous: "We don't need any bleeding-heart liberals," he said. Biologically, there has certainly been much mixture. As cultural history, however, this account is nonsense.

Legally, to be Malay is to speak Malay, as almost all Malaysians now do; to practice "Malay custom," a vague phrase that covers a wide variety of behavior; and to be Muslim. In fact, all Semai need to do to become Malays legally is to convert to Islam. The government has therefore slated Semai for conversion to Islam, and any suggestion that the people might want other options provokes an almost hysterical response from Malays. Since 1991, at enormous expense, over U.S. $7 million, the government has built almost 300 "village halls" in most settlements, including some without adequate roads, safe water supplies, or electricity. Each hall includes a Muslim chapel that is supposed to be staffed by a Malay social worker to "guide the Orang Asli toward embracing Islam." There were about 250 such workers actually in place by the end of 1997. This activity was reported in the Malay press, but got little if any notice in English-language newspapers.

In late 1997, the outgoing head of the JHEOA denied that there was a program to Islamize or assimilate Orang Asli. But in 1983, the department had circulated a secret plan in Malay, which was to cost about U.S. $5.5 million. The title was "Strategy for the Development of Islamic Religion among Orang Asli Groups," and the stated two objectives were "Islamization throughout Orang Asli society" and "Integration/Assimilation between Orang Asli and Malay society." In the Malay version of the JHEOA "Program Summary," objective 5(d) is "energizing efforts to inculcate a system of values based on Islamic values among Orang Asli societies so that they may be brought into integration with the general public, especially with Malay society." This statement is absent from the other version of the program in English.

Semai have become as furtive about their own religion as JHEOA bureaucrats are about their efforts to subvert it. It is much harder for an outsider to learn about Semai religion than it used to be. For example, there is one settlement next to which Malays have built a couple of mosques on land that used to belong to Semai. Five times a day, loudspeakers on the mosques blast out the Islamic call to prayer so loudly that sleep or conversation is impossible. But the Semai there are afraid to sing the soft chants of their traditional religion because of how angry that would make their Malay neighbors. The neighbors would complain to the police, also dominated by Malays, and the Semai would get in big trouble, people say. Or the neighbors would just beat them up, and the police would not protect them.

RESPONSE: STRUGGLES TO SURVIVE CULTURALLY

We're not like other people. We want to be friends. With other peoples—Malays, Chinese—if you do something wrong, they're not your friends any more. With us, we go into our house and avoid you for a while, but we'll love you anyway, and after a few months we're your friends again [big smile].
—Bah Apel, 1992

"Defending Our Culture"

You can have all sorts of policies towards the Orang Asli but if you don't see them as a distinct people, then you will have difficulty appreciating that they have special rights to their cultures and to their ancestral lands and resources in them. The reason for their problems now is that they are not recognised as Orang Asli by the State.
—Colin Nicholas, 1997

Americans, like Malays, have the idea of "culture" as an object that one can possess, transmit, or peddle. You can lose it, preserve it, or defend it. This is a strange idea to most Semai, who only began developing the concept that they are an "ethnic group" in the 1970s. Many Semai still deny that they have a "culture," although some young men have taken to carrying blowpipes as a defiant symbol of their non-Malay identity.

To the degree that traditional Semai are aware of themselves as having a "culture," it is as the opposite of Malays. When they tell about a custom they have, it is usually in contrast with Malay custom: "We do this, Malays do that." That is why the Semai Mrlooh talks about the difference between Malay and Semai child rearing and children, instead of just describing how Semai treat children.

Semai nonchalance plays into the stereotype Malaysians have of Orang Asli as primitive harmless people who live in the jungle like animals or even, as a 1997 editorial in the official journal of the government's prestigious Council of Language and Culture suggests, flee the houses the government builds for them in order to live in the trees like monkeys. (Of course, most Malaysians do not think about Orang Asli at all, and many people do not even recognize the term. Hardly any Malaysians have heard of "Semai.") From a Malay point of view, Orang Asli languages and manners are "crude," not really "culture" (*adat*) in the sense that Malays un-

224

derstand the term. It is not enough to "develop" Orang Asli materially, some planners say, since they obviously need "spiritual" development as well, a process that involves wiping out traditional forms of behavior, government, and systems of belief. In his August 1977 speech, the deputy head of the JHEOA said that this policy would not affect the "basic values" of people like the Semai, and a Malay anthropologist on the same platform added that "modernization" does not "break down" cultures, but lets the cultures "break out" into the world opening before them. Just what the "basic values" were that were to be allowed to "break out" was left unclear, in accordance with the general pattern of vagueness that pervades Malaysian bureaucrats' promises to fix the less fortunate results of their programs.

Since most rural or uneducated Malays, and therefore a good many Semai, think of Semai religion as not a real religion at all but just a mishmash of primitive superstitions, Semai rarely appeal to the Malaysian Constitution's religious-freedom provisions to protect their "basic values." Even if the government were prepared to treat what they officially call "animism" as a religion, any challenge to the Islamic destiny of Semai subverts the assimilationist program of the government and provokes a sort of hysteria that Semai wisely prefer to avoid. One tactic they have practiced since the 1930s is to convert to other religions, mostly Bahaism and Christianity, as a sort of prophylactic against Islam. The government's response is to discourage missionary activity by non-Islamic groups. On at least two occasions, once in 1979–80 and once in 1990–91, Malay government officials forbade Semai Christians to talk with other Semai about Christianity. The government also discourages contacts between Semai and any outsiders but Malays, saying (correctly) that the outsiders peddle cheap booze, drugs, and pornographic videos, recruit young girls as prostitutes, and so on.

Recruiting Allies

There are three reasons Semai and other Orang Asli have a hard time recruiting allies from among ecological and human-rights activists. The first is that government bureaucrats thrust Islam and Malay nationalism into any debate about their policies. This debasement of religion into a political tool not only mobilizes naive Muslims to support policies that sometimes contravene basic Islamic values but also makes Western liberals uneasy about criticizing these policies. The liberals tend to support a version of "freedom of religion" in which any criticism of any religion is taboo. It is therefore important for any critic of the Malaysian regime's policies toward the environment or toward indigenous peoples to steer clear of language that defensive bureaucrats can read, honestly or not, as blaming "Islam" or "Malays" in general for the plight of Semai and other Orang Asli. In fact, Islam in its pure form is one of the more democratic and tolerant world religions, and anyone who has ever dealt with ordinary Malays knows that most Malays most of the time are extraordinarily tolerant and courteous people. Carelessly worded critiques only justify the perversion of Islam and of Malay nationalism in which the bureaucrats can wrap themselves when criticized.

The second reason Semai get little support from environmentalists and human-rights groups is that they are not against the economic development of their communities. Indeed, their complaint is often that what the government does in the guise of economic development is just displacement and dispossession and not "real economic development." One of the most serious accusations that developers and government officials can level at protestors in Malaysia is that the protestors are "antidevelopment." As a result, almost all Semai protests about their treatment begin with the phrase "We are not against development, but . . ." A recent book detailing Orang Asli criticisms of government policy bears the Malay title *Kami Bukan Anti-Pembangunan!* (We are not anti-development!).

The third problem is that Semai protest their displacement and dispossession in ways invisible to or unacceptable by environmental and human rights organizations. For Semai, the proper response to being badly treated is to *kra'dii'*, to withdraw and sulk for a while. If your new Malay neighbors hassle you and crowd you, you move away, farther into the hills. If a government official treats you unjustly, you do not complain, but suffer in silence. But you do not hold the resentment forever, though you may wistfully remember or even dream about how the rivers sounded before the dams silenced them, or how cool it used to be in the hills before the clearing of the forest for luxury resorts raised local temperatures.

Moreover, having no input into government policies is nothing new to Semai, and the government does not enforce its policies by physical force. People do not get beaten up or enslaved or casually killed the way the old people used to talk about. The pressure is normally subtler than that. But everyone knows that the government retains overwhelming coercive power. For example, when Semai built a church on reserve land, the government sent in policemen and army reservists armed with bush knives, batons, and M-16 rifles to bulldoze the church. Because the Malaysian Constitution guarantees freedom of religion, the excuse was that the church was a permanent structure on land that did not belong to the congregation, since all land assigned to Semai by the government remains government land and does not actually belong to Semai. But the lesson about the physical danger of freely exercising one's religion was clear.

Confrontation would be dangerous. Semai know that they are outnumbered. They talk about the weapons—not just symbolic weapons but guns and helicopters—that the government has and they lack. They avoid defiance, though some people fantasize, more or less as a joke, about getting their own weapons and driving the Malays back into the sea. "I tell people," says one Semai leader, "the only action we can take is to turn our backs on them."

Withdrawal before overwhelming force is not telegenic, nor does it make the government look bad. Human-rights organizations generally refuse to become involved in cases like this because the resistance is not obvious. Moreover, it is difficult to drum up support for people who do not protest in ways that are dramatic. Semai even dress untelegenically, the way poor people do. They are "scruffy," not "authentic aboriginal."

In this context, the work of anthropologists takes on a value that in other parts of the world it has lost. Anthropologists describe the Orang Asli peoples as peoples, not as an appendix to Malays. Simply stating the obvious, that Orang Asli exist, have their own religion, were in Malaysia before the Malays, deserve respect for their cultural achievement of nonviolence, and so on, can undercut official government positions. As one Semai leader said to the author, who asked why the leader expressed gratitude to him, "You made us *known*." That is what anthropology is about.

Whatever their intent, the job anthropologists have to do makes government officials uneasy, not just in Malaysia, but everywhere. No one likes to do a touchy job with someone looking over his or her shoulder and taking notes. The Department of Indigenous People's Affairs makes it clear that foreign anthropologists who criticize government policies are not welcome. Indeed, in 1997, the retiring head of the JHEOA described foreign anthropologists' work as "half-truths, distortions, oversimplifications, conjectures, fabrications, factual errors, fact manipulation, generalization, uncorroborated evidence, and speculations." Their work is, he said predictably, part of a "deliberate design" to smear the JHEOA, the Malay people, the Malaysian government, and Islam in general. This explanation is pretty standard in Malaysian politics. A week or so earlier, the prime minister had blamed the Malaysian currency crisis on an international Jewish money-speculator conspiracy to destroy his country, a "conscious design" prompted by envy and hatred of Islam.

Since anthropologists are not aligned with the government, Orang Asli do not see ethnographers, local or foreign, as agents of the dominant peoples in the area, in contrast with the position of anthropologists in other countries like Mexico or the United States. Semai and Orang Asli therefore tend to welcome ethnographers, though not necessarily to trust them, even though ethnographers are certainly not above the sort of criticism the head of the JHEOA engages in nor that they receive from some Orang Asli.

Indigenous Organizations

The name of the Jabatan Hal Ehwal Orang Asli, the Department of Indigenous People's Affairs, is precise. It used to be the Jabatan Orang Asli, the Indigenous People's Department. When Malaysia became independent, a large percentage of the people who worked there were Orang Asli. Starting in the 1980s, that percentage dropped as people retired and were replaced by Malays. The name was changed to reflect the fact that the department was run for Orang Asli but not by them. As usual with Malaysian government statistics about Orang Asli, the numbers are not as clear as they might be: in 1993, the JHEOA told the Malaysian Parliament that 58.9 percent of the department workers were Orang Asli, but in 1997 the departing head of the JHEOA said that only 30 percent of them were Orang Asli. Most are in the lower ranks of the organization. A few Orang Asli converts to Islam run local branch offices. There are no Orang Asli in policy-making positions.

The closest approximation to a self-help organization for Orang Asli is the Persatuan Orang Asli Semenanjung Malaysia, the Peninsular Orang Asli Society of Malaysia (POASM). Orang Asli who worked for the JOA, mostly Semai, founded this organization in 1977. At first, other Orang Asli were resentful of what seemed like Semai domination of the organization, but the last couple of presidents have been non-Semai, and the mutual distrust seems to have subsided.

POASM was modeled on the dominant Malay political party, with which it was in unequal alliance, and accepted Malays (but no other Malaysians) as members. For a while in the early 1990s, the then head of the JOA was the organization's advisor. In 1996, POASM was reorganized as an ordinary self-help society, and its membership was limited to Orang Asli. All members can attend and vote at the general meetings.

The policies of the organization have varied from accommodation with government policies to a somewhat more independent stance. The leader during the most independent phase of the organization later converted to Islam. He continues as a member of POASM but is no longer active. The leadership as of 1997 seemed to be steering a middle-of-the-road course between these two poles. The issue of direct confrontation with the government has never arisen.

The Center for Orang Asli Concerns (COAC) is a shoestring operation that takes a more critical stance toward government policies. At one point, the most accommodationist head of POASM accused COAC of being a tool of foreign anthropologists, a charge that the JHEOA resurrected in late 1997. However, it is unlikely that any of the anthropologists who have worked with Orang Asli would have the gall to try to dictate to COAC, or that the people at COAC would tolerate that kind of patronizing behavior. Indeed, members of COAC have also accused foreign anthropologists of being backward-looking, interested more in the Orang Asli past than in their current struggles. That accusation is not entirely without foundation. Fortunately, Malaysian anthropologists have taken on the job of trying to focus public attention on the plight of Orang Asli. University policies have forced a couple of them who are not Malays into exile, but a Semai anthropologist, Juli Edo, remains on the faculty of the flagship University of Malaysia, and a cadre of courageous Malay anthropologists remains active.

FOOD FOR THOUGHT

The basic problem the Semai and other Orang Asli face is dispossession, the fancy word anthropologists use for situations in which one group of people takes whatever they want from another group without paying them anything close to a fair price. When governments dispossess, they usually call it "development" (meaning, for example, that land is put to new and different uses for the benefit of the new owners). When individuals dispossess, it is usually called "stealing." Whatever the legal developments of the past couple of years, the Semai have lost so much already that mere compensation is probably out of the question. Without a secure land base, the Semai will have great difficulty in maintaining their independence and their culture in the face of deliberate attacks upon it by the government agency in charge of protecting Orang Asli and inadvertent subversion of it by the seductive and commercial translational New World Order. Most of these pressures are not malevolent. The agents seek to share the spiritual comfort of their religion and the material comforts of economic progress. The question individual Semai need to answer is whether, to attain some comforts, they wish to lose all the history and cultural achievements that gave them their identity and vanish into the world's mass, rootless, impoverished majority. Among the important questions observers need to ponder are: Is economic, religious, and cultural dispossession of the very poorest people an inevitable part of economic development? Is the future of most of the world's people one of impoverishment and loss of independence? Are ethnic identity and cultural integrity valuable enough to be worth sacrificing their—and their kids'—economic and political well being? Can we observers ignore such questions? Who decides the answers to such questions? Who has the right to decide the answers?

Questions

1. One of the problems Semai and Orang Asli in general face is that they protest displacement and dispossession in ways invisible to or unacceptable by human-rights organizations. Should Semai have to dress up like "primitive people" and stage telegenic confrontations in order to have their plight recognized? They could paint their faces and wear flowery headgear the way they did for religious ceremonies; they could carry blowpipes and wear nose quills. Or is there some other way for human-rights organizations to recognize passive protest as protest?

2. The Malaysian government has dealt with the Semai as the American government has done with Native Americans: displacement, dispossession, and subtly coercive assimilation. Confronted with the appalling destruction of the Malaysian environment, the Malaysian government says, in effect, "You folks in the West did it to *your* environment, and now that you're really rich as a result, you want to tell us not to do the same thing." They could say the same thing about their policy toward the Semai. What moral standing does the West have to protest Malaysian policies?

3. A fifteen-year-old Semai youth asked a visitor the following question: "You've been around a lot, you've read a lot. Can you tell me why it is that, everywhere in the world, the original inhabitants of a country are always the poorest and most powerless people there?" How would you answer him?

4. In response to criticism, the Malaysian government always tells foreigners to look to their own countries and stay out of Malaysian affairs. Are there any people who live near you, not necessarily indigenous people, who suffer the same sorts of indignities, bigotry, dispossession, or displacement that Semai do in Malaysia? What are the similarities? What are the differences? What could you or anybody else do about it?

5. Violence is a major problem for Americans and many other people. Part of the problem may be that violence is defined only as physical violence. Physical violence is the form of violence that poor people resort to because they lack access to other sorts of power. But suppose violence is defined the way traditional Semai defined it, as any action that leaves people feeling betrayed or disrespected, as if they and their hopes and fears count for nothing, whether it is beating them up or not showing up on time for an appointment. The new definition would certainly embrace many activities Americans now actually praise and reward. What changes would have to be made if the Semai definition were accepted? Would that sort of change reduce physical violence in the United States?

6. What are the pluses and minuses of "green tourism," or "ecotourism," for host countries like Malaysia? For rural indigenous peoples like most Semai?

RESOURCE GUIDE

Published Literature

There are many good books and articles about the Semai. Unfortunately, most are hard to obtain because they are published in Malaysia or by overseas university presses, some in Malay. You should check your library for books and articles by Alberto G. Gomes, Colin Nicholas, Juli Edo, Razha bin Rashid, Clayton Robarchek, Wazir Jahan Karim and Zawawi bin Ibrahim. See also Chapter 7 by Kirk Endicott on the Batek of Malaysia.

Baer, A. *Health, Disease, and Survival: A Biomedical and Genetic Analysis of the Orang Asli of Malaysia.* Jubang Jaya, Malaysia: Center for Orang Asli Concerns, 1999. A survey of all the published material on Orang Asli biology and health, indicating that their health has not improved in the last thirty years.

Dentan, Robert Knox. *The Semai: A Nonviolent People of Malaya*. New York: Holt, Rinehart and Winston, 1979. A short, informal sketch of traditional Semai life for serious high-school seniors and college freshmen.

Dentan, Robert Knox, and Ong Hean Chooi. "Stewards of the Green and Beautiful World: A Preliminary Report on Semai Arboriculture and Its Policy Implications." In *Dimensions of Tradition and Development in Malaysia*, ed. Rokiah Talib and Tan Chee-Beng, 53–124. Kuala Lumpur: Pelanduk Publications, 1995. A technical account, with many quotes from Semai, by an anthropologist and a botanist.

Dentan, Robert Knox, Kirk Endicott, Alberto G. Gomes, and Barry Hooker. *Malaysia and the "Original People": A Case Study of the Impact of Development on Indigenous Peoples*. Boston: Allyn and Bacon, 1997. A somewhat technical description of what was happening to Semai and other Orang Asli in the early 1990s, for college undergraduates, by three anthropologists and a lawyer.

Nicholas, Colin. *Pathway to Dependence: Commodity Relations and the Dissolution of Semai Society*. Monash Papers on Southeast Asia no. 33. Clayton, Victoria, Australia: Centre of Southeast Asian Studies, Monash University, 1994. An excellent analytical account of the effects of "economic development" on Semai society, in somewhat technical language.

Robarchek, Clayton. "The Peaceful Semai." *World and I* 3, no. 7 (1988): 468–479. A brief but clear sketch of the Semai, with excellent color pictures, by the expert on Semai nonviolence.

Internet and WWW Sites

Semai ritual and economic development
http://wings.buffalo.edu/academic/department/AandL/ams

Essays on and photos of Semai children
http://www.noogenesis.com/malama/bood.html

Orang Asli list service
Oalistserv<orang-asli@massey.ac.nz>

Suaram (concerned with Orang Asli environmental and civil rights)
www.geocities.com/CapitolHill/Lobby/1577

Active Voices (an online journal that provides up-to-date short accounts of indigenous peoples' struggles)
www.cs.org

Organizations

Center for Orang Asli Concerns (COAC)
Pusat Prihatinan Orang Asli
P.O. Box 3052
47590 Subang Jaya
Malaysia

Malaysian Nature Society
P.O. Box 10750
50724 Kuala Lumpur
Malaysia
E-mail: mns@natsoc.po.my

Aliran Kesedaran Negara
P.O. Box 1049
10830 Pulau Pinang
Malaysia

Utusan Konsumer Pinang
228 Jln. Macalister
10400 Pulau Pinang
Malaysia

Barbara Nowak and Peter Laird (run Orang Asli list service, see Internet and WWW
   Sites)
Institute for Development Studies
Massey University Private Bag 11-222
Palmerston North
New Zealand

Profits from some books listed under Published Literature go to a fund for the
Orang Asli. The chair of the fund is Professor Dee Baer:

Zoology Department
3029 Cordley Hall
Oregon State University
Corvallis, OR 97331-2914

In Chapter 7, Kirk Endicott provides further information on resources available
to people interested in learning about the Orang Asli.

Chapter 14

The Uyghur of China

Dru C. Gladney

The Uyghur people are the descendants of a high civilization of Central Asian nomadic people who had a kingdom based here in Turfan. The elegant paintings and wrapping in this tomb date to the Han Dynasty (206 B.C.–220 A.D.) and are comparable in beauty and sophistication. A mummy in the Xinjiang Provincial Tombs also found in this area dates over 6,000 years old and proves the Uyghur people are even older than the Han Chinese.

—Uyghur member's view of his people's history, related at the Astana tombs in Turfan, northwestern China

CULTURAL OVERVIEW

The People

The Uyghur are an official minority nationality of China, identified as the second largest of ten Muslim peoples in China, primarily inhabiting the Xinjiang Uyghur Autonomous Region (Table 14-1). Many Uyghur in Turfan and Kashgar argue persuasively that they are the autochthonous people of this region. The fact that over 99.8 percent of the Uyghur people are located in Xinjiang, whereas the other Muslim peoples of China have significant populations in other provinces and outside the country, contributes to this important sense of belonging to the land. The Uyghur continue to conceive of their ancestors as originating in Xinjiang, claiming to outsiders that "it is our land, our territory," despite the fact that the early Uyghur kingdom was based in what is now Outer Mongolia and the present region of Xinjiang is under the control of the Chinese state.

Historians of Inner Asia also generally trace the origins of the present Uyghur to the formerly nomadic people who later settled in oases, spoke

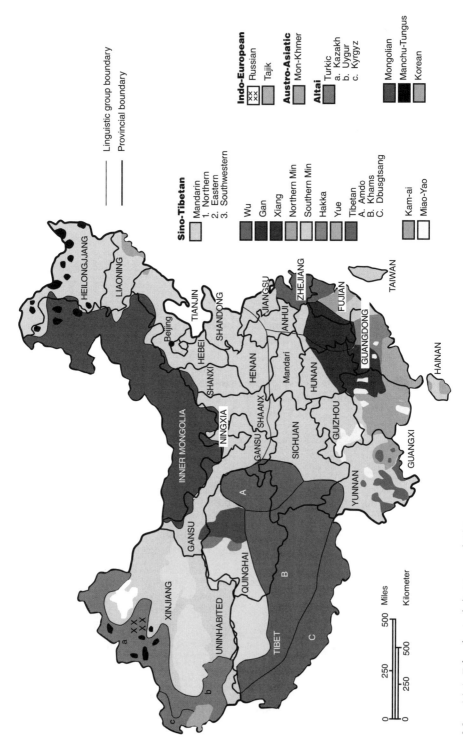

Sino-Tibetan

Mandarin
1. Northern
2. Eastern
3. Southwestern

Wu
Gan
Xiang
Northern Min
Southern Min
Hakka
Yue
Tibetan
A. Amdo
B. Khams
C. Dbusgtsang

Kam-ai
Miao-Yao

Indo-European
Russian
Tajik

Austro-Asiatic
Mon-Khmer

Altai
Turkic
a. Kazakh
b. Uygur
c. Kyrgyz

Mongolian
Manchu-Tungus
Korean

Linguistic group boundary
Provincial boundary

Map 14-1. Ethnological divisions of China.

Table 14-1
Population of Muslim Minorities in China and Xinjiang

Minority Ethnonym	Location	Language Family	1990 Census Population	Percentage in Xinjiang
Hui	All of China, especially Ningxia, Gansu, Henan, Xinjiang, Qinghai, Yunnan, Hebei, Shandong*	Sino-Tibetan	8,602,978	7.9%
Uyghur	Xinjiang	Altaic (Turkic)	7,214,431	99.8%
Kazak	Xinjiang, Gansu, Qinghai	Altaic (Turkic)	1,111,718	-
Dongxiang	Gansu, Qinghai	Altaic (Turkic)	373,872	-
Kyrgyz	Xinjiang, Heilongjiang	Altaic (Turkic)	141,549	99.1%
Salar	Qinghai, Gansu	Altaic (Turkic)	87,697	-
Tajik	Xinjiang	Indo-European	33,538	99.9%
Uzbek	Xinjiang	Altaic (Turkic)	14,502	99.8%
Baonan	Gansu	Altaic (Mongolian)	12,212	-
Tatar	Xinjiang	Altaic (Turkic)	4,873	99.9%

*Listed in order of size.

Source: Gladney, Muslim Chinese: 20.

a Turkic dialect, and formed the Uyghur Kingdom based in Karakoram (745–840 A.D.) A provocative theory argues that the designation "Uyghur" derives from the influence of Soviet advisors in Xinjiang in the 1930s, fresh from their experience of making official designations of the Soviet central Asian populations. In addition to the shifting use of the term "Uyghur" and its disappearance and revitalization after 500 years, the people referred to by that name are now primarily identified as a "Muslim" people. Yet a brief look at the history of the Uyghur will reveal a transition from traditional central Asian shamanistic nomads to Manichaean and then to Buddhist and Nestorian Christian believers. From the tenth to the fifteenth century, the term "Muslim" designated all those peoples who were specifically not Uyghur, as the term "Uyghur" specifically referred to those Buddhist and Nestorian oasis dwellers of the Tarim basin in Southern Xinjiang who did not convert to Islam until the mid-fifteenth century. Tracing the evolution of Uyghur identity from steppe nomad tribal confederation to settled seminomadic kingdom, to dispersed oasis traders, and, finally, to a minority nationality of the People's Republic of China is a story of ethnic change that reveals much about minority-state relations and cultural survival in the modern nation-state.

The Setting

While a collection of nomadic steppe peoples known as the "Uyghur" has existed since before the eighth century, this identity has evolved through radically changing sociopolitical contexts. Any attempt to understand the cultural survival of contemporary Uyghur and their recent political activism must place that survival in these contexts. It was not until the fall of the Turkish Khanate (552–744 A.D.) to a people reported by the Chinese historians as Hui-he or Hui-hu that the beginnings of the Uyghur Empire are found in written history. At this time the Uyghur were but one collection of nine nomadic tribes who initially, in confederation with other Basmil and Karlukh nomads, defeated the Second Turkish Khanate and then dominated the federation under the leadership of Koli Beile in 742.

The gradual settling down of the Uyghur and their defeat of the Turkish Khanate occurred precisely when trade with the unified Tang state became especially lucrative. The high Uyghur civilization that became, in one anthropologist's words, "a bridge between the world of the nomads and surrounding civilizations" (Barfield 1989) resulted from their extorting the Tang state, which the Chinese historians justified as "tribute." It was in the Uyghur Empire's interest to assist the Tang state in order to maintain a profitable relationship because the Uyghur were more interested in exploitation than expansion.

Sedentarization of the Uyghur and interaction with the Chinese state were accompanied by socioreligious change: the traditional shamanistic Turkic-speaking Uyghur came increasingly under the influence of Persian Manichaeanism. Trade and military alliances with the Chinese state developed to the extent that the Uyghur gradually adopted cultural, dress, and even agricultural practices of the Chinese. The Uyghur capital of Karabalghasun in Mongolia was conquered by the nomadic Kyrgyz in 840 without rescue from the Tang, who by then may have become intimidated by the wealthy Uyghur Empire.

According to some scholars, the Uyghur were dispersed across China into three main branches. One collection of thirteen tribes fled southeast from the Mongolian steppes to just beyond the Great Wall and then later disappeared from historical record, presumably assimilating into the Northern Han population. The rest of the Uyghur, composed of some fifteen tribes, dispersed west and southwest from Mongolia throughout northwest China, forming the basis for the second and third branches. The second branch eventually migrated to what is now Jiuquan, in Gansu, and became the ancestors of the people currently identified as the Yugur nationality, concentrated primarily in the Gannan Yugur Autonomous County. The third branch was dispersed in the oases surrounding the Tarim basin of the Taklamakan Desert, including Turfan, Karashahr, and Kashgar, where the Uyghur may previously have had dependencies. This group took advantage of the unique socioecology of the glacier-fed oases surrounding the Takla-makan Desert, and were able to preserve their merchant and limited agrarian practices, gradually establishing Khocho or Gaochang, the great Uyghur city-state based in Turfan for four centuries (850–1250). It is interesting that while this group is culturally reckoned as the direct ancestors of the present-day Uyghur, and the region it inhabited became known as Uyghuristan, its members added Buddhist and Nestorian Christian beliefs to their Manichaean religious practice and were the very last of the Uyghur in the Taklamakan oases to convert to Islam. Even today, like Muslims elsewhere, many Uyghur mix a wide variety of local practices into their Islamic rituals extending from this long history.

Traditional Subsistence Strategies

By the middle of the ninth century, the people now known as the Uyghur had become farmers and completely sedentarized. Excavations reveal a wealthy aristocratic civilization that rivaled the highly developed Tang and Song courts in its artistic and material sophistication, as well as a long history of interaction and migration from throughout Eurasia. Rather than possessing any linguistic uniformity—by this time the Uyghur people maintained their Turkish dialect while their elite had adopted Persian with an ancient Sogdian script—the disparate Uyghur peoples took on identities based on their separate oases. The gradual Islamization of the Uyghur from the tenth to the sixteenth centuries displaced their Buddhist religion but did little to bridge these oasis-based loyalties. With the conversion of the ruler Sadik Boghra Khan in 950 A.D., the peoples of the western Takla-makan oases, especially Kashgar, rejected their Buddhist and other central Asian religious traditions in favor of the more politically and perhaps symbolically advantageous ideology of Islam. From that time on, the people of Uyghuristan centered in the Turfan depression who resisted Islamic conversion until the mid-fifteenth century were the only people known as Uyghur. The others were known only by their oasis or by the generic term of Muslims.

Once again, ethnic and religious change for the Uyghur was precipitated by sociopolitical incorporation. In this case, the expansion of Islamic rule led to the gradual displacement of the Buddhist, Manichaean, and Nestorian Uyghurs by an Islamic identity alien and in opposition to the traditional Uyghur identity to the extent that the name "Uyghur" was dropped as people became Muslim. Under the Buddhist Kara-Kitai (1137–1210 A.D.) and Mongol (1209–1368) empires, Buddhist and Nestorian Uyghur scribes and administrators were heavily relied upon. With the fall of the Mongol Empire, the decline of the overland trade routes, and the expansion of trade relationships with the Ming, Turfan gradually turned toward the Islamic Moghuls and, perhaps in opposition to the growing Chinese

Empire, adopted Islam by the mid-fifteenth century. The Uyghurs, who were identified as the non-Muslim, mainly Buddhist rulers of Turfan, converted, and the local inhabitants no longer preferred to be known by the non-Islamic term. Instead, there was a proliferation of such localisms as "yerlik" (persons of the land) and "sart" (caravaneer). There was no significant unification of these disparate oasis populations until the late Qing Empire conquered the Mongolian Zungarian rule (1653–1754 A.D.). Until this time, the Tarim basin was riven with political succession struggles among the Moghul leaders and religious disputes. During the seventeenth and eighteenth centuries a brief period of unification of eastern Xinjiang under the Yarkant Khanate was broken up when religious and political factionalism between two competing central Asian Sufi orders, the "White Mountain" Afaqiyya in Kashgar and the "Black Mountain" Ishiqiyya in Yarkant, led to intervention by the Mongolian Zungars in the late seventeenth century.

Social and Political Organization

The Yaqub Beg rebellion that established the thirteen-year Kashgar Emirate (1864–1877) crystallized Uyghur resistance against what they perceived to be a cultural as well as political Chinese threat to their identity. While the Uyghur involved in this rebellion were divided into the local, ideological, and socioeconomic factions that usually disunited them, it nevertheless played an important role in setting all Uyghur apart from the Chinese state. While these peoples were divided internally among themselves during periods of oppression and revolt, many of them later began to conceive of themselves as united vis-à-vis the dominant powers. During the republican period in the first half of the twentieth century, Uyghur identity was again marked by factionalism along locality, religious, and political lines.

Prior to the mid-nineteenth century, the Qing government was mainly interested in pacifying the region by setting up military outposts that supported a vassal-state relationship. Colonization began with the migrations of the Han in the mid-nineteenth century, but this was cut short by the Yaqub Beg rebellion in the second half of the nineteenth century, the fall of the Qing Empire in 1910, and the ensuing warlord era that dismembered the region until its incorporation as part of the People's Republic of China in 1949. Competition for the loyalties of the peoples of the oases in the "great game" played between China, Russia, and Britain further contributed to divisions among the Uyghur along political, religious, and military lines. The peoples of the oases, until the challenge of incorporation into the nation-state, lacked any coherent sense of identity.

Incorporation of Xinjiang for the first time into a nation-state required unprecedented delineation of the so-called nations involved. The reemergence of the label "Uyghur," though arguably inappropriate because it had last been used 500 years previously to describe the largely Buddhist population of the Turfan basin, stuck as the name for the settled Turkish-speaking Muslim oasis dwellers. It has never been disputed by the people themselves or the states involved. There is too much at stake for the people labeled as such to wish to challenge that identification.

Religion and World View

That Islam became an important, but not exclusive, cultural marker of Uyghur identity is not surprising, given the sociopolitical oppositions with which the Uyghur were confronted. The Uyghurs are Sunni Muslims, the main school of most Muslims, practicing Islamic traditions similar to their coreligionists in the region (Figure 14-1). In addition, many of them are Sufi, adhering to mystical traditions related to Central Asian Sufism. However, it is also important to note that Islam was only one of several unifying markers for Uyghur identity, and that their lives are just as marked by their oasis-based agrarian and trading practices. Most profoundly, modern Uyghurs, especially those living in larger towns and urban areas, are most marked by Chinese influence and incorporation. Islamic traditions often become the focal point for Uyghur efforts to preserve their culture and history. One such popular tradition that has resurfaced in recent years is that of the Mashrap (or "prayer gathering"), where Uyghurs, mostly young people, gather to recite poetry and sing songs (often of folk or religious content), dance, and share traditional foods. These evening events have often become focal points for Uyghur resistance to Chinese rule in recent years.

THREATS TO SURVIVAL

Unforeseen sociopolitical integration of Xinjiang into the Chinese nation-state has taken place in the last forty years. While Xinjiang has been under Chinese political domination since the defeat of the Zungar in 1754, until the middle of the twentieth century it was but loosely incorporated into China proper. The extent of the incorporation of the Xinjiang Region into China is indicated by Han migration, communication, education, and occupational shifts since the 1940s.

Han migration into Xinjiang has swelled the local population to an incredible twenty-six times over the 1940 level, with an annual growth of 8.1 percent (see Table 14-2). The increase of the Han population has been accompanied by the growth and delineation of other Muslim groups in addition to the Uyghur. A dramatic increase in the Hui (Dungan, or mainly Chinese-speaking Muslim) population can also be seen. While the Hui pop-

Figure 14-1. Uyghur Muslim at prayer, Idgah Mosque, Kashgar, Xinjiang Uyghur Autonomous Region, May 16, 1993. Courtesy of Dru C. Gladney.

ulation in Xinjiang in 1982 had grown to over six times the level in 1940 (averaging an annual growth rate of 4.5 percent), the Uyghur population has followed a more natural biological growth rate of 1.7 percent.

Chinese incorporation of Xinjiang has led to a further development of ethnic socioeconomic niches. Whereas earlier travelers reported little distinction in labor and education among Muslims other than that between settled and nomadic peoples, the 1982 census revealed vast differences in socioeconomic structure (Table 14-3).

A disparity is also reflected in reports on education among Muslim minorities in China. The Uyghur are about average in terms of university graduates and illiteracy in China as compared with other ethnic groups (0.2 and 45 percent, respectively). The Tatar achieve the highest representation of university graduates among Muslims (39 percent) as well as the lowest percentage of illiteracy (9 percent), far below the average for all of China (32 percent). The main drawback of these figures is that they reflect only what is regarded by the state as education, namely, training in the Chinese language and the sciences. However, among the elderly elite, there continues to be a high standard of traditional expertise in Persian, Arabic, and the Islamic sciences, which are not considered part of Chinese "culture" and education. Although elementary and secondary education is offered in the Uyghur language, Mandarin has become the language of upward mobility in Xinjiang as well as the rest of China. Many Uyghur

Table 14-2
Muslim and Chinese Population Growth in Xinjiang, 1940–1982

Ethnic Group	1940–1941	1953	1982
Uyghur	2,941,000	3,640,000	5,950,000
Kazak	319,000	492,000	904,000
Hui	92,000	150,000	571,000
Kyrgyz	65,000	68,000	113,000
Tajik	9,000	14,000	26,000
Uzbek	5,000	14,000	12,000
Tatar	6,900	6,900	4,100
Han	202,000	—	5,287,000
Total Population	—	4,874,000	13,082,000

Source: Gladney, *Muslim Chinese*: 224.

have been trained in the thirteen Nationalities Colleges scattered throughout China since they were established in the 1950s. These secular intellectuals trained in Chinese schools are asserting political leadership in Xinjiang, as opposed to traditional religious elites. Many Uyghurs in Urumqi point to the establishment of the Uyghur Traditional Medicine Hospital and Madrassah complex in 1987 as an initial counterbalance to this emphasis on Han education. However, many Uyghur believe that their history and traditional culture continue to be downplayed in the state schools and must be privately reemphasized to their children. It is through the elementary schools that Uyghur children first participate formally in the Chinese nation-state, dominated by Han history and language, and most fully enter into the Chinese world. The predominant educational practice of teaching a centralized, mainly Han subject content, despite the widespread use of minority languages, continues to drive a wedge between the Uyghur and their traditions, inducting them further into the Han Chinese milieu.

The increased incorporation of Xinjiang into the political sphere of China has not only led to the further migration of Han and Hui into the region, but opened China to an unprecedented extent for the Uyghur. Uyghur men are heavily involved in long-distance trade throughout China. They go to Tianjin and Shanghai for manufactured clothes and textiles, Hangzhou and Suzhou for silk, and Guangzhou and Hainan for electronic goods and motorcycles brought in from Hong Kong. In every place, especially Beijing, due to the large foreign population, they trade local currency (renminbi) for foreign exchange certificates (*waihuijuan*). Appearing more like foreigners than the local Han, they are often less suspect. "We use the hard currency to go on the Hajj [pilgrimage to Mecca]," one young Uyghur in the central market square of Kunming, Yunnan Province, said in 1985. "Allah will protect you if you exchange money with me." While some may save for the Hajj, most purchase imported or luxury goods with their hard

Table 14-3
Occupational Structure of Muslim Minorities in China (Percentage), 1982

Occupation	Hui	Uyghur	Kazak	Dongxiang	Kyrgyz	Salar	Tajik	Uzbek	Baonan	Tatar	All Ethnic Groups
Scientific technical staff	5.75	4.25	11.25	1.00	7.00	3.25	5.75	17.25	1.50	23.50	4.00
Administration	1.75	.75	2.00	.25	1.50	.75	2.75	3.75	2.25	4.50	1.00
Office and related workers	1.75	1.00	2.00	.25	1.75	.75	2.00	3.25	.75	4.25	1.00
Commercial workers	3.50	1.50	1.25	.25	.75	.75	.50	10.75	.50	5.25	1.25
Service workers	4.00	1.50	1.50	.25	1.00	.75	.75	6.50	.50	4.50	1.25
Farming, forestry, fishing, and animal husbandry	60.75	84.00	74.50	96.75	84.00	90.50	85.75	31.50	92.25	8.50	84.00
Production and transport	22.25	7.00	7.50	1.25	4.00	3.25	2.50	27.00	2.25	19.25	7.50
Others	.25	—	—	—	—	—	—	—	—	.25	—

Source: Adapted from Population Atlas of China, Oxford University Press, 1987, xxx, 28.

currency and take them back to Xinjiang, selling or trading them for a profit—a practice that keeps them away from home six months out of the year. As Uyghur continue to travel throughout China, they return to Xinjiang with a firmer sense of their own pan-Uyghur identity vis-à-vis the Han and the other minorities they encounter on their travels.

International travel has also resumed for the Uyghur. An important development in recent years has been the opening of a rail line between China and Kazakhstan through the Ili corridor to Almaty, as well as the opening of several official gateways to the surrounding, nations on China's borders. With the resumption of normal Sino–central Asian relations in 1991, trade and personal contacts have expanded enormously. This expansion has led many Uyghur to see themselves as important players in the improved Sino–central Asian exchanges. An example of the new freedom is that many of the imported Hong Kong–made electronic goods purchased by Uyghur with hard currency in Canton and Shenzhen have found their way into the marketplace and the hands of relatives across the border in Almaty who are also identified by the Kazakhstan state as Uyghur.

RESPONSE: STRUGGLES TO SURVIVE CULTURALLY

Increasing integration with China has not been smooth. Many Uyghur resent the threats to their cultural survival and have resorted to violence. After denying them for decades and stressing instead China's "national unity," official reports have recently detailed Tibetan and Muslim conflicts in the border regions of Tibet, Yunnan, Xinjiang, Ningxia, and Inner Mongolia. After the March 7, 1997, bus bombings in Beijing, widely attributed (though without verification) to Uyghur separatists, coupled with the Urumqi bus bombings on the day of Chinese leader Deng Xiaoping's 1997 memorial on February 25, which killed nine people, Beijing can no longer keep such conflicts secret. The Yining uprising on February 7, 1997, that left at least nine dead and hundreds injured, with seven Uyghur suspects now arrested and most probably slated for execution, has been heavily covered by the world's media. This distinguishes the last few events from ongoing problems in the region in the mid-1980s that have previously met with little media coverage.

In 1996, the *Xinjiang Daily* reported five serious incidents since February 1996, with a crackdown that rounded up 2,773 terrorist suspects, 6,000 pounds of explosives, and 31,000 rounds of ammunition. Overseas Uyghur groups have claimed that over 10,000 have been arrested in the roundup, with over 1,000 killed. The largest protest on February 2–8, 1996, was sparked by a Chinese raid on an evening Mashrap cultural meeting. The protests to the arrests made during the meeting led to 120 deaths and over 2,500 arrests. On March 2, 1996, the progovernment mullah of Kashgar's Idgah mosque and his son were stabbed by knife-wielding Uyghur militants;

on May 27, there was another attack on a senior government official; and in September, six Uyghur government officials were killed by other Uyghurs in Yecheng.

The government has responded with a host of random arrests and new policy announcements. In the spring of 1998, the National Peoples Congress passed a New Criminal Law that redefined "counterrevolutionary" crimes to be "crimes against the state," subject to severe prison terms and even execution. Included in "crimes against the state" were any actions considered to involve "ethnic discrimination" or "stirring up antiethnic sentiment." Many human-rights activists have argued that this is a thinly veiled attempt to criminalize "political" actions and to make them appear as illegal as traffic violations, supporting China's claims that it holds "no political prisoners." Since any minority activity could be regarded as stirring "antiethnic feeling," many ethnic activists are concerned that the New Criminal Law will be easily turned against them.

On June 12, 1998, the *Xinjiang Daily* reported "rampant activities by splittists inside and outside China" that contributed to the closure of ten "unauthorized" places of worship, the punishment of mullahs who had preached illegally outside their mosques, and the execution of three people on May 29 in Aksu County (an area that is 99 percent Uyghur), allegedly for murder, robbery, rape, and other violent crimes. Troop movements to the area have reportedly been the largest since the suppression of the Baren Township insurrection in April 1990, perhaps related to that year's nationwide "Strike Hard" campaign. This campaign, launched in Beijing in April, was originally intended to clamp down on crime and corruption but has now been turned against "splittists" (separatists) in Xinjiang, calling for the building of a "great wall of steel" against them. The *Xinjiang Daily* on December 16, 1996, contained the following declaration by Wang Lequan, the region's first party secretary: "We must oppose separatism and illegal religious activities in a clear and comprehensive manner, striking hard and effectively against our enemies."

The People's Republic of China, as one of five permanent voting members of the United Nations Security Council, and as a significant exporter of military hardware to the Middle East, has become a recognized player in Middle Eastern affairs. With the decline in trade with most Western nations after the Tiananmen Square massacre in the early 1990s, the importance of China's Middle Eastern trading partners (all of them Muslim, since China did not have relations with Israel until recently), increased considerably. This may account for the fact that China established diplomatic relations with Saudi Arabia in August 1990, with the first direct Sino-Saudi exchanges since 1949 taking place (Saudi Arabia canceled its long-standing diplomatic relationship with Taiwan and withdrew its ambassador, despite a lucrative trade history). In the face of a long-term friendship with Iraq, China went along with most of the United Nations resolutions in the war against Iraq. Although it abstained from Resolution 678 on supporting the ground war, making it unlikely that Chinese workers will be welcomed back into Kuwait, China enjoys a fairly stable reputation in the Middle East as an untarnished source of low-grade weaponry and cheap reliable labor. Recent press accounts have noted an increase in China's exports of military hardware to the Middle East since the Persian Gulf War, perhaps due to a need to balance its growing imports of Persian Gulf oil required to fuel its overheated economy. Unlike its Tibet problem, China can thus ill afford to ignore its Muslim problem. The warning by the Saudi Arabian official newspaper *al-Bilad* to China about the "suffering of [its] Muslims whose human rights are violated" over the February 7, 1997, crackdown in Yining will certainly not be taken lightly by the Chinese Foreign Ministry.

Chinese authorities are correct that increasing international attention to the plight of indigenous border peoples has put pressure on the regions. Notably, the 1997 elected chair of the Unrepresented Nations and Peoples Organisation (UNPO) based in The Hague is a Uyghur, Erkin Alptekin, son of the Uyghur Nationalist leader Isa Yusuf Alptekin, who died in December 1996 in Istanbul, where there is now a park dedicated to his memory. At least five international organizations, based in Amsterdam, Munich, Istanbul, Melbourne, and New York, are working for the independence of Xinjiang, known as Eastern Turkestan. Clearly, with Xinjiang representing the last Muslim region under communism, Chinese authorities have more to be concerned about than just international support for Tibetan independence.

The real question is, why call attention to these Tibetan and Muslim activities and external organizations now? The Istanbul-based groups have existed since the 1950s, and the Tibetan spiritual leader, the Dalai Lama, has been active since his exile in 1959. Separatist actions have taken place on a small but regular basis since the expansion of market and trade policies in China, and with the opening of six overland gateways to Xinjiang, in addition to the Trans-Eurasian Railway since 1991, there seems to be no chance of closing up shop. In his 1994 visit to the newly independent nations of central Asia, Premier Li Peng called for the opening of a "new Silk Road." This was a clear attempt to calm fears in the newly established central Asian states over Chinese expansionism, as was the April 1996 Shanghai communiqué that solidified the existing Sino–central Asian borders. This was perhaps the most recent and clearest example of Chinese government efforts to finally solidify and fully map its "internal colonies."

Practically speaking, China is not threatened by internal dismemberment. China's separatists are small in number, poorly equipped, loosely linked, and vastly outgunned by the People's Liberation Army and People's Police. Local support for separatist activities, particularly in Xinjiang, is ambivalent and ambiguous at best, given the economic disparity between these regions and their foreign neighbors, which are generally much poorer and, in some cases, such as Tadjikistan, torn by civil war. Memories in the region are strong of mass starvation and widespread destruction during the Sino-Japanese and civil wars in the first half of the twentieth century, not to mention the chaotic horrors of the Cultural Revolution, which ended in the 1970s. International support for Tibetan causes has done little to shake Beijing's grip on the region. Many local activists are not calling for complete separatism or real independence, but more often express concerns over environmental degradation, nuclear testing, religious freedom, overtaxation, and recently imposed limits on childbearing. Many ethnic leaders are simply calling for "real" autonomy according to Chinese law for the five autonomous regions, which are each currently led by first party secretaries who are all Han Chinese controlled by Beijing. Extending the "Strike Hard" campaign to Xinjiang, Wang Lequan, the party secretary for Xinjiang, recently declared, "There will be no compromise between us and the separatists."

Beijing's official publication of the separatist issue may have more to do with domestic politics than any real internal or external threat. Recent moves suggest efforts to promote Chinese nationalism as a "unifying ideology" that will prove more attractive than communism and more manageable than capitalism. By highlighting separatist threats and external intervention, China can divert attention away from its own domestic instabilities of natural disasters (especially the recent flooding), economic crises (such as the Asian economic downturn's drag on China's currency), rising inflation, increased income disparity, displaced "floating populations," Hong Kong reunification, and the many other internal and external problems facing Jiang Zemin's government. Perhaps nationalism will be the only "unifying ideology" left to a Chinese nation that has begun to distance itself from communism, as it has from Confucianism, Buddhism, and Daoism in the past. Perhaps this is why religiously based nationalisms, like Islamic fundamentalism and Tibetan Buddhism, are targeted by Beijing, while the rise of shamanism and popular religion goes unchecked. At the same time, a firm lid on Muslim activism in China sends a message to foreign Muslim militant organizations to stay out of China's internal affairs, and to the Taliban to stay well within their Afghan borders. Although it is hard to gauge the extent of support for Uyghur separatism among the broader population, it is clear that cultural survival is a critical concern for many, and significant attempts to preserve Uyghur culture are being made, assisted to some extent by international tourism and the state's attempts to demonstrate its goodwill toward its restive Muslim population.

FOOD FOR THOUGHT

The continued incorporation of Xinjiang into China has become inexorable and perhaps irreversible. The need for the oil and mineral resources of the region since China became an oil-importing nation in 1993 means that Chinese influence will only grow. To be sure, the Uyghur are still oriented culturally and historically toward central Asia in terms of religion, language, and ethnic custom, and interaction has increased in recent years due to the opening of the roads to Pakistan and Almaty. Certainly, pan-Turkism was appealing to some, but not all, Uyghurs during the early part of the twentieth century. Historical ties to central Asia are strong. Turkey's late Prime Minister Turgut Ozal espoused a popular Turkish belief when, on his first visit to Beijing in 1985, which sought to open a consulate there, he commented that the Turkish nation originated in what is now China. Yet separatist notions, given the current political incorporation of Xinjiang into China, while perhaps present, are not practical. To a question regarding political separation, one prominent Uyghur in a *Los Angeles Times* interview responded, "Some people would like to, but there is no hope."

The opening of China to the outside world has meant much for the Uyghur, who may easily travel beyond China's borders through Pakistan along the Karakoram highway, through the Ili valley into Kazakhstan, or by several China Airlines flights to Istanbul from Urumqi. Uyghur pilgrims travelling on the Hajj to Mecca have increased 300 percent. These contacts have allowed the Uyghur to see themselves as participants in the broader Islamic brotherhood while at the same time being Muslim citizens of the Chinese nation-state. As they return from the Hajj, many Uyghur who generally travel together as a group have said that they gained a greater sense of affinity with their own as one people than with the other multiethnic members of the international Islamic community.

State-promoted tourism of foreign Muslims and tourists to Muslim areas in China in hopes of stimulating economic investment is also an important trend related to this opening of Xinjiang and its borders. Urumqi, a largely Han city constructed in the last fifty years, is undergoing an Islamic facelift with the official endorsement of central Asian and Islamic architecture that serves to impress many visiting foreign Muslim dignitaries. A local Soviet customs official said that more than fifty groups had crossed from Kazakhstan into Xinjiang through the Sino-Soviet border near Panfilov in 1988. In Kashgar in 1988, so many Pakistanis were staying in the Qinibake Hotel, formerly Chini Bagh, the old British Consulate, that there was almost no room for other foreigners, most of whom stay in the Seman Hotel, the former Russian Consulate, or the newer Kashgar Guest House. Most of these foreigners come to see the colorful minorities and the traditional dances and costumes by which their ethnicity is portrayed in Chinese and foreign travel brochures. One Japanese tourist in Kashgar who had just arrived by bicycle from Pakistan across the Karakoram highway said that a tourist brochure told him that the real Uyghurs could only be found in Kashgar, whereas most Uyghur believe that Turfan is the center of their cultural universe. Yet many of these Kashgaris will in the same breath argue that much of traditional Uyghur culture has been lost to Han influence in Turfan and that since they themselves are the repositories of the more unspoiled "Uyghur" traditions, tourists should spend their time and money in Kashgar.

This search for the so-called real Uyghur confirms that the nationality statistics and tourism agencies have succeeded. The re-creation of Uyghur ethnicity has come full circle: the Chinese nation-state has identified a people who in the last forty years have taken on that assigned identity as their own, and in the process, those who have accepted that identity have sought to define it and exploit it on their own terms. The Uyghur believe that they have a 6,000-year cultural and physical history in the region. They are not likely to let it go.

Questions

1. China is generally thought to be a monocultural society—one people, the Chinese, speaking one language, Chinese. Why is this assumption false?
2. Why do you think that China would choose to recognize fifty-six separate nationalities?
3. Why do you think the Chinese government recognized the Uyghur as an official nationality?
4. Why do you think the Uyghur people are more politically active than other Muslim minorities? What are their demands?
5. What do you think the future holds for the Uyghurs, Tibetans, and other minority peoples in China?

RESOURCE GUIDE

Published Literature

Barat, Kahar. "Discovery of History: The Burial Site of Kashgarli Muhammad."*AACAR Bulletin* 2, no. 3 (1989).

Barfield, Thomas. *The Perilous Frontier: Nomadic Empires and China.* Cambridge, MA: Basil Blackwell, 1989.

Chen, Jack. *The Sinkiang Story.* New York: Macmillan, 1977.

Dorian, James P., Brett Wigdortz, and Dru Gladney. "Central Asia and Xinjiang, China: Emerging Energy, Economic, and Ethnic Relations." *Central Asian Survey* 16, no. 4 (1997): 461–486.

Forbes, Andrew D. W. *Warlords and Muslims in Chinese Central Asia.* Cambridge: Cambridge University Press, 1986.

Franke, Herbert, and Denis Twitchett. *The Cambridge History of China.* Vol. 6, *Alien Regimes and Border States, 907–1368.* Cambridge: Cambridge University Press, 1994.

Gladney, Dru C. "The Ethnogenesis of the Uyghur." *Central Asian Survey* 9, (1990): 1–28.

———. *Muslim Chinese: Ethnic Nationalism in the People's Republic.* 1st ed., 1991. Cambridge, MA: Harvard University Press, 2nd ed., 1996.

———. "Relational Alterity: Constructing Dungan (Hui), Uygur, and Kazakh Identities across China, Central Asia, and Turkey." *History and Anthropology* 9, no. 4. (1996): 445–477.

Lattimore, Owen. *Pivot of Asia: Sinkiang and the Inner Asian Frontiers of China and Russia.* Boston: Little, Brown, 1950.

Mackerras, Colin. *China's Minorities: Integration and Modernization in the Twentieth Century.* New York: Oxford University Press, 1994.

Rudelson, Justin Jon. *Oasis Identities: Uyghur Nationalism along China's Silk Road.* New York: Columbia University Press, 1997.

Films and Videos

The Silk Road. 6-part film. NHK/CCTV. 6 hours. 1991.
Waiting for Uyghuristan: A Documentary by Sean R. Roberts. 50 minutes. 1997.
Xinjiang Mummies. With Dr. Victor Mair. NOVA/PBS. 60 minutes. 1998.

Internet and WWW Sites

Brief history of the Uyghers

http://www.geocities.com/capitolhill/1730/buh.html

Turkish World Home Page

http://www.turkiye.net/sota/sota.html

Organizations

Central Asian Uighur Information and Project Center
Nurmuhammed Kenji, director
22, Microdistrict 11, Apt. 66
720060, Bishkek
Kyrghyz Republic
Phone: (3312) 460-909
Fax: (3312) 235-735
E-mail: nurkenji@cauipc.freenet.bishkek.su

Eastern Turkistan Information Center
Lindwurmstr 99, 80337 Munich, Germany
Mr. Abduljelil, director
Phone: 49-89-904-5340
Fax: 49-89-904-6155
E-mail: 0899046155-0001@t-online.de

(SOTA) Research Centre for Turkestan, Azerbaijan, Crimea, Caucasus, and Siberia
P.O. Box 9642
2003 LP Haarlem
The Netherlands

Turkistan News and Information Network
TURKISTAN-N@VM.EGE.EDU.TR

Chapter 15

The Yi of China

Margaret Byrne Swain

I contend that even though "Yi" is a constructed official term, the majority
of the "Yi" population share many cultural elements and a common ideology.
—Wugashinnuimo Louwu, Nuosu Yi, Liangshan

CULTURAL OVERVIEW

The People

The Yi are one of China's largest ethnic minorities at the end of the twentieth century, but they did not exist as a group until the early 1950s. How
this came about is a tale of language and culture, state intervention, identity, and political economy. The name "Yi" is now used to indicate an
ethnic unit composed of diverse Tibeto-Burman groups living in southwest
China. In their own languages, none of these people called themselves "Yi,"
nor was there any organization or name for a greater ethnic group. The
term "Yi," a Chinese word used through history with a pejorative meaning
of non-Chinese "barbarian," was an outsiders' label applied to some of
these groups' purported ancestors. The new group name is pronounced the
same but is written as a different character.

While over 90 percent of China's population is Han Chinese, minority
people live in some 60 percent of China's land mass that is difficult to work
but is rich in resources and located in strategic frontier zones. After the
1949 Communist Revolution, the Chinese state embarked on a program of
categorizing and quantifying non–Han Chinese people for administration
in special "autonomous" regions, propaganda, and defense purposes.[2]

Minority groups perceived by government experts to have significant

251

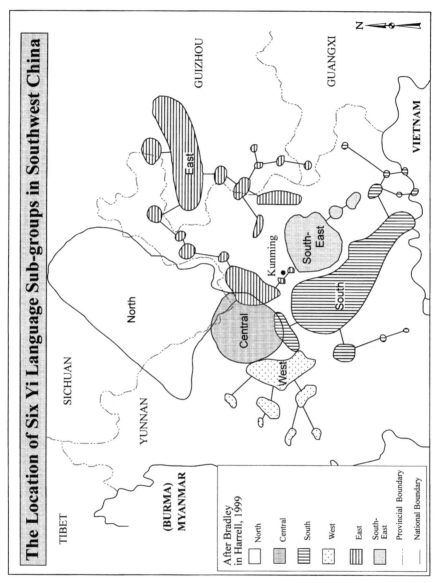

Map 15-1. Courtesy of Maryann Brent.

common elements were declared to be separate nationalities (*minzu*). This was the case for twenty-eight cultures that were recognized as branches of the Yi nationality, even though their social structures and spoken languages are quite distinct from each other, and they are geographically spread over a range of environments.[3]

A unified Yi history, constructed by scholars in China to demonstrate that this nationality has endured through time, links origin stories with current language use and geographic location. It is based on an epic told in some Yi groups that relates how six clans migrated in different directions out of the central plateau of Yunnan, forming the basis of today's Yi population. Contemporary Yi are thus classified into six subgroups, four of which have histories of using a related writing system, and two of which do not.

The Setting

Southwest China has tremendous geographical diversity. The region extends from the southeast corner of semitropical hills and river valleys located by the Vietnam border up to the northwest's high, dry mountains toward Tibet. Migration throughout the area makes it difficult to label many peoples as locally "indigenous," but there is no question that regional settlement has been shaped by centuries of Chinese internal colonization and resource competition.

The Northern Yi or Nuosu are settled in compact communities in the cool Liangshan mountain ranges of up to 11,482 feet elevation along the Sichuan-Yunnan border. Further south, Yi communities are often somewhat intermixed with other ethnic groups, living in a variety of environments. The Eastern Yi or Nasu are composed of many branches scattered across northeast Yunnan, western Guizhou, and into northwest Guangxi. The Southeastern Yi are all located in eastern Yunnan and are categorized into four major branches, including the Sani. The Southern Yi or Nisu, located in south central Yunnan, are linguistically and culturally very diverse.[4] The Central and Western Yi subgroups do not have a history of using Yi script. They are located toward the west and to the southwest of Yunnan's central plateau and are linguistically more related to neighboring non-Yi groups.

Traditional Subsistence Strategies

These diverse environments support a range of subsistence activities among Yi groups. A variety of crops are cultivated by slash-and-burn methods. At the higher elevations, buckwheat used to be a major staple and is still grown, along with the introduced crops of potatoes and maize. Rice is an important staple for some Yi peoples. Crops of hemp fiber and tobacco, gathered firewood, mushrooms, and medicinal herbs are processed both for home use and the market. Animal husbandry includes pasturage of sheep, goats, and cattle, raised for wool or hides, meat, and milk; and household livestock of pigs and chickens for food, and oxen and horses for labor. Livestock and their products are bartered and sold at market.

Social and Political Organization

Before 1949, most of the Yi in Yunnan, Guizhou, and Guangxi were under direct or indirect control of the central government, while the Nuosu were isolated from Chinese society and organized in a quasi-caste system of clans. A Nuosu, Ma Erzi, explained that among Nuosu, "the clan structure can be compared to a three-story building. . . . Each unit of each floor contains one clan. . . . It transgressed limits of time, space, wealth, poverty, weakness and strength. The clans usually had a political, military, and judicial function. It upheld the benefits of the members, which were the order and class relations of the old Liangshan Yi society."[5] There were also two named groups of people outside of the class system who over time might become incorporated individually into the lowest ranks: people, perhaps non-Nuosu captives, owned by others as slaves, and laborers or tenants affiliated to a landlord master.

Intermarriage between these castelike classes was forbidden and policed by the clans. The general rule was to marry outside of one's patriclan, but inside one's class. The practice of marriage exchange between clans (two clan groups dictating marriage-partner choice to maintain clan alliances) is changing, but cross-cousin marriage (a man marries his mother's brother's daughter or father's sister's daughter) is still prevalent. Elderly parents were supposed to live with their youngest son, who inherited the house.

Arranged marriages between clans were the norm within many Yi groups, but with more flexibility and less hierarchy than in the Nuosu class system. Among the Sani, a Southeastern Yi branch, individual choice of marriage partners was an idealized norm that is still practiced. Responsibility for the care of elderly parents was still rotated among resident children (male or female) in the late twentieth century. Marriage of a man into a woman's family to continue a family line, alternating her and his (Chinese) surnames by generation, as well as cross-cousin marriage, is found in Sani communities.

At the community level among some non-Nuosu groups, legal, political, and ritual functions were controlled by a rotating headmanship system. Most of these groups were incorporated into the Chinese state by a system of appointed hereditary local leaders who had ultimate local control in intercommunity politics and law.

Family, clan, community, and ethnic-group affiliations were thus negotiated in distinct ways among Nuosu and non-Nuosu groups. Despite such local social, linguistic, cultural, and historical variation, people labeled "Yi" by the government recognize that the multiple identities they negotiate now include this very real category as well. There is a Yi ethnic consciousness, accepted by some and contested by others.

Religion and World View

Yi peoples have in common some religious beliefs, rituals, and annual celebrations such as the torch festival. The torch festival celebrates the end of the summer harvest with music, dancing, wrestling, and bullfighting contests as well as the burning of torches and bonfires at night. Two major types of religious practitioners may be found in Yi communities: a priest (almost always a man), called *bimo* in Chinese translation, who officiates at rituals (birth, marriage, death, and community needs) and bases his knowledge on Yi written texts passed down in family lines; and a shaman, who communicates with spirits and acts for his or her clients to diagnose illness, find lost objects, and foretell fortune. Belief in natural spirits, ghosts, and ancestral spirits who inhabit a supernatural world that affects humans is sometimes augmented with imported belief systems, including popular Chinese religion and Christianity. Rites of passage from birth to death vary considerably.

THREATS TO SURVIVAL

In modern history, Yi culture has experienced two major setbacks. First [from the 1300s into this century] . . . the government made a policy to expand local garrisons and use the troops to open up areas for immigration. This resulted in the slaughter of many Yi people. . . . The second setback was the Cultural Revolution [1966–76]. . . . The destruction caused during this time left the Yi culture in an extremely miserable situation.

—Li Yongxiang, Niesu Yi, Yunnan[6]

Demographic Trends

The Yi numbered just over 6.5 million people in the 1990 national census, with over 1.5 million Northern Yi comprising the largest single group. By province, the most Yi people lived in Yunnan (over 4 million) (Fig. 15-1), followed by Sichuan (1.8 million), Guizhou (700,000), and Guangxi (7,000). Just under 3 percent of these Yi lived in cities except in Guizhou (21 percent urban), and there were some 16,000 Yi who lived in other, primarily urban, areas of China outside of the southwest.[7] In general, the Yi, like many minorities living in fairly remote mountainous areas, had higher levels of fertility and mortality than the national average. The Yi growth rate (increase in population) of 2.3 percent per year, higher than a

Figure 15-1. Xiaoliang Shan Xi men at home, Hei Shui, Lijiang County, Yunnan, 1993. Courtesy of Margaret Byrne Swain.

national average of 1.5 percent, was also reflected in a younger age structure: 35 percent of Yi were under fifteen years old, compared to 28 percent nationally. Yi women on average had 3.01 children, compared to the national fertility rate of 2.16 children. The average death rate for the Yi was 136 percent of the national rate, and the infant mortality rate was more than double the national rate of 28.7 deaths per 1,000 live births.[8]

A comparison of the category "Yi" with the national census total gives some insight into conditions of poverty and average relative gender equity. The Yi fertility level is possibly explainable by the desire for surviving children in response to infant mortality and the limited availability of health services, adequate nutrition, and education. The Yi sex ratio (number of males to 100 females) was 105, more balanced than the national figure of 110, for children zero to four years old. One interpretation could be that more equal care was given to small Yi children.

Education levels indicate that overall, Yi rates were much lower compared to national averages, and that fewer Yi females than males attended school or became literate. Of all Yi over the age of fifteen, 50.3 percent were literate in Chinese, compared to a national rate of 77.8 percent. By gender, 35.2 percent of Yi women were literate, compared to 68.1 percent nationally, and 65.2 percent of Yi men were literate, compared to 87.1 percent nationally. Of all Yi students attending school, 39 percent were female. Girls are often kept home to help with domestic work. With regard to occupations, 93.7 percent of Yi were in agriculture, compared to 72.2 percent nationally, with roughly equal numbers of women and men in both populations.

Current Events and Conditions

National policies after the 1949 revolution such as the 1958 Great Leap Forward and the 1966–76 Cultural Revolution had devastating economic and cultural effects specifically on national minorities. For example, government policies to foster grain production led to the forced introduction of rice cultivation in unsustainable mountain areas by people unaccustomed to rice. Cultural Revolution policies tried to stamp out "superstitions" and all old ways, including language and dress deviations from national norms, and disregarded environmental impacts in favor of exploitation. Since the 1980 reform era began, government attempts to address minority-nationality inequities with affirmative-action policies for population control, education, and economic development have had mixed results.

Environmental Crisis

Various threats to the environment from poverty and public policy can be illustrated by looking at deforestation among two very distinct Yi populations in Yunnan: the Sani settled in Lunan County and the Nuosu living in Ninglang County. In the past, the Sani's need for firewood production led to deforestation, while the Ninglang Nuosu now face significant deforestation problems due to government-sanctioned practices.

The Sani's ancestral lands are in and around the famous Stone Forest tourist site, composed of deeply weathered limestone. In a nearby Sani village, the slogan "Protect the forests for future use" is painted on various buildings. This is ignored by a daily parade of Sani women walking by with heavy loads of kindling. Such a split between law and behavior can be explained by conditions of the moment. Over the past hundred years, firewood gathering moved from just being a subsistence activity to also being a cash source, as Sani women cut and transported firewood to market. Contrary to the general assertion that deforestation in China's limestone regions was a post-1958 phenomenon, the area around the Stone Forest was completely devoid of trees by 1954 when government reforestation efforts began.

In 1993, Lau Huang, a seventy-three-year-old woman, recalled vividly in an interview that before 1955 women walked east from her village near the Stone Forest for more than an hour to areas where they could find wood to harvest. Through the years, she was pregnant fifteen times, bearing nine live children. Her family was poor and needed money, so her children would accompany her, carrying other children or their own burdens of kindling. To sell the wood, Lau Huang and her family would walk at least one hour to the west to the market town. Now things are very different. They can go nearby to the reforested county land to find kindling, pine needles, and cones, her family also uses coal, and they have electricity.

Around her village, tufted trees are a common sight: all lower branches have been stripped off for firewood by people who lack an alternate source of energy. Although the cutting of large trees for lumber is strictly controlled, subsistence gathering of branches, cones, and needles, also theoretically restricted, is allowed by the Forestry Bureau. The contest for usable land for forest, farming, grazing, and now tourism is significant. Fields have decreased rapidly to the point that some households no longer do agricultural work, and all supplement their subsistence activities with cash income. As many Sani women's economic roles change from horticulturist and gatherer to international tourism entrepreneur, some forest-conservation goals are being sacrificed, while a long-term solution is being sought in a different economic base.

The Ninglang Nuosu Yi region is situated on the other side of Yunnan Province near the Sichuan border, in a sedimentary mountain range with mixed-conifer forest cover. Deep erosion is evident throughout the region due to widespread county- and provincial-government clear-cutting of forests. Forest consumption is an activity that many communities are beginning to protest as the effects on farming land, pasture, and water supply are felt.

For Nuosu, like the Sani and many other mountain folk, the procuring of firewood is a major use of women's time. Women in some regions use more than four hours a day to secure firewood. In Ninglang, it is also evident that lumber is used heavily in house construction (wood walls and roof shingles), and wood is used for eating utensils and other household articles, all manufactured by men. Extraction of timber by village men is a regular, usually illegal, pursuit. The time to take out lumber is when the guard station is regularly closed. It is a cat-and-mouse game. Local firewood sources have become problematic as the nearby lands controlled by the county and province are clear-cut, and reforestation efforts are minimal. Regional resistance to this continued practice has ranged from dynamiting logging roads to replanting government trees upside down in traditional pasturage declared by the government to be new "reforested" lands.

Sociocultural Crisis

Poverty and social change threaten the survival of Yi societies in many ways. In a Ninglang Nuosu community, an interview with sixty-three-year-old Jazi Naska illustrates some of the issues in a poor family. She is taking care of a one-year-old baby on her back and is cooking food for pigs and roasting potatoes, the local staple. Her possessions are few, there is no furniture, and the stone hearth is the only stove. Her husband died when she was forty years old, so she lives with her youngest son. He has ended up in jail for stealing. His twenty-one-year-old illiterate wife is the only labor force of the family, working outside in the fields.

Jazi Naska says that she and her daughter-in-law rely on each other. She takes care of the household so her son's wife does not have a double burden, but "just" works like a man. Jazi Naska gestures, pushing her hat back up on her head, and says that sometimes her daughter-in-law is angry that her baby's father is in jail, and it is hard to know how to deal with it. The young mother comes home for the day and cuddles her baby with her field-rough hands. Jazi Naska comments that besides working their land, her son's wife sometimes helps other families in their fields. They will help out each other, for example, by sending over some beans when needed. She agrees that women's cooperatives would be very useful. There are feelings of hardship, but there is no government support for women's cooperatives. They just talk about it among themselves.

Women in this community need government support for their efforts to help themselves. In order to change their living conditions, the cycle of keeping girls out of school to help their overworked mothers must be broken. Education of women is critical for their future, as are opportunities to use that education. Individual women's success as apple growers or tourism entrepreneurs is a positive first step, but it does little to improve the overall well-being of Ninglang Nuosu women like Jazi Naska and their families who have no capital to start a business.

RESPONSE: STRUGGLES TO SURVIVE CULTURALLY

Attempts by Chinese government affirmative-action policies since the 1980s to promote more equitable conditions for minority nationalities have had very mixed results. In the 1990s, government efforts have been augmented by international aid programs, impacted by the global economy, and challenged by local self-help efforts to promote cultural survival, as can be seen among Yi groups.

Health and Well-Being

Government birth-control restrictions from 1979 until 1991 were generally less stringent in minority areas, with three or more births tolerated for some minority women, while Han Chinese neighbors were restricted to one or two. Reports of forced sterilizations and abortions, however, have been made across ethnic boundaries. During the 1990s, regional population policies such as those in Yunnan have incorporated minority groups into the regulations of one child for urban residents, two children for rural

259

residents. Theoretically, Yi growth rates should now go down as the average number of allowed children decreases from three to two, and if health conditions do not improve, the rate will be lower.

The Ford Foundation's Women's Reproductive Health and Development Program in Yunnan was started in 1991 to address rural low-income women's health needs. One of the project's most impoverished sites has been an Eastern Yi village where the project identified disparities in existing health care systems and facilitated changes to address these needs. For example, family planning was relatively effective, but there was no information about hygiene or disease prevention and little treatment available for these villagers. The project worked very successfully to involve local women in their own well-being, dramatically improving health of mothers and children, education, women's advocacy, and grassroots poverty alleviation.

Economic Development

Many mountain Yi farmers live below the poverty line, which by 1995 government standards was an income of less that 300 yuan (U.S. $36) and 500 jin (551 pounds) of grain per person per year. National and provincial financial aid programs for all people living below this level are allocated through county systems. Some twenty-one minority-nationality autonomous administration units (prefectures and counties) with Yi populations in southwest China use these resources for economic development in impoverished districts. These autonomous regions have specific policies for the promotion of minority officials and involvement in decision making.

Tourism is a form of development with a number of environmental impacts, economic consequences, and cultural issues for local minority nationalities that is being promoted in Yi areas. Economic schemes boom and crash, such as the government plan to encourage horseback packing for tourists by local Nuosu from Ninglang that was then undercut by a ski lift to the "Love-Suicide Meadow." Communities settled in scenic areas have been moved because the regional center of Lijiang was awarded United Nations World Heritage Site status in 1998. Now there is a struggle between recreational development and environmental protection in the whole region.

Integration into global and national systems and relative prosperity also brings social problems, including new intergeneration and class disparities. During the past decade in some Sani villages, formal education has become universal for all children through sixth grade, with many students now continuing on in school. Most of these children's mothers are illiterate, and fathers often have minimal literacy skills.

Young girls who a generation ago would have been preparing for marriage into a farm family began planning their lives as tourist guides and entrepreneurs. Their reputations' reflection on the community became a

Figure 15-2. Sani Yi women artisan peddlers
in the streets of Kunming, Yunnan, 1997.
Courtesy of Margaret Byrne Swain.

concern that required constant negotiation as some young women contributed almost all of the cash income for their families. Sani women artisans
built an informal handicraft souvenir industry in Lunan during the early
1980s. This led to circular migration to sell their wares in the city of Kunming, and now countrywide, as some Sani became involved in the national
and international handicrafts trade (Figure 15-2).

Sani class disparity was growing during the 1990s. In the village closest
to the Stone Forest Park entrance, resident household annual income
ranged from 400 renminbi (RMB; one RMB was worth from U.S. $0.10
to 0.15) for a widower and two young children, to 40,000 RMB reported
by a family that owns a guest house. This huge difference was graphically
illustrated by relatives living side by side in old decrepit earth houses and
new Chinese-style modern brick houses. Local family obligations and welfare practices eased some disparity, but these changes may be at least as
dramatic as previous state-mandated projects with the communist revolution that reinforced a formerly egalitarian Sani community life.

New global goods like boomboxes, videocassette recorders, cars, and motorcycles are both symbols of modernity and sources of inequalities and resentments. In Lunan, karaoke music blares and video nights at the largest Sani-owned guest house show Hong Kong kung fu movies. Televisions in many homes are tuned to national programming and local advertisements, some of which feature images of Stone Forest Park and nameless Sani costumed as "generic exotic ethnics."

Education and Cultural Renaissance

Yi people saw gratifying aspects of the new situation and government during the renaissance of folk customs at the beginning of the 1980s. But with the passage of time, and the policy of reforming and opening to the outside world, the traditional culture of the Yi is now faced with many new problems which lead to contradictions and difficult positions. These problems are associated with the tourist industry, modern propaganda mediums, new pastimes, thoughts, ideas, behavior models, and language disappearance.
—Li Yongxiang, Niesu Yi, Yunnan

The Yi are faced with a serious choice whether or not to abandon their tradition so as to enjoy "modernity."
—Pan Jiao, Nuosu, Liangshan

Along with disparities of physical well-being, cultural issues such as the commodification of identity, language death, and modernity have severely affected the survival of Yi peoples. The Chinese Constitution and the Law of Regional National Autonomy grant minorities the right to use their own language and writing system in their autonomous regions. However, government affirmative action in education has generally been skewed toward assimilation into the modern Chinese nation. This has meant lower standards for minority students competing for a place in the national education system, "bilingual" education of the youngest students in their native language to ease them into all-Chinese instruction, and specialized state educational institutions for minority nationalities. However, as Yi intellectuals become active in cultural politics, cultural revival may become more of a norm for urban and rural Yi. Individual and community responses have made it clear that with change comes reinvention and a desire for cultural continuity.

Bilingual education in Liangshan Yi Autonomous Prefecture has used two models since 1984: teaching in spoken and written Nuosu Yi with Chinese as a subject, and teaching in Chinese with Yi as a subject. The first model with Yi textbooks, teacher training, and research for primary through secondary instruction has a greater success rate of keeping students in school, but Yi-taught schools are few, and the whole system is underenrolled and has high dropout rates. Some Nuosu scholars believe that there is now a solid base in this model from which to expand bilingual education,[9] even though "the founders of this system have no intention to send their children to this kind of school"[10] due to concerns about the quality of education and the children's prospects in the job market.

Other groups with a Yi writing system may not even have this choice to make. Among the Sani, basic linguistic research and a Chinese-Sani dictionary have been available since the mid-1980s, but there is no instruction in the schools. According to Zeng Guopin, a Sani, "There are only a few people over seventy who understand the Yi characters . . . so the Yi characters of the Sani branch in Lunnan are in danger of disappearing."[11]

Most of the older people in any community who can read Yi writing are religious leaders or *bimo*. These practitioners were severely persecuted during the Cultural Revolution, and the "rehabilitation" of this profession has occurred with varying amounts of government assistance emphasizing cultural preservation. In Liangshan, the revival of *bimo* included the following:

The practice of *bimo* religious rituals by Yi professionals living in cities (such as ghost dispelling and cattle sacrifice)

The dramatic increase in young children studying to be *bimo*

The new modern applications of *bimo* ritual such as praying for college entrance, cursing the use of drugs, or avoiding traffic accidents

The higher income and standard of living of *bimo* professionals than their rural neighbors.[12]

Among the Sani, *bimo* practice in communities along with women shamans (*shima*). Sani religion adjusts to Chinese modernity and also competes with Catholicism, which has survived in some communities for over a hundred years since French missionaries first colonized Lunan. Some Sani *bimo* have become involved in efforts by other intellectuals to revive and reinvent their heritage. Such projects in the late 1990s included the Lunan County's Cultural History Center; the Stone Forest Tourism Bureau's Cultural Arts Center; and a private, independent project with past funding from UNESCO and plans for the future. This last project paired elderly *bimo* with several trained Sani linguists who were translating Sani Yi texts into the international phonetic system, Chinese, and English.

Another project of note for "self-conservation of Yi culture" was implemented at a primary school by researcher Li Yongxiang in his native Neisu Yi village. Three courses in music, dance, and writing taught by local *bimo* and artists were introduced into the curriculum. The community response was so positive that the project is now expanding and has gained government support.

The cultural renaissance can also be seen in the marketplace, where heritage and modernity merge. In both Nuosu and Sani regions, "traditional" artifacts, singing, and dancing are produced for tourist consumers, but there is also a great deal of local consumption of modern ethnic culture. Popular Yi music tapes and CDs, from nostalgic folk songs to a Nuosu heavy-metal band, are played in homes and on the streets. Factory-produced handicrafts such as Nuosu lacquer ware, Sani embroidered bags, and standardized "traditional" clothing are locally purchased and used. While the transformation of ethnic dress to special-use costumes indicates cultural loss, it is also a sign of continuity in new conditions. In the recent past for many Yi people, the possibility of openly celebrating their religious and artistic heritage would have seemed impossible. Now, as Yi and as members of their own cultures, they are confronting citizenship in modern China with its restrictions, disparities, and inequalities as well as its possibilities for the future.

FOOD FOR THOUGHT

We cannot stop the process of modernization, and it is necessary as many Yi people are still living in terrible conditions. They have to develop their economy so that they will no longer be hungry and cold. But we should do careful research so that we protect our traditional culture as we develop the economy.... I want to emphasize that Yi cultural protection and conservation should be done by those people who are Yi, and who care about Yi. Also it should not be done in isolation from the native land and Yi community.... Yi culture conservation should be started from childhood. To conserve the history and culture of the Yi people for following generations, it should be included in regular education.

—Li Yongxiang, Niesu Yi, Yunnan

These issues, raised by various Yi intellectuals cited in this chapter, are faced by endangered peoples world-wide. Specific problems for Yi peoples are marked by local conditions and cultural variation. Data on the Yi from government and field research sources as well as analysis by Yi and other scholars document problems of physical and cultural survival. The state in China has had a very active role in defining/creating, suppressing, and maintaining the Yi and other ethnic groups during the second half of the twentieth century. We have seen the legacies of colonial conquest and the effects of contemporary government schemes of identification, resettlement, and affirmative action policies for Yi peoples. The response of the Yi themselves, as Li Yongxiang writes above, is critical for survival. Yi peoples at the beginning of the twenty-first century must deal with problems from government policies, local disparities (especially ethnic, gender, age, and class), and the global economy. They have rich unique cultural resources to draw strength from and protect.

Questions

1. In the quotation by Li, what does his statement that Yi cultural conservation "should be done by those people who are Yi, and who care about Yi" mean in terms of ethnic relations? Why does it matter to him that such conservation "should not be done in isolation from the native land and Yi community"?

2. If Native American peoples in the U.S. Southwest are compared with Yi peoples in southwest China, what parallels might you find in government policies of ethnic classification, settlement, administration, and education for native peoples on national frontiers? Why would there be parallels between these "democratic" and "Communist" systems?

3. What could Pan Jiao mean about Yi people's choices between tradition and modernity when he comments about bilingual education that "the founders of this system have no intention to send their children to this kind of school"?

4. How might constructed identities such as the "Yi" be beneficial or harmful for forming political alliances by endangered peoples? Does it make a difference to such alliances if this type of identity is imposed or self-generated, or if there are multiple histories or one unified historical narrative?

5. If Yi peoples were to be socially integrated rather than culturally assimilated or absorbed into the nation-state, what might this mean for local education, tourism development, and religious practice? How could government policies of affirmative action and autonomous areas be involved?

6. Li is concerned that "the traditional culture of the Yi is now faced with many new problems . . . associated with the tourist industry, modern propaganda mediums, [and] new pastimes." Give examples of problems that Yi peoples have faced from incorporation into a global economy, environmental change, local ethnic identity, and national culture to either support or refute his statement.

NOTES

1. Wugashinnuimo, L., "Discovering and Re-Discovering Yi Identity: Shared Identity Narratives from the Classics of Yunnan, Sichuan, Guizhou, and Guangxi," in Heberer's unpublished collection of papers on the 1998 proceedings of the Second International Conference on Yi Studies in Trier, Germany.

2. Pan Jiao, "Theories of Ethnic Identity and the Making of the Yi," in Heberer.

3. Lu Hui, "Multiple Identity of the Yi Nationality in China," in Heberer.

4. D. Bradley, "Language Policy for the Yi," in *Yi Society and Culture*, ed. Stevan Harrell (Berkeley: University of California Press, 1999).

5. Ma Erzi, "Recognizing the Old Liang Shan Yi Social Structure," in Heberer.

6. Li Yongxiang, "Self Conservation and Protection of Yi-Culture in Social Changes," in Heberer.

7. *Tabulation of the 1990 Census, Vol. 1, 1993* (State Statistical Bureau, People's Republic of China, 1993). Some interpretation of these figures by the author, unless otherwise noted.

8. See F. Yusuf and M. Byrnes, *Ethnic Mosaic of Modern China*, Research Paper 374 (Macquarie University, School of Economic and Financial Studies, 1993).

9. Tiexi Qumu, "The Bilingual Education in Liangshan Yi Ethnic Group," in Heberer.

10. Pan Jiao, "Theories of Ethnic Identity and the Making of the Yi," in Heberer.

11. Zeng Guopin, "Bilingual Education in Lunan," in Heberer.

12. Bamo Ayi, "The Bi-mox in the Liangshan Yi Society," in Heberer.

RESOURCE GUIDE

Harrell, Stevan. "The History of the History of the Yi." In *Cultural Encounters on China's Ethnic Frontiers*, ed. Stevan Harrell, 63–91. Seattle: University of Washington Press, 1995.

———, ed. *Perspectives on the Yi.* Berkeley: University of California Press, 2000.

Heberer, Thomas, ed. *Proceedings, The Second International Conference on Yi Studies: Processes of Social Change, Rising Ethnic Identity, and Ethnicity among the Yi Nationality in China.* 1998 in Trier, Germany. Unpublished.

Lin, Yaohua. *The Lolo of Liang Shan.* Translated by Ju-shu Pan from Liangshan Yijia. New Haven, CT: HRAF Press, 1961 (1947).

Swain, Margaret Byrne. "Père Vial and the Gni-P'a: Orientalist Scholarship and the Christian Project." In *Cultural Encounters on China's Ethnic Frontiers*, ed. Stevan Harrell, 140–185. Seattle: University of Washington Press, 1995.

Glossary

Age-grade system. Organizing a society based on grouping together individuals of a similar age.

Animism. A belief that natural objects and forces have souls or spirits.

Austronesian. A Malayo-Polynesian language grouping for languages spoken in Oceania, Malaya, and Madagascar.

Autochthonous. A synonym for "aboriginal," "indigenous," or "native."

Biodiversity. The variety of life forms, the number of different species in an ecosystem.

Cassava. A starchy tuber grown in the tropics.

Copal. The dried fiber from a coconut shell.

Endogamy. Marriage within a particular group with which one is identified.

Endogenous. Growing from within.

Ethnogenesis. The development of an ethnic identity of a group in contrast to other ethnic groups within a multiethnic or plural society.

Exogamy. Marriage outside of a particular group with which one is identified.

Foraging. The gathering of wild plant foods and hunting and fishing.

Gazetting. The process of legally establishing ownership of land through registration in government archives.

Generalized reciprocity. Informal gift giving for which no accounts are kept and no immediate or specific return is expected.

Indigenous people. The descendants of the original people in a region who share a common culture, history, and homeland.

Matriclan. A group that claims but cannot trace descent through the female line from a common female ancestor.

Matrilocal. The residence of a married couple with or near the wife's kin.

Megatrend. A major trend over the long term in biological or cultural evolution.

Monocrop. A single species or variety of domesticated plant in a garden as contrasted with multiple species or varieties, as in a polycrop.

Negrito. A person of short stature and dark skin color who is recognized as distinctive from other populations in a region.

Niche differentiation. A process in which two different populations or species diverge in their specializations into two different niches, resulting in reduction in direct competition.

Nongovernmental organization. A group or organization working outside the government to meet or address social needs.

Patriclan. A group that claims but cannot trace descent through the male line from a common male ancestor.

Patrilocal. The residence of a married couple with or near the husband's kin.

Savanna. Tropical grasslands.

Sedentarization. The practice of establishing more permanent or fixed settlements or villages.

Shamanism. The belief in the powers of a shaman, a medium of the supernatural who purportedly possesses unique curing, divining, or magical capabilities.

Swidden. A system of food production in which natural vegetation is cut, the debris is left to dry and is then burned, and a garden is planted in the ashes. Plots must be abandoned after a few years because of loss of soil fertility or invasion of vegetation from the surrounding forest.

General Bibliography

BOOKS

Asia

Barnes, R. H., Andrew Gray, and Benedict Kingsbury, eds. *Indigenous Peoples of Asia*. Ann Arbor, MI: Association for Asian Studies, 1995.

Carrier, J., ed. *Occidentalism: Images of the West*. Oxford: Clarendon Press, 1995.

Evans, Grant, ed. *Asia's Cultural Mosaic: An Anthropological Introduction*. Englewood Cliffs, NJ: Prentice Hall, 1993.

Hockings, Paul, ed. *Encyclopedia of World Cultures*. Vol. 5, *East and Southeast Asia*. Boston: G. K. Hall, 1990.

Mackerras, Colin, ed. *East and Southeast Asia: A Multidisciplinary Survey*. Boulder, CO: Lynne Rienner, 1995.

Nicholas, Colin, and Raajen Singh, eds. *Indigenous Peoples of Asia: Many Peoples, One Struggle*. Bangkok: Asia Indigenous Peoples Pact, 1996.

Said, Edward. *Orientalism*. New York: Routledge and Kegan Paul, 1985.

Tweddell, Colin E., and Linda Amy Kimball. *Introduction to the Peoples and Cultures of Asia*. Englewood Cliffs, NJ: Prentice Hall, 1985.

Colonization

Bodley, John H. *Victims of Progress*. 4th ed. Mountain View, CA: Mayfield, 1999.

Coedes, G. *The Indianized States of Southeast Asia*. Honolulu: East-West Center and the University Press of Hawaii, 1975.

Dentan, Robert Knox, Kirk Endicott, Albert G. Gomes, and M. B. Hooker. *Malaysia and the "Original People": A Case Study of the Impact of Development on Indigenous Peoples*. Boston: Allyn and Bacon, 1997.

269

Dove, Michael R., ed. *The Real and Imagined Role of Culture in Development: Case Studies from Indonesia.* Honolulu: University of Hawaii Press, 1988.

Geertz, Clifford. *Agricultural Involution: The Processes of Ecological Change in Indonesia.* Berkeley: University of California Press, 1963.

Maybury-Lewis, David. *Indigenous Peoples, Ethnic Groups, and the State.* Boston: Allyn and Bacon, 1997.

Conflicts and Wars

Bilton, Michael, and Kevin Sim. *Four Hours in My Lai.* New York: Penguin, 1992.

Deac, Wilfrid P. *Road to the Killing Fields: The Cambodian War of 1970–1975.* College Station: Texas A&M University Press, 1997.

Glossop, Ronald J. *Confronting War: An Examination of Humanity's Most Pressing Problem.* 3rd ed. Jefferson, NC: McFarland, 1994.

Hachiya, Michihiko. *Hiroshima Diary: The Journal of a Japanese Physician, August 6–September 30, 1945.* London: Victor Gollancz, 1955.

Hicks, George, ed. *The Broken Mirror: China after Tiananmen.* New York: Longman, 1990.

Horowitz, Donald L. *Ethnic Groups in Conflict.* Berkeley: University of California Press, 1985.

Kaplan, Robert. *The Ends of the Earth: A Journey at the Dawn of the 21st Century.* New York: Random House, 1996.

Lifton, Robert Jay. *Hiroshima in America: A Half Century of Denial.* New York: Avon, 1996.

Martin, Marie Alexandrine. *Cambodia: A Shattered Society.* Berkeley: University of California Press, 1994.

Smith, Dan. *The State of War and Peace Atlas.* 3rd ed. New York: Penguin, 1997.

Stevens, Richard L. *The Trail: A History of the Ho Chi Minh Trail and the Role of Nature in the War in Viet Nam.* New York: Garland, 1993.

Taylor, J. G. *Indonesia's Forgotten War: The Hidden History of East Timor.* London: Zed Books, 1991.

East Asia

Ahern, Emily Martin, and Hill Gates, eds. *The Anthropology of Taiwanese Society.* Stanford, CA: Stanford University Press, 1981.

Bowring, Richard, and Peter Kornicki, eds. *The Cambridge Encyclopedia of Japan.* New York: Cambridge University Press, 1993.

Chang, Kwang-chih. *The Archaeology of Ancient China.* 4th ed. New Haven, CT: Yale University Press, 1986.

Chiao, Chien, and N. Tapp. *Ethnicity and Ethnic Groups in China.* New Territories: Chinese University of Hong Kong, 1994.

Dernberger, Robert F., ed. *The Chinese: Adapting the Past, Building the Future.* Ann Arbor: University of Michigan Center for Chinese Studies, 1986.

Ebrey, Patricia, ed. *Chinese Civilization and Society: A Sourcebook.* New York: Free Press, 1981.

Fei, Hsiao Tung. *Toward a People's Anthropology*. Beijing: New World Press, 1981.

Friedrich, Paul, and Norma Diamond, eds. *Encyclopedia of World Cultures*. Vol. 6, *Russia and Eurasia/China*. Boston: G. K. Hall, 1994.

Gladney, Dru. *Muslim Chinese: Ethnic Nationalism in the People's Republic*. Cambridge, MA: Harvard University Press, 1991.

Harrell, Stevan, ed. *Cultural Encounters on China's Ethnic Frontiers*. Seattle: University of Washington Press, 1995.

Heberer, T. *China and Its National Minorities: Autonomy or Assimilation?* Armonk, NY: M. E. Sharpe, 1989.

Hendry, J. *Understanding Japanese Society*. 2nd ed. New York: Routledge, 1995.

Hook, Brian, ed. *The Cambridge Encyclopedia of China*. New York: Cambridge University Press, 1982.

Ma Yin, ed. *China's Minority Nationalities*. Beijing: Foreign Languages Press, 1989.

Mackerras, Colin, and Amanda Yorke. *The Cambridge Handbook of Contemporary China*. New York: Cambridge University Press, 1991.

Moser, Leo J. *The Chinese Mosaic: The Peoples and Provinces of China*. Boulder, CO: Westview Press, 1985.

Nakane, Chie. *Japanese Society*. Berkeley: University of California Press, 1970.

Norbeck, Edward G. *Changing Japan*. New York: Holt, Rinehart and Winston, 1976.

Ramsey, S. Robert. *The Languages of China*. Princeton, NJ: Princeton University Press, 1987.

Shepherd, J. R. *Statecraft and Political Economy on the Taiwan Frontier, 1600–1800*. Stanford, CA: Stanford University Press, 1993.

Smith, Christopher J. *China: People and Places in the Land of One Billion*. Boulder, CO: Westview Press, 1991.

Ward, Barbara E. *Through Other Eyes: Essays in Understanding "Conscious Models," Mostly in Hong Kong*. Hong Kong: Chinese University Press, 1985.

Weiner, Michael, ed. *Japan's Minorities: The Illusion of Homogeneity*. New York: Routledge, 1997.

Environment

Brookfield, Harold, and Yvonne Byron, eds. *South-East Asia's Environmental Future: The Search for Sustainability*. New York: Oxford University Press, 1993.

Bruun, Ole, and Arne Kalland, eds. *Asian Perceptions of Nature: A Critical Approach*. Richmond, England: Curzon Press, 1995.

Callicott, J. Baird, and Roger T. Ames, eds. *Nature in Asian Traditions of Thought: Essays in Environmental Philosophy*. Albany: State University of New York Press, 1989.

Conklin, Harold. *Hanunoo Agriculture*. Rome: Food and Agriculture Organization, 1957.

Donner, Wolf. *Land Use and Environment in Indonesia*. Honolulu: University of Hawaii Press, 1987.

Gyallay-Pap, Peter, and Ruth Bottomley, eds. *Towards an Environmental Ethic in Southeast Asia*. Phnom Penh: Buddhist Institute, 1998.

Hurst, Philip. *Rainforest Politics: Ecological Destruction in South-East Asia.* London: Zed Books, 1990.

Leslie, John. *The End of the World: The Science and Ethics of Human Extinction.* New York: Routledge, 1996.

MacKinnon, John. *Wild China.* Cambridge, MA: MIT Press, 1996.

McNeely, Jeffrey A., Kenton R. Miller, Walter V. Reid, Russell A. Mittermeier, and Timothy B. Werner. *Conserving the World's Biological Diversity.* Gland, Switzerland: International Union for the Conservation of Nature, 1990.

McNeely, Jeffrey A., and Paul Spencer Sochaczewski. *Soul of the Tiger: Searching for Nature's Answers in Southeast Asia.* Honolulu: University of Hawaii Press, 1995.

McNeely, Jeffrey A., and Sunthad Somchevita, eds. *Biodiversity in Asia: Challenges and Opportunities for the Scientific Community.* Bangkok: Thailand Ministry of Science, Technology, and Environment, Office of Environmental Policy and Planning, 1996.

Myers, Norman. *Ultimate Security: The Environmental Basis of Political Stability.* Washington, DC: Island Press, 1996.

Parnwell, Michael J. G., and Raymond L. Bryant, eds. *Environmental Change in South-East Asia: People, Politics, and Sustainable Development.* New York: Routledge, 1996.

Payne, Junaidi. *Wild Malaysia: The Wildlife and Scenery of Peninsular Malaysia.* Cambridge, MA: MIT Press, 1990.

Ponting, Clive. *A Green History of the World: The Environment and the Collapse of Great Civilizations.* New York: Penguin, 1993.

Rambo, A. Terry, Kathleen Gillogly, and Karl L. Hutterer, eds. *Ethnic Diversity and the Control of Natural Resources in Southeast Asia.* Ann Arbor: University of Michigan Center for South and Southeast Asian Studies, 1988.

Renner, Michael. *Fighting for Survival: Environmental Decline, Social Conflict, and the New Age of Insecurity,* New York: W. W. Norton, 1996.

Rigg, Jonathan, ed. *Counting the Costs: Economic Growth and Environmental Change in Thailand.* Singapore: Institute of Southeast Asian Studies, 1995.

Smil, Vaclav. *China's Environmental Crisis: An Inquiry into the Limits of National Development.* Armonk, NY: M. E. Sharpe, 1993.

Stewart-Cox, Belinda. *Wild Thailand.* Cambridge, MA: MIT Press, 1995.

Whitten, Tony, and Jane Whitten. *Wild Indonesia: The Wildlife and Scenery of the Indonesian Archipelago.* Cambridge, MA: MIT Press, 1992.

Wilson, Edward O. *The Diversity of Life.* Cambridge, MA: Belknap Press of Harvard University Press, 1992.

World Resources Institute. *World Resources, 1998–99.* Washington, DC: World Resources Institute, 1999.

Human Rights

Blaustein, Albert P., Roger S. Clark, and Jay A. Sigler, eds. *Human Rights Sourcebook.* New York: Paragon House, 1987.

Burger, Julian. *Report from the Frontier: The State of the World's Indigenous Peoples.* Cambridge, MA: Cultural Survival, 1987.

Johnston, Barbara Rose, ed. *Who Pays the Price? The Sociocultural Context of Environmental Crisis*. Washington, DC: Island Press, 1994.

———. *Life and Death Matters: Human Rights and the Environment at the End of the Millennium*. Walnut Creek, CA: Altamira Press, 1997.

Lawson, Edward, ed. *Encyclopedia of Human Rights*. Bristol: Taylor and Francis, 1991.

Miller, Marc S., ed. *State of the Peoples: A Global Human Rights Report on Societies in Danger*. Boston: Beacon Press, 1993.

Rand McNally. *World Facts and Maps*. Chicago: Rand McNally, 1999.

Religion

Einarsen, John, ed. *The Sacred Mountains of Asia*. Boston: Shambhala, 1995.

Hue-Tam Ho Tai. *Millenarianism and Peasant Politics in Vietnam*. Cambridge, MA: Harvard University Press, 1983.

Kinsley, David. *Ecology and Religion: Ecological Spirituality in Cross-Cultural Perspective*. Englewood Cliffs, NJ: Prentice Hall, 1995.

Lansing, J. Stephen. *Priests and Programmers: Technologies of Power in the Engineered Landscape of Bali*. Princeton, NJ: Princeton University Press, 1991.

Matthews, Warren. *World Religions*. 3rd ed. Belmont, CA: Wadsworth, 1999.

Mehden, Fred von der. *Religion and Modernization in Southeast Asia*. Syracuse: Syracuse University Press, 1986.

Palmer, Martin. *Travels through Sacred China*. San Francisco: Thorsons, 1996.

Swearer, Donald K. *The Buddhist World of Southeast Asia*. Albany: State University of New York Press, 1995.

Weller, Robert P. *Unities and Diversities in Chinese Religion*. Seattle: University of Washington Press, 1987.

Wolf, Arthur P., ed. *Religion and Ritual in Chinese Society*. Stanford, CA: Stanford University Press, 1974.

Southeast Asia

Bellwood, Peter. *Prehistory of the Indo-Malaysian Archipelago*. New York: Academic Press, 1985.

Coedes, George. *The Indianized States of Southeast Asia*. Honolulu: East-West Center, 1968.

Cultural Survival. *Southeast Asian Tribal Groups and Ethnic Minorities*. Cambridge, MA: Cultural Survival, 1987.

Dutt, Ashok, ed. *Southeast Asia: Realm of Contrasts*. 3rd ed. Boulder, CO: Westview Press, 1985.

Hall, K. R. *Maritime Trade and State Development in Early Southeast Asia*. Boston: Allen and Unwin, 1985.

Higham, Charles. *The Archaeology of Mainland Southeast Asia*. New York: Cambridge University Press, 1989.

Keyes, Charles F. *The Golden Peninsula: Culture and Adaptation in Mainland Southeast Asia*. Honolulu: University of Hawaii Press, 1995.

————. *Thailand: Buddhist Kingdom as Modern Nation-State*. Boulder, CO: Westview Press, 1987.

Magallanes, Catherine, J. Iorns, and Malcolm Hollick, eds. *Land Conflicts in Southeast Asia: Indigenous Peoples, Environment and International Law*. Bangkok, Thailand: White Lotus Press, 1998.

Reid, Anthony. *Southeast Asia in the Age of Commerce, 1450–1680*. 2 vols. New Haven, CT: Yale University Press, 1990, 1993.

Rigg, Jonathan. *Southeast Asia: A Region in Transition*. New York: Routledge, 1994.

SarDesai, D. R. *Southeast Asia, Past and Present*. Boulder, CO: Westview Press, 1997.

————. *Vietnam, Past and Present*. Boulder, CO: Westview Press, 1998.

Wijeyewardene, Gehan, ed. *Ethnic Groups across National Boundaries in Mainland Southeast Asia*. Singapore: Institute of Southeast Asian Studies, 1990.

VIDEOS

China: Beyond the Clouds. Washington, DC: National Geographic Society, 1994.

Festivals of Asia. Tokyo: Asian Cultural Center for UNESCO, 1998.

The Heart of the Dragon (China). New York: Ambrose Video Publishing, 1988.

Japan: Land of the Rising Sun. Las Vegas: Library Distributors of America, 1992.

Japan Past and Present. Princeton, NJ: Films for the Humanities, 1989.

Japan 2000. Princeton, NJ: Films for the Humanities and Sciences, 1998.

Mini Dragons (Indonesia, Malaysia, Thailand). New York: Ambrose Video Publishing, 1993.

Portrait of Japan. New York: Ambrose Video Publishing, 1992.

Raise the Bamboo Curtain (Burma, Cambodia, Vietnam). Chicago: Questar Video, 1995.

Slow Boat from Surabaya: Through South East Asia with Jack Pizzey. Falls Church, VA: Phillip Emmanuel Productions, 1992.

South Korea: Land of Morning Calm. San Ramon, CA: International Video Network, 1996.

The Wisdom of Faith (survey of major world religions). Princeton, NJ: Films for the Humanities and Sciences, 1994.

ORGANIZATION

Cultural Survival, Inc.

96 Mount Auburn St.

Cambridge, MA 02138

Web site: www.cs.org

Index

About the Contributors

GEORGE N. APPELL is Senior Research Associate, Department of Anthropology, Brandeis University, Waltham, Massachusetts.

SUSAN M. DARLINGTON is Associate Professor of Anthropology and Asian Studies at the School of Social Sciences, Hampshire College, Amherst, Massachusetts.

ROBERT K. DENTAN is Professor of Anthropology in the Departments of Anthropology and American Studies, State University of New York/University at Buffalo, New York.

JAMES F. EDER is Professor of Anthropology, Department of Anthropology, Arizona State University, Tempe, Arizona.

KIRK ENDICOTT is Professor of Anthropology, Department of Anthropology, Dartmouth College, Hanover, New Hampshire.

DRU C. GLADNEY is Dean of Academics, Asia-Pacific Center, Honolulu, currently on leave from his position as Professor of Asian Studies, University of Hawaii.

YOKO HAYAMI is Research Associate at the Graduate School for Asian and African Area Studies, Kyoto University, Kyoto, Japan.

HSIANG-MEI CHENG is Assistant Professor in the Institute of Anthropology, Tzu Chi University, Hualien, Taiwan.

MASAMI IWASAKI-GOODMAN is Associate Professor of Anthropology, Department of Humanities, Hokkai Gakuen University, Toyohira-ku, Japan.

CORNELIA ANN KAMMERER is Senior Researcher at Health and Addictions Research, Inc., in Boston, Massachusetts, and Affiliated Scholar in the Women's Studies Program, Brandeis University, Waltham, Massachusetts.

GERARD A. PERSOON is Head of the Program on Environment and Development, Centre for Environmental Sciences, Leiden University, The Netherlands.

JAMES E. ROBERSON is Visiting Assistant Professor of Anthropology at the College of William and Mary, Williamsburg, Virginia.

RICHARD SIDDLE is Director of the Centre for Japanese Studies at the University of Sheffield, Sheffield, England.

LESLIE E. SPONSEL is Professor of Anthropology, Department of Anthropology, University of Hawaii, Honolulu, Hawaii.

MARGARET BYRNE SWAIN is Professor of Anthropology, Department of Anthropology, University of California, Davis, California.